WHO DO THE'

Photo by: Unboxed Vision

The Vindication of Minister Louis Farrakhan

A never before seen compilation of high profile and prominent people throughout society whose testimonies serve as character witnesses for the Honorable Minister Louis Farrakhan. Read commentaries from Elected Officials, Celebrities, Journalists, Religious Leaders, Pastors, Professors and Organizations who testify to the Character, Impact and Immeasurable Value of The Honorable Minister Louis Farrakhan

By Brother Demetric Muhammad
Expanded 2nd Edition

Cover Art: Jahleel Muhammad
Photo Credit Cover Image: Hannibal Muhammad

ResearchMinister.Com
P.O. Box 613117
Memphis, TN 38101
www.ResearchMinister.Com

Ordering Information:
Quantity sales. Special discounts are available on quantity purchases by corporations, associations, and others. For details, contact the publisher at the address above.
Printed in the Nation of Islam

ISBN: 978-0-9965156-1-0

Table of Contents

5

Foreword by Dr. Boyce Watkins

The world is changing, and we owe most of this change to the Internet. Ideas are being spread at lightning speed, and people have faster and more immediate access to perspectives and information than ever before.

In the age of the Internet, it's also become more and more difficult to defend a lie, unless it happens to be a lie with which you're most comfortable. In other words, the web is a place where you can either hunt down the truth or bury your head in the sand. This is one of the reasons that our nation hasn't been this divided since the Civil War.

One lie that was well-protected for many decades is the idea of Minister Louis Farrakhan as an anti-Semitic extremist. Some have even used terms like reverse racist, which are designed to alleviate America of the guilt of what's been done to black people for the last 400 years.

The release of important books like "The New Jim Crow" by Michelle Alexander and "Black Labor, White Wealth" by Dr. Claude Anderson, have unveiled the depth of abuse that black people have endured since slavery, and how these transgressions impact our society today.

One of the few leaders capable of connecting the struggles of our community with the trauma of the past is Minister Farrakhan. Farrakhan is one of the few members of the black community who is respected by both his friends and enemies. He's served well as a thinker, builder, orator, spiritual guide, mentor, father-figure and spokesperson for a community that has had to redefine its leadership over the last five years.

When rappers refuse to speak to one another, they respond to Farrakhan's call for reconciliation.

When the people of Baltimore and Ferguson refused to talk to most old school civil rights leaders, they still paid close attention to the words of Farrakhan.

When Farrakhan has appeared on media outlets such as The Breakfast Club, the largest urban radio show in the country, the world stood still to hear what he had to say. When Farrakhan asked a million black men to come to Washington, they came in droves and did it again 10 and 20 years later.

The minister can go into the darkest and most dangerous parts of any city in America and be fully protected by men of all age groups and socioeconomic backgrounds. No politician, advocate or police officer in the world can say the same thing. The reason Farrakhan is respected, especially by black men, is that he gives us love in a society that is designed to hate, emasculate, criminalize and destroy us. For many of us, he's all we've got.

In some ways, Minister Farrakhan might be considered the president of the black community. Of course, not everyone loves the minister. But even his harshest critics have a tough time thinking of anything the minister has done in the last 30 years that has been anything short of productive and uplifting for black people.

If a critic is asked to quote any hateful remark Farrakhan has made over the last 30 years, they are left grasping for whatever they can, like a desperate drug addict trying to find money for crack. They are addicted to hating Farrakhan, even if there is little reason to do so, even if they've never heard him speak for more than 30 seconds. Brainwashing is difficult to overcome and it might be more painful to acknowledge the truth than it is to keep taking his words out of context.

Farrakhan's greatest strength is his authenticity. He and The Nation of Islam have shown a type of unconditional love for black people that even the black community itself cannot comprehend. They stand by us when we are at our worst, and have been arguably the most consistent and self-determined institution in our community. The Nation of Islam shows us that black people can prosper with dignity, and without begging others to save us. The capacity of members of the nation to forgive and accept us for who we are is an extraordinary breath of fresh air in a world where we are taught to hate everything about our dark skin and ambiguous culture. Farrakhan and his organization make us PROUD.

When the police, government and educational systems have abandoned us, The Nation of Islam was always there. When we've needed an economic program, they've worked to put one together. When our role models were being shipped away to American slave camps (aka prisons), the men of The Nation of Islam were the cleanest, sharpest, most articulate and polite men in the entire neighborhood.

It is because Farrakhan and The Nation of Islam are so beloved and respected that many of us have a difficult time understanding why mainstream media has worked so hard to paint the minister in ways that are not in the least bit accurate. The fact that a man can be so loved by black people and hated by whites is yet another reminder of just how deep the racial divide remains in America.

The use of propaganda to defame one of the most respected men in the African American community wins absolutely no friends for the Anti-Defamation League. Their insistence that Farrakhan is not even worthy of a meeting is insulting and hurtful to The African American community and indicative of disrespect for the black community as a whole. It is also reflective of a fear that revealing the truth through a direct meeting with the minister would undermine many decades of propaganda that have been used to paint him as some kind of deranged and violent bigot.

The same was done to The Black Panthers.

The same was done to Malcolm X.

The same was done to Marcus Garvey.

The list goes on and on.

How can you judge a man so harshly when you refuse to even hear him speak? What are you afraid of?

This century is the first time in American or world history that black people have been able to communicate with one another without going through media filters controlled by somebody else. We aren't learning about Minister Farrakhan through CBS news or reading about him in the New York Times. We are hearing from him directly on the Internet, which means that his 20-plus year blackball from mainstream media outlets has come to an end.

My own meetings with the minister included a three-hour conversation in which he and I sat knee-to-knee in his office, discussing every topic under the sun, from the state of the educational system to issues in American politics. The entire time, I felt like I was speaking to my own grandfather, and it was a relief to hear from a senior black man who didn't live his life in fear, but at the same time, was able to possess enough love in his heart to forgive his enemies.

Farrakhan is certainly NOT the hate-filled caricature that has been created in mainstream media. Such a fictional portrayal of one of black America's most respected leaders is not only one that is easily disproven by the minister's own YouTube channel, but it's one that causes all of us to question the credibility of those who seek to feed such a lie to the American public.

The ADL and other groups must realize that stubbornly refusing to meet with Minister Farrakhan does not reduce the impact of his legacy. It only speaks to the kind of arrogance that white supremacy creates in a world where black people are perceived to be second-class citizens. The minister is strong, even if you want to pretend that he does not exist. He is the elephant in your room, and it's better to coordinate with the elephant's strength than to try to sweep him under a rug.

Jewish leaders, even when they are at their most extreme, are respected by the American government and the black community. Black public figures deserve the same respect. I cannot speak for Minister Farrakhan, but I highly doubt that there is any member of ADL leadership who would not be invited into his home for dinner and be treated with complete respect.

The truth can set us free, but it also indicts those who've sought to protect a lie. It's time to either start telling the truth about Farrakhan, or allow him to speak for himself. You can't call a man anti-Semitic for 30 years without at least hearing what he has to say. Such behavior is deeply disturbing, counter-productive and perhaps even fraudulent. It's time for bridges to be built and for seasons to change.

It's also time to start telling the TRUTH about Farrakhan.

Dr. Boyce Watkins is a Finance PhD. and founder of The Black Economic Empowerment Tour, designed to share ideas on Economic Empowerment throughout the world. To learn more, please visit BoyceWatkins.com.

Introduction
Character Witnesses, Character Assassination & Crucifixion

On April 26, 2016, the artist and performer known as Prince (aka Prince Rogers Nelson) passed away. His death was so stunning and shocking most who were his fans and supporters are still struggling to process the fact that he is gone.

Prince's music and movies are a part of my childhood. I am one of the millions who enjoyed his music and artistry. Prince's risqué lyrics and performances pushed the envelope during the early 1980's, of what was deemed appropriate and safe for both television and live audiences. It is no secret that much of his appeal to the young was the sexually charged nature of his music and his embracing of taboo subjects.

But over the years, it became rather clear that as most of us where growing and aging chronologically, Prince was growing and maturing as a person and as a conscientious member of the Black community. So much so that at the time of his passing, many who knew of his work behind the scenes have rightly heralded him as a music revolutionary and warrior businessman who forged the way for artists to have a greater measure of control over their music.

The passing of Prince and his evolution into being a socially conscious and Black conscious artist who enjoyed a universal appeal and fan base has caused many in the Black community to suspect that the strange circumstances surrounding his death might be as a direct result of his revolutionary and Black Nationalist tendencies.

In 1995 he wrote a song entitled "We March" for the Million Man March called for by the Honorable Minister Louis Farrakhan. In the year 2000 as the Honorable Minister Louis Farrakhan was preparing for the 5-year anniversary of the Million Man March-the Million Family March- Prince donated $50,000 to help make the march a success.

Prince and his private support for the Honorable Minister Louis Farrakhan is an important lead in into this second volume of the pioneering book **Who Do They Say I Am: The Vindication of The Honorable Minister Louis Farrakhan.**

Prince and his support for the work and ministry of the Honorable Minister Louis Farrakhan is one example of the powerful examples that we have documented within the pages of this book entitled **Who Do They Say I Am: The Vindication of the Honorable Minister Louis Farrakhan Expanded 2nd Edition.** Due to the history of Minister Farrakhan and his value to Black people in and outside of America, we feel it vitally necessary to present the testimonies of a host of diverse men, women and groups that make up a strong and unmatched treasure of character witnesses on behalf of Minister Farrakhan's defense in the court of public opinion.

Prince, Michael Jackson and Whitney Houston are arguably the most popular and highest earning artists in music history. Their celebrity power looms so large even after their death that it is hard to quantify. Yet one of the most unspoken of things that they all have in common is their close relationship with the most controversial Black man in America-the **Honorable Minister Louis Farrakhan.** Michael Jackson was a friend of Minister Farrakhan who also sought out the Minister for wise counsel and advice. He donated more than $100, 000 to the Million Man March. Over the years he felt comfortable and safe during critical moments of his career due to his usage of Nation of Islam security personnel. Whitney Houston and Bobby Brown were also supporters of Minister Farrakhan's work. They utilized Nation of Islam security personnel and made a public appearance at the Million Family March in the year 2000 to show their support for the Minister and his call to strengthen the Black family.

These high-profile celebrities all died at relatively young ages and all with mysterious circumstances. Their unusual deaths have fed countless "conspiracy theories" in the minds of many within the Black community. Yet the one real and credible thing that would have angered the most powerful in the music and entertainment industry-and therefore offer legitimacy to a conspiracy theory- is their sharing of their celebrity status with the Honorable Minister Louis Farrakhan.

At this point the reader must be made aware of a denial objective and strategy that was proposed and carried out by the notorious and nefarious group called the ADL. The Anti-Defamation League of B'Nai B'rith has made it one of their top priorities to "dog the trail" of the Honorable Minister Louis Farrakhan with falsehoods and slander to destroy the character and reputation of our beloved Minister. They really want him dead.

In 1994 the ADL drafted a briefing paper called ***Mainstreaming Anti-Semitism: The Legitimation of Louis Farrakhan*** wherein they lamented that "mainstream" Black leaders and organizations were embracing their own Black brother-the Honorable Minister Louis Farrakhan. Written by Steven Freeman in January of 1994, the document begins by noting that

> "Minister Louis Farrakhan, leader of the Nation of Islam (NOI) and long a voice of religious intolerance and racial divisiveness in this country, has recently **attained a new level of acceptance** among certain mainstream Black organizations and leaders. His "legitimation" has been reflected most notably by his participation last summer in the Parliament of the World's Religions, his obtaining federal funds for NOI's anti-AIDS efforts and the security services it has been providing at several federal housing projects, and his warm reception at the annual legislative meeting of the Congressional Black Caucus (CBC) last fall....the black community in this country is wrestling with a desperate crisis situation in our inner cities--and when Farrakhan's NOI is arguably filling a void for that community... "

Spectacularly after acknowledging that Minister Farrakhan and the Nation of Islam *fill a void in the crisis stricken Black community*, the ADL goes on to propose punishing all in the Black community who would recognize and give support to the good work that the Minister and the Nation of Islam provided! In coded language Freeman writes:

> "What we can and should do is **impose an obligation** on those who deal with him, or, as in the case of universities, give him a platform."

I ask the question, is the ADL plot to punish (***impose and obligation on***) popular celebrities and leaders who "legitimate" Minister Louis Farrakhan connected to the untimely demise of Prince, Michael Jackson and Whitney Houston?

16

I believe that it is at the root of the mystery and secrecy and shocking departure from life of these magnificent entertainers who were magnets for public affection and adoration. The forces who control the world of entertainment are largely of the Jewish community. Neal Gabler wrote a book about the Jewish influence in the world of entertainment from its very start called **An Empire of Their Own: How Jews Invented Hollywood**. Jewish hegemony of Black talent has been a longstanding reality. It is easy to see that their watchdog group, the ADL, signals to their Hollywood brethren those whom should be deemed *persona non-grata*. So, they didn't want Prince's fans and Whitney's fans and Michael's fans to simultaneously become Farrakhan fans.

In one sense persons, such as Prince, Michael Jackson, Whiney Houston and even Bill Cosby are like Lazarus was in the Bible. Lazarus was a man that Jesus impacted in a mighty way. Jesus raised Lazarus from the dead. And according to the New Testament scriptures, many people began to believe in Jesus because of Lazarus. So, the Jewish Sanhedrin determined that they must crucify Jesus and that they must also crucify Lazarus.

> "Meanwhile a large crowd of Jews found out that Jesus was there and came, not only because of him but also to see Lazarus, whom he had raised from the dead. So, the chief priests made plans to kill Lazarus as well, for on account of him many of the Jews were going over to Jesus and believing in him."
> -John 12: 9-11

The modern Sanhedrin (Jewish leadership) hate the fact that Blacks and Black groups that they either fund, control or influence would develop and affinity and public relationship with Minister Louis Farrakhan. For each time a prominent Black celebrity or Black organization embraces Minister Farrakhan, a door is opened for the Minister to access and influence the fans of that celebrity and the members of that organization. The Minister's strong message of truth among the masses of Black people is considered a feared contagion by Jewish groups who have long situated themselves within the Black community for the purposes of control and exploitation.

In another sense, the Minister's celebrity friends and acquaintances have been like the enchanters of Pharaoh. Pharaoh's enchanters were workers in his employ whom he used to cast a spell over the people. But over time and after certain proofs had been made manifest to them they, against the will of Pharaoh, expressed a belief in the God of Moses and Aaron. This caused Pharaoh to promise to crucify them for their disobedience.

> "So the enchanters fell down prostrate, saying: We believe in the Lord of Aaron and Moses. (Pharaoh) said: You believe in him before I give you leave! Surely he is your chief who taught you enchantment. So, I shall cut off your hands and your feet on opposite sides and I shall crucify you on the trunks of palm-trees, and you shall certainly know which of us can give the severer and the more abiding chastisement."
> -Holy Qur'an 20:70-71

Again, we see the scripture's portrayal of a powerful ruler or ruling class react in violent condemnation to those whom they have controlled and used when they come under the influence of one who is considered dangerous and threatening to the continued rule of the powerful, yet wicked, rulers.

This has played out in the life of the Honorable Minister Louis Farrakhan when high-profile, prominent Black people (or those of other races) have dared to share a platform with him, give him accolades or be associated with him in any way. They are made to recant or do something to show their condemnation of the Minister. If they refuse to condemn the Minister or persist in having a relationship with him they are threatened with the crucifixion of their reputations which in the case of athletes and entertainers is a direct threat to their ability to earn a living. For a politician, it can be political suicide to publicly support or embrace Minister Farrakhan.

Rev. Jesse Jackson Sr. was forced to repudiate the Minister when the Minister was serving as surrogate speaker for him in the early 1980s.

> Jesse L. Jackson yesterday denounced as "reprehensible and morally indefensible" Nation of Islam leader Louis Farrakhan's most recent

18

controversial comments on Jews and supporters of Israel, amid swelling criticism of Farrakhan by Democratic and Republican leaders, including Vice President Bush.

"Such statements and thoughts have no place in my own thinking or in this campaign, and I call upon all of my supporters to join me in speaking out in support of my stand," Jackson said in a statement issued by his Democratic presidential campaign advisers here as he was winding up his trip to Cuba and Central America.

"I will not permit Minister Farrakhan's words, wittingly or unwittingly, to divide the Democratic Party. Neither anti-Semitism nor anti-black statements have any place in our party," he said.

Jackson has been under intense criticism from prominent Democrats and Jewish leaders for his failure to repudiate Farrakhan, his one-time political associate, since the remarks in a speech broadcast last Sunday. Jackson's fellow presidential candidates, Walter F. Mondale, the prospective nominee, and Sen. Gary Hart (D-Colo.), were under similar pressure.

Jackson's campaign manager, Arnold Pinkney, said he and other advisers told Jackson by telephone yesterday that they had concluded that the controversy enveloping him "would not go away" unless such a statement was issued.

Farrakhan, meanwhile, said "a rebuke by my brother" would be "well worth it" if the repudiation permitted Jackson "to go to the Democratic National convention and represent the 85 percent of the black vote that he earned and represent the locked-out of the Democratic Party."

(Jackson Denounces Farrakhan: Martin Schram, Milton Coleman and Washington Post Staff Writers; staff researcher Maralee Schwartz contributed to this report June 29, 1984, WASHINGTON POST)

Bruce Willis was forced to recant kind words that he said about the Minister in 1996.

Good thing Bruce Willis got survival training in those *Die Hard* movies because the action hero has wandered into a minefield.

The movie star today sought to distance himself from a controversial *George* magazine profile in which *The Last Boy Scout* popped off about politics, in general, and Nation of Islam leader Louis Farrakhan, in particular.

"Unfortunately, what I said to *George* magazine was taken entirely out of context," Willis said in a statement.

"Never was it my intention to aggravate, insult or hurt anyone. Please understand that once I say something, I have no control over how a publication will run that material."

A spokesperson for *George* said the John F. Kennedy Jr.-edited magazine stands by its reporting.

Willis, 43, has a vested interest in not ticking off too many people this summer.

His latest big-budget movie, *Armageddon*, opens July 1.

The actor's recantation comes a day after the Anti-Defamation League shot off a letter to the actor, taking exception with his much-publicized *George* rant: "I'll tell you something, if I were black, I'd be with Farrakhan, too."

Added Willis, in the magazine: "A lot of people feel Louis Farrakhan stands for a lot of negative things. But he is raising his voice against inequality. Anyone who stands up against injustice is a hero of mine."

(Bruce Willis Backs Away from Farrakhan: Joal Ryan, June 18, 1998, E! NEWS)

Senator Barack Obama was forced to condemn the Minister during his run for the presidency by Hilary Clinton in 2008.

Sen. Barack Obama denounced the recent support for his candidacy expressed Sunday by controversial minister and Nation of Islam leader Louis Farrakhan.

"I have been very clear in my denunciation" of Farrakhan's history of anti-Semitic remarks, Obama said at the Democratic debate in Cleveland, "I did not solicit his support." Obama said he "cannot censor" individual endorsements but said there is no affiliation with his campaign and Farrakhan. "I can't say to somebody that he can't say that he thinks I'm a good guy," Obama said, citing his support among Jewish Americans and stating that he would make it a priority to soothe historically tense ties between the African-American and Jewish communities in the nation. "I have some of the strongest support from the Jewish community in my hometown of Chicago and in this campaign," he said, describing himself as a "stalwart" on supporting Israel.

Sen. Hillary Clinton suggested Obama's comments weren't good enough, citing her own record of rejecting controversial support in her 2000 Senate bid. "There's a difference between denouncing and rejecting," she countered, "And I made it very clear that I did not want their support, I rejected it," she said, "I would not be associated with people" that make such comments.

Obama quickly responded. "I'm happy to concede the point and I would reject and denounce," he said. "Good, good," replied Clinton. **(Obama Denounces Farrakhan Endorsement: Editor, Susan Davis, February 26, 2008, WALL ST. JOURNAL)**

NBA star and world Champion Craig Hodges's relationship with Minister Farrakhan was seen as a primary reason why the league leading 3-point shooter was not re-signed by the Bulls after a championship season in 1992.

It seems appropriate then to consider the case of the Federal lawsuit recently filed in Chicago: Craig Hodges vs. the National Basketball Association, in which Hodges said that "the owners and operators of the 29 N.B.A. member franchises have participated as co-conspirators" in "blackballing" Hodges from the league "because of his outspoken political nature as an African-American man."

In 1992, after 10 seasons in the N.B.A., Craig Hodges, at age 32, was not re-signed by the team he had played with for the previous four seasons, the Chicago Bulls, who had just won their second straight championship. Hodges had been a backup shooting guard for the Bulls, and was still considered one of the better 3-point shooters in the league.

When the team went to the White House after an invitation from President Bush, Hodges wore a dashiki, and handed the President a letter that asked him to do more to end injustice toward the African-American community.

The lawsuit alleges that the incident embarrassed the N.B.A. It alleges that Hodges's work to curb "the breakdown of the African-American family" with Louis Farrakhan and the Nation of Islam was also seen as inimical by the N.B.A. As was Hodges's public criticism of "African-American professional athletes who failed to use their considerable wealth and influence to assist the poor and disenfranchised."

Hodges, meanwhile, was fired two weeks ago as the head coach at Chicago State University, as he seemed to be giving more time to his lawsuit and community affairs than to campus duties while his team went 8-51 in a little more than two seasons.

"After the 1992 season," Hodges said, "I or my agent had called every team in the N.B.A. and not one would even give me a tryout, let alone sign me."

The Bulls didn't re-sign him, according to one team official who asked for anonymity, "because he was on his last legs as a player."

"He couldn't guard a post," the official said, "and everyone knew it." In his last season for the Bulls, Hodges played in only 53 of the team's 82 regular-season games. The Bulls signed Trent Tucker, a better defender than Hodges and a higher percentage 3-point shooter.

"I thought we improved ourselves there," said Phil Jackson, the Bulls' coach. "I had the highest regard for Craig, though. He was a great team player, never caused any problems and I respected his views. I'm a spiritual man, and so is he. But I also found it strange that not a single team called to inquire about him. Usually, I get at least one call about a player we've decided not to sign. And yes, he couldn't play much defense, but a lot of guys in the league can't, but not many can shoot from his range, either."

(The Case of Hodges Vs. the N.B.A.: Ira Berkow, December 25, 1996, NEW YORK TIMES)

And who can forget the subject of many a barbershop, beauty salon conversations over the ending of the **Arsenio Hall** show. Arsenio told VLAD TV that he had actually resigned long before he booked Minister Farrakhan on his show. He actually desired to take time away from the grueling schedule of his Late Night show to be a better father to his son. But Jewish groups pounced upon him and expressed their fears that the huge platform of Arsenio would be used to "legitimize" the Minister.

> The scheduled appearance tonight of Nation of Islam leader Louis Farrakhan on "The Arsenio Hall Show" has sparked protests from religious and gay organizations who fear Farrakhan will be given an uncontested forum to put forth his controversial views on whites, Jews and gays.
>
> The Simon Wiesenthal Center has urged KCOP-TV Channel 13 and other stations around the country not to broadcast the program. Rabbi Abraham Cooper, associate dean of the Los Angeles-based center, said in a letter to the stations that "we do not believe that an entertainer hosting an entertainment program should provide Louis Farrakhan a comfortable, cozy and legitimizing platform at a time when Farrakhan and his followers are busy spreading their divisive rhetoric."
>
> The Anti-Defamation League, the L.A. Gay and Lesbian Community Services Center, the Catholic League for Religious and Civil Rights and the Gay and Lesbian Alliance Against Defamation/L.A. also criticized the appearance in a full-page ad in Thursday's Daily Variety. **(Farrakhan Appearance on 'Arsenio' Sparks Furor: Greg Braxton, February 25, 1994, L.A. TIMES)**

And many believe the current "astro-turf" led campaign to destroy the reputation and legacy of Bill Cosby is because of his praise of Minister Farrakhan's Black Muslims in his 2013 Op-ed piece for the New York Post.

This book is designed to refute the wicked charges of the ADL and SPLC and all who besmirch the noble name and person of the Honorable Minister Louis Farrakhan. It is also an encouragement for the prominent members of society to unite and tell the truth about our beloved Minister.

For in as much as Minister Farrakhan can be viewed in the light of great historical Black champions of our people's liberation. The clearest light to see him is in the light of scripture. And based on his strong opposition by Jewish groups, his visage is strongly resembling of Jesus in the Bible.

Thusly, this book is aimed at interfering with the plan to crucify the Minister's character. Especially as we see and understand that character assassination of this type is the preliminary stages of physical assassination.

It is an assembly of those who have been so impacted by him that their true, honest and unprovoked feelings forced their own testimonies that reveal Farrakhan as a good man, a noble man, a man of high morals and a man of spiritual ability and prowess.

In the face of these powerful testimonies, the court of public opinion must vindicate the Minister and allow him to teach unhindered and unbothered.

Demetric Muhammad, November 6, 2016

Foreword to First Edition

Brother Demetric Muhammad through the written word and visual presentation has provided us with powerful insight into the impact of the words, work, sacrifice and humility of the Honorable Minister Louis Farrakhan. His skillful weaving together of the recorded testimony of those who have openly opposed Minister Farrakhan and the Nation of Islam as well as others who admire and love him is one of the finest defenses of Truth anyone could develop. For those who only know Minister Farrakhan through second-hand sources, sound-bites, propaganda and half-truths, *Who Do They Say I Am: The Vindication of Minister Louis Farrakhan* not only clears up misinformation, it also provides a path directly into the *heart* of a human being who has touched every walk of life.

The Most Honored Elijah Muhammad wrote that the religious class and those most educated and accomplished in this world would be most opposed to his work of the resurrection of Black and oppressed people in America, the Western Hemisphere and all over the world, *yet* a critical mass of these *same* persons would eventually be persuaded by His Message and provide some of the greatest help possible to further and establish it during an especially dark hour.

As this prediction becomes manifestly true it is important that we understand the evolution of the conflicted thinking of such persons - initially blinded out of ignorance and genuine misunderstanding or envy, jealousy and vanity – but who are now able to see Minister Farrakhan more and more as Allah (God) and His Christ do; an essential man standing as both bridge and door between two worlds. As more and more of the brightest 'stars' of this world look up to Minister Farrakhan it paves the way for those who follow them to do the same. *Who Do They Say I Am: The Vindication of Minister Louis Farrakhan* uniquely chronicles and displays aspects of the hidden and secret thinking at work in all of us who wrestle with finding a balance between our hopes and fears and the consequences of our choices on ourselves, our families, our professional lives and our status in society. Many of us it seems, could and would accept Minister Farrakhan, if only we could overcome our fear of loss.

Allah (God) says in the Holy Qur'an, **"Never did We send a Warner to a population but the wealthy ones among them said: 'We believe not in the (Message) with which ye have been sent.'"** Certainly, it is those who have been blessed with the wealth of finance; the wealth of knowledge; and the wealth of ability who are often slowest to respond to the message of truth. But when they finally do - their belief, hard work and pursuit of righteousness provides one of the most powerful forms of witness on behalf of both the Message and the Messenger. This wonderful book is but a snapshot of this phenomenon as well as the confluence of forces which produce it.

As one who has picked up his cross, as a disciple of Christ, Minister Farrakhan in lifting up His Teacher, has unintentionally moved to the core of a magnetic process, as it reads in the Book of John, "And I, if I be lifted up from the earth, will draw all men unto me." In compiling *Who Do They Say I Am: The Vindication of Minister Louis Farrakhan* Student Minister Demetric Muhammad is assisting in this process, described in I Peter 3:15, "…Always be prepared to give an answer to everyone who asks you to give the reason for the hope that you have. But do this with gentleness and respect." His approach not only brings to clear view the fire and courage of Minister Farrakhan in defending the truth but also the gentleness and respect which characterizes his treatment of people, regardless of their creed, class and color. And understanding *both* the words and character of Minister Farrakhan are an essential part of God's merciful plan of salvation, which requires courage and patient perseverance through much suffering.

The Honorable Elijah Muhammad taught that the worst famine in history was coming to America. As his National Representative, Minister Farrakhan has been the foremost instrument of God in the extension of this Warning. In the 105th Psalms it reads, "*He called down famine on the land and destroyed all their supplies of food; and he sent a man before them— Joseph, sold as a slave. They bruised his feet with shackles, his neck was put in irons, till what he foretold came to pass, till the word of the LORD proved him true. The king sent and released him, the ruler of peoples set him free. He made him master of his household, ruler over all he possessed, to instruct his princes as he pleased and teach his elders wisdom.*" This book of witness - *Who Do They Say I Am: The Vindication of Minister Louis Farrakhan* - represents overwhelming evidence of this work in progress – the spiritual ascent and elevation of Minister Farrakhan in the minds of *both* the classes and the masses - in fulfillment of one of the most important prophecies in all of divine scripture.

Allah (God) says in the Holy Qur'an in part, "**Ye have indeed in the Messenger of Allah a beautiful pattern (of conduct) for any one whose hope is in Allah and the Final Day, and who engages much in the Praise of Allah.**" In Part 28 of his 'The Time and What Must Be Done' series, Minister Farrakhan revealed that when he was last in the Holy City of Medina - at the Mosque and Tomb of Prophet Muhammad (Peace Be Upon Him) - he uttered a prayer to Allah (God) that he be given a *double* portion of the spirit of Muhammad.

The moving testimony contained within *Who Do They Say I Am: The Vindication of Minister Louis Farrakhan* indicates that the Lord of The Worlds both heard and answered the prayer of this Servant of God.

There can only be a Divine explanation for what you are about to read.

Brother Cedric Muhammad
July 31, 2013

Brother Cedric Muhammad is an economist and economic advisor to the African Union. He is a member of the Nation of Islam Research Group and founder of Blackelectorate.com and AfricaPreBrief.com. He is the author of the excellent 3 volume series of books entitled The Entrepreneurial Secret.

Preface to First Edition
Allah (God) bears witness to his Messenger

"When the hypocrites come to thee, they say: We bear witness that thou art indeed Allah's messenger. **And Allah knows thou art indeed His Messenger.** *And Allah bears witness that the hypocrites are surely liars."*
(Al-Munafiqun: The Hypocrites. Chapter 63, verse 1)

It is a great honor, a humbling experience and profound privilege to be asked by the author, my Brother Demetric Muhammad, to offer my testimony in support of his new scholarship, ***"Who Do They Say I Am? The Vindication of Minister Louis Farrakhan."***

CONTEXT

This statement "Who do they say I am?" arises in the **context** of Jesus talking with his disciples as they were traveling to different areas in Palestine where Jesus performed his many miracles. *(Matthew 16:13-20 KJV)*. It also is the basis for Peter's confession that Jesus is the Christ.

His disciples' answers to the question were varied. But the question is, "Why did Jesus have to ask his disciples who do they, the people, say I am?" Jesus performed many miracles; cleansing the leper, healing the woman with the issue of blood, and raising Lazarus from the dead. He would often tell those that he healed to not speak of it. Why? What did Jesus know about the talk that was circulating about him, that he wanted see if his disciples were aware. He also wanted to know how they saw him.

Many of the Jewish sects of that day, the scribes and Pharisees were attempting to trap Jesus into saying something that would violate Roman law, and thus cause him to be brought up on false charges., especially the charge of sedition which was ultimately leveled against him. Jesus hearing them and knowing their thoughts would never be trapped by their skillful and deceptive questions. So, his enemies began circulating among the people to create a false reputation of Jesus and his good works. The Bible speaks of this in the Book of Revelations as the Serpent casting out of his mouth water as a flood after the woman (the Messenger of God), that he might cause her to be carried away of the flood. *(Rev. 12:15 KJV)*

When Jesus was falsely charged with sedition, speaking and acting against the authority of Rome, and mockingly charged with saying that he was the "king of the Jews" none of his disciples came forward to defend him. In fact, the disciples denied him before the courts of Pontius Pilate.

The wicked frame mischief by means of the law. It is always the tactic, strategy and method of the wicked to create false charges. To use the law falsely against the prophets and Messengers of God. Because the wicked fear the people, who have a view of the Messenger as a man of great character and reputation, the wicked must first destroy the character and good reputation of the Messenger of God in the minds of the people.

This is so, that when they bring the Messenger of God before their courts with their false charges, the people will believe the false charges to be true and not rise up to oppose the unrighteous acts of the wicked and their government.

These events and circumstances of the past, in the time of Jesus, are unfolding today in our time, regarding the modern scribes and Pharisees and the modern example of Jesus today in the person of the Hon. Minister Louis Farrakhan. If we carefully studied scriptural history that we have shared a portion of in this writing, and overlay the facts and circumstances of yesterday with today, you will clearly see the same pattern. This is why such a book is necessary, because today the disciples should not deny the good character and reputation of a man who has given us all spiritual life. We must come forward to defend God's anointed servant, as it is our salvation to do so. Jesus was silent in the face of his accusers, because the trial was not really his, the trial was ours.

This book is purposed to present an answer to the question, who do the people say that Farrakhan is? Since at least 1984, the Hon. Minister Louis Farrakhan has been falsely charged by the modern scribes and Pharisees, the Synagogue of Satan, with being mad, anti-Semitic, anti-white, homophobic, and a hater. Nothing could be further from the Truth.

The wicked have spewed their negative flood of propaganda against the Hon. Minister Louis Farrakhan for the last 29 years through the mass media of publications and broadcasting that they have an inordinate ownership and control over. This book will help the earth (the people) to open their mouths, and swallow the flood, the negative and false propaganda of the synagogue of Satan against the anointed servant of Allah (God), the Hon. Minister Louis Farrakhan. *(Rev. 12:16 KJV)*. The aim of these wicked acts on the part of the Synagogue of Satan are to destroy the good name, good character, and good reputation of the Hon. Minister Louis Farrakhan in the minds of the people. This is so, when they use their courts of law to bring false charges against the Hon. Minister Louis Farrakhan and the Nation of Islam, their hope is that there will be no outcry against this wickedness by the people whom they fear.

CHARACTER AND REPUTATION

What is character and what is reputation? Character is defined as *the aggregate of features and traits that form the individual nature of some person or thing, moral or ethical quality, qualities of honesty, courage, or the like; integrity.* This definition perfectly fits the character of the Hon. Minister Louis Farrakhan. The Holy Quran defends the character of the Messenger by stating that the Messenger has sublime morals. *(Al-Qalam: The Pen: Chapter 68, verse 4)*.

My venerable evidence professor and dean from law school taught us that in a court of law, especially in the criminal context, character evidence is really not evidence of a person's character at all. Character is an intrinsic trait, such that only God, and maybe the person, actually knows the character of the self.

He taught us that it is actually testimony about the reputation of the person that is offered to give an indication of what the character of the individual may be.

Reputation is defined as the *estimation in which a person or thing is held, especially by the community or the public generally.* Thus, the Synagogue of Satan works in this area to slander and defame the good name and reputation of the Messenger of God in the minds of people. This they have attempted to accomplish against the Honorable Minister Louis Farrakhan up to the very minute of the writing of this testimony.

They have not been successful, and they will not be successful. As the Holy Qur'an teaches, the Messenger of Allah (God) is an excellent example for any believer who hopes in Allah and the latter day, and remembers Allah much. *(Al-Ahzab: The Allies: Chapter 33 verse 21)*.

The reputation of the Hon. Minister Louis Farrakhan is as different as the night is from the day, and as far away as the Sun is from the planet Pluto, depending upon who you talk with. Among the people whom he is anointed to serve, which is black people, and all oppressed people and humanity itself, he is seen as a man of truth, a lover of humanity, one who speaks truth to power, and hates the wicked actions not only of Satan and his Synagogue, but also those of us who may individually engage in wicked practices, regardless to creed or class or color. He is first and foremost a lover of Almighty God and His Truth, and the Mission of His Messenger Messiah. He loves his people, which he has demonstrated by sacrificing his life to see human beings made better. The Bible teaches us that no greater love than this, that a man would lay down his life for his friends. *(John 15:13)*. The Minister has proved this to see us free, justified and equal, and to return humanity back to the oneness of Allah (God).

He proves among us each day the bible's teachings, that you should love god with all your heart, soul, mind and strength and love your neighbor as yourself. These are the two great commandments given by Jesus to his disciples. *(Matt. 22:37-40)*

THE REBUILDING

It is necessary that we retrace our footsteps, and review the demonstration of the good character and reputation of the Hon. Minister Louis Farrakhan, as well as some of the attacks of the wicked. In hopes that we will not continue to make mistakes in our understanding and view of Allah (God's) blessing to us by his presence among us. The Most Honorable Elijah Muhammad said that History is best qualified to reward our research. It develops the springs and motives of Human Conduct. If our conduct and behavior is to be rightly guided, then the scripture teaches us "how can they know, except they have a teacher, and how can they have a teacher except he be sent" *(Rom. 10:14-15)*

During the first or second week of September 1977, the scales fell from the Hon. Minister Louis Farrakhan's eyes, and he accepted the assignment to rebuild the work of the Hon. Elijah Muhammad, as scripture prophesied he would.

Jesus had prayed for Peter, that his faith would not fail him altogether, and when he returned to Christ, then he should go and strengthen his brethren. *(Luke 22:31-32).*

The Hon. Elijah Muhammad promised the Minister that *"there will be two backing you up Brother, Allah and Myself."* The journey that led to this event in September of 1977 involves Bro. Akbar Muhammad and Bro. Jabril Muhammad, among others. Both men have magnificent testimonies on these events. I have heard the Hon. Minister Louis Farrakhan relate some of these events, however the beauty and magnificence of Allah (God) working in and through his anointed servant, requires an exactness of recitation that will require further research and exploration. Of course, the Hon. Minister Louis Farrakhan is best at explaining the actual facts of those events

For seven years, the Hon. Minister Louis Farrakhan traveled throughout America, and especially among the youth on college campuses to reestablish the teachings of the Hon. Elijah Muhammad. In 1979 I became one of those college students that he met and taught as I went to see him at Coppin State teacher's college in Baltimore Maryland.

The Minister would not do interviews with the media. He shared with me that the Hon. Elijah Muhammad taught him that when a seed is germinating in the earth, that it sends its roots down deep into the earth, long before it sends a reed up through the earth. And even though the reed may look weak, it is firmly rooted in the earth. The Hon. Minister Louis Farrakhan worked quietly like this building study groups among college students and in individual homes. There would be several study groups studying the teachings of the Hon. Elijah Muhammad in the same city and they would not know the existence of each other. This led to our first Saviours' Day in the Rebirth of the Nation of Islam.

Although it is commonly believed that the Most Honorable Elijah Muhammad is physically dead, The Honorable Minister Louis Farrakhan declared in his first Saviours' Day Message in the rebuilding of the Nation of Islam on February 22, 1981 at the Auditorium Theater in Chicago before thousands of persons, that the Honorable Elijah Muhammad was physically alive, and that He had escaped a death plot, and was with His Sender Master Fard Muhammad on the Wheel. A giant mechanical object that the Honorable Elijah Muhammad said fulfilled Ezekiel's vision of a wheel within a wheel. *(Ezekiel1:1-28)*

The Honorable Minister Louis Farrakhan though vilified, maligned, and evil spoken of, even by his own people, for his assertion that he believed that the Honorable Elijah Muhammad was in fact alive, traveled the Country on a 43-city speaking tour, teaching on the spiritual subjects "The Time and What Must be Done" and "In Christ, All Things Are Possible".

In 1983 the Honorable Minister Louis went on another speaking tour entitled, 'Christ's Imminent Return: He Makes All Things New". Many of these teachings were at Christian Churches, which surprised many Christians who assumed that Muslims did not believe in Jesus Christ. In 1984, The Honorable Minister Louis Farrakhan announced his support for the Presidential Candidacy of the Reverend Jesse L. Jackson, Sr. When Rev. Jesse Jackson embraced Yassir Arafat and the struggle of the Palestinian people, he began to receive death threats from some Jewish groups.

When the Minister warned certain members of the Jewish community about the consequences of their death threats against the life of Reverend Jackson, he was called a Black Hitler. When he defended himself against such false charges, the wicked scribes (which are the writers and broadcasters of the press) falsely accused the Minister of praising Hitler and later also falsely accused the Minister of calling Judaism a "gutter religion". In 1985, after his address at the Forum in Los Angeles before 19,000 people, the cry among the members of the Jewish community was that they wanted The Honorable Minister Louis Farrakhan dead.

MORE THAN A VISION

It was in this murderous climate that after his speech he left Los Angeles and went into Mexico, and there he and his wife Mother Khadijah were in a hotel in Tepoztlan, where he had on many occasions climbed the mountain and visited a temple built on top of that mountain in honor of Quetzalcoatl the Christ figure of Mezzo America or Central America. On the night of September 17th 1985 he had a *"more than a vision experience,"* and in that experience he was transported to the Wheel by a little baby plane that singled him out from among a group of persons, and took him to the Mother Wheel where he was ushered into a room. He saw a scroll roll down in front of him with cursive writing and when he went to read the writing it disappeared and then he heard the voice of his Teacher, the Most Honorable Elijah Muhammad telling him of plans made by the President and his joint Chiefs of Staff in early September 1985, that the President (Reagan) had planned a war. The Minister was never told where the war would be, or who it would be against, but he was told in that communication to hold a Press Conference and make the President's plan known. The Hon. Elijah Muhammad instructed the Minister as follows; *"and tell them, you got it from me, Elijah Muhammad on the Wheel."* The Minister was then told by the Hon. Elijah Muhammad, that he had one more thing to do, and when that was completed, he could come again to the Wheel where he would be allowed to see him face to face.

When the Minister awakened, he did not remember this experience and it wasn't until an earthquake hit Mexico City on September 19[th]that affected Tepoztlan that his experience on the night of September 17th came back to him and he shared it for the first time with his wife Mother Khadijah and Mother Tynetta Muhammad, the wife of the Honorable Elijah Muhammad.

Fresh from that experience, the Minister went to New York City to hold our first Saviours' Day in honor of the birth of the Most Honorable Elijah Muhammad, on October 7, 1985, where 50,000 people tried to get into Madison Square Garden to hear the Honorable Minister Louis Farrakhan. Every seat was taken and even the aisles had people in them and the adjunct building the Felt Forum was filled, and 20,000 more people were in the streets trying to get in to hear the message. Once again the climate of hate created by the Anti-Defamation League (ADL), and the Jewish Defense League (JDL) and the press, incited protesters from the Jewish Defense League who were chanting in frenzy, "Who do you want?" Farrakhan! "How Do You Want Him? Dead!

In December 1985, the Minister started his first World Friendship Tour in the Virgin Islands, he went to Jamaica, Barbados and from Barbados to Panama where he was rejected in several hotels, due to Jewish pressure. He was banned from traveling to Bermuda, the island where his mother grew up and where his grandmother and grandfather are buried. That ban was subsequently lifted by the work of Minister Byron Muhammad known as Hamid Abdullah. The Minister was also banned from the United Kingdom (England) and that ban still exists today.

In Panama Brother Minister Akbar Muhammad, our International Representative had made reservations at the Marriott Hotel and they were rejected; they were rejected at a second hotel, and at a third hotel reservations were made under an alias, but when the Hotel found out that it was the Minister and his delegation, they were asked to leave but refused. This happened because of the hatred that was falsely projected against him by the Synagogue of Satan, which had been spread throughout the world.

The Honorable Minister Louis Farrakhan went on to speak in Panama in Colon and from there he went to Honduras, and while he was in Belize City, President Ronald Reagan came on television and issued an executive order that stopped all Americans from traveling to and doing business with Libya. The Executive Order also directed that any American traveling to Libya would be fined and sentenced up to 10 years in federal prison.

The Honorable Minister Louis Farrakhan then came back to the United States to prepare for the second leg of the journey and in early February 1986 he was visited by Kwame Ture (formerly known as Stokely Carmichael) and he asked the Minister if he would hold a Press Conference at the National Press Club in Washington D.C. where there were 15 groups that would stand with him to say *"hands off Libya."* The Minister agreed and flew to Washington and wrote the speech that he would give at the National Press Club which was approved by Kwame Ture and four other groups that were willing to stand with The Minister during that time in delivering this speech. At the press conference as the Minister saw all of the camera's bright lights flashing in the back of the room, it reminded him of his experience. And it crystalized for him that the war was against Libya and its Leader Muammar Gadhafi.

Notwithstanding the Executive order banning travel to Libya, the Hon. Minister Louis Farrakhan showing his character and courage, went to Libya, and based upon his *"more than a vision experience"* shared his belief that President Reagan planned attack Libya. This saved the life of President Muammar Gadhafi, when President Reagan bombed Libya in 1986. The Attorney General of the United States, Edwin Meese in a news article, threatened to arrest the Minister on his return to the United States. A law firm hired by the Nation under the direction of Attorney Ava Muhammad filed a lawsuit against President Reagan and his Secretary of State George Schultz, and Attorney General Edwin Meese. The government backed away from their claim to arrest the Minister and the court dismissed the case.

Also during this period in the late 1980's President Reagan, as a staunch anti-communist, felt that Nicaragua could not fall to a socialist regime, and since Congress had not allocated any of the tax payer's money, to fund opposition against a socialist regime coming to power, he went around Congress to fight the war. Saudi Arabia gave financial assistance to the Reagan Administration to fund a War against the Contras. It was also during the Reagan administration, that a counter Whitehouse was set up in the basement by Col. Oliver North to sell drugs among black people in the Ghettos of America to fund the War in Nicaragua.

During this time in History, tens of thousands were flocking to hear the message of the Honorable Minister Louis Farrakhan. Why was this War waged by an American Administration in Nicaragua significant? It is because every time there is a major rising of the consciousness in the Black Community, it is followed by the introduction of drugs into the community. The money generated from this government run drug trafficking enterprise in the Black Community was used to fund the War in Nicaragua. In the 1960's there was Heroin introduced into the black community as a response to the rise of Consciousness and militancy among Black people. This was primarily due to the teachings of the Hon. Elijah Muhammad and his principal student Malcolm X. In the 1980's there was crack cocaine. This was the beginning of the crack cocaine epidemic that swept the West Coast through our unknowing Brother "Freeway" Rick Ross. And just as opium was used to drug the Chinese and bring silver out of China, the same strategy has been used here to rob the Black community of 400 billion dollars generated by our Black economy by bringing crack in the U.S. and taking money out of the Black community to finance a war in Central America. This

36

epidemic swept through the Ghettos of America like a cancer, and we saw the emergence of the "New Jack City" era.

From 1984 on the Minister was under vicious assault by some in the Jewish community who were bitterly angry with Him for his defense of the Reverend Jesse Jackson. He was referred to by them as a "Black Hitler," which made members of the Jewish community afraid, and of the mind that a new Hitler had to be dealt with before he became powerful.

It is also interesting that the 17th Chapter of the Holy Qur'an is called the Israelites and on the night of the 17th of September the Honorable Minister Louis Farrakhan had his experience, and in this Chapter of the Holy Qur'an it opens referring to the night vision of Prophet Muhammad.

The Minister came to understand that the war planned by the President had two aspects; a Muslim leader and county in the East, but also on this side in America a Muslim Leader with Black American youth. With gang warfare spreading, you had the Crips and the Bloods, and Minister Farrakhan immediately went on tour speaking to Black people about Stop the Killing. After this tour the Minister began the Men's only Meetings.

He was told by a Nigerian, do not do that because the government might think that you are trying to raise an army and this will bring the wrath of the government down upon you. He listened but also remembering the experience on the wheel, he went into major cities speaking to tens and hundreds of thousands of Black men and that inspired the Million Man March.

As the night vision of Prophet Muhammad created division among Muslims. They wanted to know, did he go in reality or was it a vision? This set a division among the Muslims, because it might make people think the Prophet was crazy, silly or mad. So, it is with the Hon. Minister Louis Farrakhan's *more than a vision experience.* There are mixed feelings and controversy around the subject. The Holy Qur'an vindicates the Messenger of God against the false charge that he is mad, and assures him that his reward will never be cut off by the wicked. *(Al-Qalam: The Pen Chapter 86 verses 1-6)*

In 1989 the Hon. Minister Louis Farrakhan held a press conference at the Marriott, Hotel in Washington D.C. In following the instructions of the Hon. Elijah Muhammad, he made the announcement concerning his experience. The Minister warned the Government of America *"that before you can make mockery of me you will see these things [wheels] over major cities."* That night in Washington Fifteen Squadrons of 4 of these Wheels were seen in Washington over the U. S. Capitol and White House, proving the power of Allah (God) that was backing his servant, the Honorable Minister Louis Farrakhan. The Minister was also accompanied by the wheels after his speech in New York.

Every succeeding President has had an altercation with the Muslim World. In his experience the Minister was never given a name, he was told, "the President" and each President has planned some aspect of war with the Muslim World, but the biggest of all at that time was President George W. Bush.

DIVINE WARNER

On May 3rd, 2004, the Honorable Minister Louis Farrakhan, held a press conference at the National Press Club in Washington D.C. entitled "Guidance in A Time of Trouble: To America and the World." At this press conference the Honorable Minister Louis Farrakhan shared with the World, the guidance he shared with President Bush, based on his experience.

What the Honorable Minister Louis Farrakhan told President George W. Bush in his letters of December 1, 2001 and October 30, 2002, is the consequences he would face, if he carried out what Allah (God) had revealed to him was in the mind of President Bush about going to War in Iraq. President Bush did not heed the guidance and ran right into those consequences, and it destroyed his presidency, as he left being considered the worst President in U.S. History.

The Minister has come to understand more deeply the meaning of his *"more than a vision experience."* The experience is such a part of his DNA that every time he has spoken of his experience, he has told it the exact same way. This bears witness to the reality of his experience. It started in the second term of President Ronald Reagan, who has passed away, and his bombing of Libya. From the Minister's *"more than a vision experience"* we have had five Presidents. Mr. Reagan for 8 years, George H. W. Bush for 4 years, William Jefferson Clinton for

8 years, George W. Bush for 8 years, and now President Barack Obama for 5 years. It has been 28 years since The Honorable Minister Louis Farrakhan received this revelation, and the things that he has been able to see from the communication and from the experience that he had on the wheel with the Hon. Elijah Muhammad, is what has led to the Stop the Killing Tours, the Men Only Meetings, and ultimately the Million Man March in 1995, the Million Family March in 2000 and the Millions More Movement in 2005. He saw a war being planned against Black youth, especially the black male in the United States. In 2012 he has led the FOI and MGT back into the streets to save our people from the evil of the genocidal plans against them.

This writer believes that we may be reaching the fulfillment of the meaning of the experience of the Hon. Minister Louis Farrakhan during the Presidency of Barack Obama, and in the revealing of the Synagogue of Satan in the yearlong broadcasts of "The Time and What Must Be Done". The Minister attempted to give guidance to President Obama on his actions in Libya at a press conference on March 31, 2011 at Mosque Maryam. He also warned the U.N. in a press conference on June 15, 2011 at the UN Plaza Hotel about NATO's aggression against the people of Libya based upon the wicked propaganda from our government. Such advice went unheeded which resulted in the death of President Muammar Gadhafi, and the American Ambassador to Libya.

This is some of the record of good works of the Hon. Minister Louis Farrakhan. We must remember, defend and uphold his good character, reputation and morals. Allah (God) has already promised us the victory. Let us always be ready to defend him and the truth that he represents. As the Holy Qur'an tells us of the Hon. Minister Louis Farrakhan in the 53rd Chapter, called *Al-Najm-The Star.*

"In the name of Allah, the Beneficent, the Merciful. By the Star when it sets! Your companion errs not, nor does he deviate. Nor does he speak out of desire. It is naught but revelation that is revealed. One Mighty in Power has taught him. The Lord of Strength. So, he attained to perfection. And he is in the highest part of the horizon. Then he drew near, drew nearer yet, So he was the measure of two bows or closer still. So, He revealed to His servant what He revealed. The heart

was not untrue in seeing what he saw." (Al-Najm: The Star Chapter 53 verses 1-11)

Let us not be untrue to what we see of a man of good character, reputation and morals. He is already vindicated with Allah (God). We should take Allah's coloring.

Abdul Arif Muhammad
August 12, 2013

Abdul Arif Muhammad is a helper of the Hon. Minister Louis Farrakhan, a Student in the Ministry, an attorney, historian, researcher, writer, lecturer and former Editor-in-Chief of The Final Call newspaper. He also serves as General Counsel of the Nation of Islam and is a member of the Nation of Islam Research Group

Introduction to First Edition
Mixed Feelings and Controversy
Examining the Pattern of Reaction to The Ministry of The Honorable Minister Louis Farrakhan As the Struggle Against Prophetic and Revolutionary Magnetism

In the name of Allah, the Beneficent, the Merciful.
(By) the inkstand and the pen and that which they write! By the grace of thy Lord thou art not mad. And surely thine is a reward never to be cut off. And surely thou hast sublime morals. So, thou wilt see, and they (too) will see, Which of you is mad. Surely thy Lord knows best who is erring from His way, and He knows best those who go aright. So, obey not the rejecters. They wish that thou shouldst be pliant, so they (too) would be pliant. And obey not any mean swearer, Defamer, going about with slander, Hinderer of good, outstepping the limits, sinful, Ignoble, besides all that, notoriously mischievous -Surah 68:1-13

It has been such a great joy for me to research, study and reflect over the tremendous life and work of the Honorable Minister Louis Farrakhan during the production of this book. This book began as part of an assignment that I received while serving as a member of Minister Farrakhan's research team. The assignment involved preparing research material that would educate and prepare a small team of Muslim marketing professionals, who would work together to help promote the wide spread distribution of the Honorable Minister Louis Farrakhan's message using modern marketing tools. What I discovered in the process of carrying out that assignment is that there had not been any serious examination of the Minister's impact on groups and persons outside of the Nation of Islam.

At the root of this lack of research emphasis is that The Minister for more than 36 years has been the target of hate filled slander and strategic propaganda coming from various Jewish groups who have an economic interest in opposing the Self-Help message of Minister Farrakhan. Their propaganda and slander against Minister Farrakhan has produced something of a veritable prison of public opinion that the Minister is inside of. And those of us who love The Minister continue to write, educate, inform and otherwise seek to influence

41

public opinion with our own fact-filled counter- narrative to what is widely distributed through the major media sources on behalf of groups who are anti-Farrakhan. But as a member of the Nation of Islam under Minister Farrakhan's direct leadership, it is rather an expected response that I and others would extol the Minister's many virtues and noble character. What is not necessarily expected is those outside of the Nation of Islam's membership expressing love, admiration and respect for such a much maligned man-the man who is affectionately known as "The Minister."

So this book begins with a profound compilation of quotes from an eclectic and diverse group that includes elected officials, celebrities, religious leaders, professors, and journalists whose words and expressions about Minister Farrakhan are not what one might expect, especially if you have only known of The Minister through sound bites and the routinely doctored snippets taken from hours long lectures. This compilation is a very substantial amount of praise, admiration, gratitude, respect and love. It is of such quantity, it causes one to see it as very "weighty" evidence in support of The Minister who is frequently tried in the court of public opinion. These quotes therefore are real testimonies from what we can consider The Minister's character witnesses. This kind of testimony and "witness bearing" is very important. It is so important because it foils the various efforts at the character assassination of The Minister.

The history of both Prophets and Revolutionaries is replete with the recorded attempts of their enemies to assassinate their character. When the corrupt rulers and religious leaders, who are the frequent object of the prophet's and revolutionary's protest and condemnation, can assassinate their character, they then carry out their planned physical assassination with ease. Their muddying the reputation and good name of the Prophets and Revolutionaries ensures that the masses of the people will neither protest nor rise to defend the Prophets and Revolutionaries during the hour of their persecution.

As you read these statements and observations, it will become easy to see that Minister Louis Farrakhan is the inheritor of the legacy, tradition, spirit, mind and will of the scripture's Prophets and history's revolutionaries. He is therefore epitomized in this way; he is unique and special in this way. And in my opinion, Minister Farrakhan's impact, value and character cannot be fully and accurately determined without due consideration of how he, in the most critical of time periods, embodies prophets and revolutionaries. This is critical because Minister Farrakhan represents how the perfect harmony or balance between the sacred and the secular is achieved. What I mean by this is that there are certain human beings who exist as the embodiment of what other human beings who lived long before them desired and expected. These kinds of human beings we could say are born with a pre-determined idea; some would consider them to be "seeds of yearning." The Prophets of religion have often been such persons. The Scientists and Inventors have been such persons. The political Revolutionaries and social reformers have been such persons.

These special individuals fulfill and answer certain problems that existed before them. They fill gaps and voids. Such individuals contain in them what history wanted, what the present needs and what the future will comprised of. They are exemplars, emblems and models.

This aspect of who and what Minister Farrakhan is explains how he is more than a Black leader, great orator and activist religious leader. This aspect of who and what Minister Farrakhan is, also explains why he is more than a prophet or messenger from God and more than a political Revolutionary. He is unique. Perhaps the best historical figure to provide similitude to who and what the Minister Farrakhan is, is the Jesus of the Gospels, who was, according to scholars, both prophet and revolutionary. And like Jesus, Minister Farrakhan proves that the root of the religious prophet and secular (non-religious) revolutionary is the same frustration, exasperation and pain over the present condition of the world and its people--the same ancient universal yearning for balance, perfection and completion. So in Minister Farrakhan we see Jesus, but we also see Nat Turner; we see Muhammad but we also see Martin Luther; we see Aaron, Elisha and Paul, but we also see Garvey, MLK and Brother Malcolm. His leadership therefore eliminates the false choice of "either or;" his is a synthesis that provides for our people "and both," on the question of the secular or the sacred path toward liberation.

In his voice is a characteristic musical and harmonious delivery of mighty truths and profound wisdom. But his messages are not just musical in cadence, tone and effect; the content of his messages harmonize and synthesize the best wisdom of all leaders, sages, prophets, and revolutionaries who lived before him.

This aspect of his role and his ability is in similitude to the book of scripture of the Muslims called the Holy Qur'an. For in the Qur'an is essential truths that have been by Allah (God) revealed so that the Qur'an as the last of the revelatory books, would itself be a harmonious synthesis of the best wisdom and teachings of all scriptures that were revealed before it. And what one hears in the epic and august messages of Minister Farrakhan of the voices and strategies of the best of history's heroes.

So, much of what these "witnesses" have declared regarding The Minister is borne of their examining the very curious phenomenon that The Minister has become. They have examined him through the lens of their profession, their educational background, their race, their political orientation and their hopes and expectations. Their examination of Minister Farrakhan that we have compiled here deserves great study. In the study of the natural world, the field of Chemistry emphasized the study of "reactions." This is of note because human interactions are often described as having "Chemistry" or not having "Chemistry." An old Arab proverb suggests that reactions are of special merit in determining the relative strength or importance of a man. That proverb states that "you don't judge a man by who his friends are, but by who his enemies are." In fact, often are prominent Black people polled and examined to determine if and to what degree they have been affected by what could be termed as the "Farrakhan reagent" that is present in the atmosphere. This occurrence is often referred to as "The Farrakhan Litmus Test." Litmus tests are used in chemical reactions and are defined as being *a coloring material (obtained from lichens) that turns red in acid solutions and blue in alkaline solutions; used as a very rough acid-base indicator.* The idea of The Farrakhan Litmus Test is therefore to identify to what degree has Minister Farrakhan's message and ideas saturated the hearts and minds of the Blacks who occupy prominent positions within American society. It is to determine if such persons have become "acidic" or consciously averse to the reigning idea of "white supremacy" that has ill-effected every institution and every sphere of public and professional life. And all who fail The Farrakhan Litmus Test are forced to pay a price. Many endure and suffer great loss as a result of possessing a favorable opinion of The Honorable Minister Louis Farrakhan. This is a reality that must come to an end!

At this point in my continuing study of what these courageous "witnesses" have provided for us in the way of defending the character and reputation of The Minister, I find a very interesting trend of reactions. It might be considered something of a "moth to a flame" reaction.

Like a moth to a flame, the elite, the mighty, the wealthy and the famous are frequently attracted to the phenomenal presence of the Honorable Minister Louis Farrakhan. Consider the flame for a moment. The source of the flame's attractive power is its warmth, color, light, movement and energy. The flame then, has aesthetics, substance, purpose and a beneficial function. As the moth comes closer it risks becoming consumed by the flame that has so attracted it. In the case of these prominent persons who have examined The Minister, we find a certain excitement and enthusiasm with The Minister's ability to do things that others simply cannot do. Specifically, his ability to accurately identify problems in the Black community and address them in a way no one else can. They admire his ability to attract and draw crowds in the tens of thousands, even at what is considered in today's world, an advanced age. They marvel at how he can reform Black people who have previously been destroyed by the effects of institutional racism and what it produces of self-destructive life-styles. He is regularly cited for his oration and preaching ability that is exceptionally better than any who one would consider as his peers. Some have examined him from a close distance and comment on his humility, sincerity and great appetite for learning. Other are awe-struck over his beautiful appearance and courage to "speak truth to power," for he is the most beautiful of revolutionaries.

Invariably however, these human "moths" feel the need to stay at a safe distance so as not to become fully consumed with The Minister's message and its revolutionary ideas. We find this demonstrated when there are complimentary expressions regarding The Minister mixed with "complain-itory" expressions about The Minister. And this is quite intriguing. For it suggests that who The Minister is and what he says draws and pulls on his examiner on a deep level, but they often feel conflicted internally because what he says and does, that they are naturally drawn to and are affected by, does violence to the ideas and previously held beliefs that they hold on to in their minds. So they are drawn in to him because their heart is in agreement with him; but what is in their head is in opposition to him because their mind has been formed and fashioned by a whole host of life experiences in the hostile American environment where the philosophy of white supremacy and black inferiority continue to dominate the Black American zeitgeist.

So what follows is as much about Minister Farrakhan's great magnetism as it is about prominent and powerful persons wrestling with being magnetically drawn to a man that they are expected to loathe and hate. These mixed feelings surrounding the controversial presence of Minister Louis Farrakhan are similar, and in many instances identical, to the mixed feelings surrounding scripture's prophets.

The prophets were mocked by the "chiefs and leaders" of the people. They were called mad. The Arabic word *majnun* is translated as "mad" in the English translation of the Holy Qur'an. The word *majnun* is from the root word *janna,* which is the same root as the word *jinn*. In Islamic cultures the jinn are believed to be hidden beings who oppose mankind whenever he strays from the path of righteous. The root word *janna* means "to be mad, dark, covered or hidden." This suggests that the prophet's alleged "madness" was coming from a hidden source or that there was much "more than what meets the eye." This is exactly the case where The Minister is concerned. His passion and bold forthright condemnation of racism and injustice do in fact emerge from a hidden source. But that hidden source is not evil or malicious.

Minister Farrakhan has been called anti-Semitic, anti-White, homophobic, anti-American and a teacher of hate. These are all the modern manifestations of the ancient scriptures foretelling and forth telling of the prophets of Allah (God) being labeled as "mad."

Allah (God) Himself is described in the Holy Qur'an as being hidden. In Arabic, Allah's (God's) hiddenness is denoted by the use of the Arabic word *ghaib,* which is oft-times loosely translated as "unseen." And it is the unseen or hidden Allah who raises from among troubled and deviant societies a man that he makes into a prophet (nabi and rasul).The English translation of the Holy Qur'an approximately 49 times refers to these prophets as *warners.*

These divine warners to corrupt and wayward governments and peoples bring good news of Allah's concern over the condition of the people; but they warn these societies that if they continue with the business of sin as usual, that Allah (God) will chastise them for their wicked practices. And since warnings seek to prevent the loss of life and property it is not done in a common ordinary tone. Warnings are delivered with a sense of urgency. Warnings are meant to be alarming. Warnings and warners are meant to offend. Therefore, a divine warner who has been commissioned by Allah (God) to warn a people whose evil outweighs their good has an alarming, unnerving and controversial presence. Consider the following verse of scripture from the Holy Qur'an:

> Corruption has appeared in the land and the sea on account of that which men's hands have wrought, that He may make them taste a part of that which they have done, so that they may return. Surah30:41

Prophets, messengers and divine warners historically have been a source of agitation to the ruling class and to the wealthy of corrupt nations. Even the Hebrew word for prophet, *naba,* is suggests the warner delivers his warning with passion, spontaneity and force. The Old Testament being translated into English from Hebrew translates the word *naba* as *prophet. Naba* means *"To prophesy, to bubble up, to gush forth, to pour forth or to chant"*.

So while the corrupt rulers of America, have painted a picture of Minister Farrakhan as a madman, it is Minister Farrakhan's similitude to the prophets of the scriptures that perfectly explains his function, behavior and the reaction of the people to him.

The testimonies that follow provide a powerful never before seen counter-narrative to the propaganda that has been used to keep The Minister in a prison of public opinion. These are the authentic, honest reactions to Minister Farrakhan's noble character, beneficial impact and indispensable value to Black people, to America and all of humanity.

It is my sincere prayer that what we offer in this volume will free Minister Farrakhan from being negatively thought of by the American people. We pray that college students will be free to invite him and his representatives to speak on their campuses. We pray that pastors and ministers will see the value in opening the doors of their houses of worship to Minister Farrakhan's ministry.

We pray that the Islamic world will unite with The Minister in building a model Muslim ummah in America. We pray that Black professionals will seek ways to offer their expertise and skills to aid The Minister solve the problems of the Black masses.

It is late in the evening for America. Minister Louis Farrakhan is the last prophetic voice that America will receive. He is a manifestation of God's willingness to extend mercy to America in spite of her great and unmatched sins. I encourage to read, reflect, and act.

May Allah bless you and your family with the light of understanding

Brother Demetric Muhammad, 8-14-2013

CHARACTER

WITNESSES

In the court of public opinion that has sought to prosecute and crucify the noble name, work and character of the Honorable Minister Louis Farrakhan we call to the witness stand an array of diverse men and women of all races and persuasions who have gone on record to testify of the great value of Minister Farrakhan and how he has impacted their lives, inspired their accomplishments, and been a rare source of truth and courage in a critical period of American and world history.

Nina Simone, Singer

A while later I met Louis Farrakhan, too, through a friend of mine who had converted, Pearl Reynolds Bryce. Reverend Farrakhan sent a message through her that I was his favourite singer and that my song Consummation was his all-time favourite. He invited me to meet him at a temple in New York, so I had a special hat and dress made for the occasion and went along. We chatted a little and I invited him home with me. We got back to Mount Vernon and he sat in the living room and started talking about separatism, Islam and the need to convert the whole of black America to his way of thinking. He talked for hours and I sat across from him, drinking gin and nodding my head, trying to take it all in.

The night got longer, the gin took effect and I got a little distracted, especially by his feet, which were tiny. I'd never seen feet that small, and I wondered if his mother had bound them when he was a baby like the Chinese used to do with their daughters. Minister Farrakhan talked on into the small hours and I sat staring at his shoes, sipping my gin and wondering what he'd say if I invited him upstairs. He kept giving me these looks as if he knew what I was thinking. At last I couldn't stand it any longer and came out and asked him. It was more out of mischief than anything else, but he spoilt the fun by turning me down; he just started talking politics again and I was too tired for that, so I sent him home. Afterwards I got messages saying he was still interested in me and would like to meet some time, but we didn't see each other again. So he didn't manage to convert me and I didn't convert him; an honourable draw. I respected him for that. (Simone 2003)

Michelle Ford, Anti-Vaccine Activist

The Honorable Minister Louis Farrakhan is going to go down in history as the person who saved humanity. He is the lover of all people, all people. and I hear the rhetoric and I hear the drama that they put out about him on social media and what not I don't believe a word of it. That man is the unifier, he is the voice of truth, he is the peacemaker and …I really honor you for standing by a man who has been so vilified and so marginalized. He deserves so much more than what this world has been giving him. (H. M. Farrakhan, Holy Day of Atonement 2016)

Rabbi Bruce E. Kahn, Temple Shalom

I am White. I am a rabbi. I attended the Million Man March where I stood hour after hour in the midst of a sea of excited, highly principled, welcoming Black men. I listened to the speeches and shared in the grandeur of an extraordinary moment in history. Mostly, it was privilege to bear witness to how important this gathering was to the African Americans who were present.

On that Monday, I was enveloped in an overwhelming sense of joy, pride, responsibility, thoughtfulness, hope and love. Yet, no one seemed to dodge one bit an awareness of what is wrong and what needs repair in the Black neighborhoods across America. Speaker after speaker, especially Minister Louis Farrakhan, confronted self-destructive behavior by too many Black males in a hard hitting, no nonsense, clearly defined and agonizingly descriptive fashion. The people around me did the same. No cover-ups. But there was so much more that made this day unique. It was a day of atonement and affirmation. This was a day for recognizing that most Black men in America care about their families, work hard, have a love of God and country, and possess a strong and positive moral code which embraces confession and atonement. That is not a message that is perceived by the media or transmitted by it....

When it comes to reporting on African Americans in general and Minister Louis Farrakhan and the Nation of Islam in particular, this weakness[of the media] is most pronounced. Reporters are driven to take the quotes that will antagonize the reader and do not let go of those words. Convey a negative impression and generate conflict, regardless of how out of line that is with the point and mass of a presentation. There seems to be a mission, conscious or subconscious, to put before the American people as much bad stuff about Blacks as possible. Proportionality is lost. Responsibility for the impact of what is reported is not assumed. The overall shaping of attitudes of viewers and readers of the news is, at best, disregarded. Make the story sizzle. Get people going. Make a splash. These seem to be the goals.

I can say with reasonable assurance that my intense contacts over the years with members of the African-American community, especially clergy, tell me that the White community has no understanding whatever of the suffering endured by African Americans over history or now. The role of systems controlled by White America in perpetuating that suffering is something most worthy of in depth and continuous reporting. But doing that takes a different agenda from that which seems to motivate reportage today. That agenda of disservice will prevent us from ever understanding Minister Farrakhan or the Nation of Islam....

There is only one Black American who could have pulled off the Million Man March. Give him the credit he deserves for doing so. It was one of the single most positive events in the social history of our country. The people who were there attended for several reasons, not all of which had to do with Minister Farrakhan. But without him the March would not have been envisioned nor would it have succeeded. It did succeed. If it did nothing more than give a huge boost to the trampled upon ego of the Black American male, it succeeded....

It seems clear to me that despite what I consider to be the horrifying insults that have issued from the Minister, the people who listen to him do not go chasing down Jews, or gays or Whites or Koreans to beat them and murder them. They do not do that for two reasons:

First, he warns them against such violent behavior. Second, these verbal onslaughts do not constitute the main thrust of his message. As unacceptable as they are, they are also tangential. His listeners know that. They are sufferers who know how tough it is to get a fair shake as Black people. They want that to change. They hear in Minister Farrakhan's words inspiration and instructions to begin to bring about that change. That is the message on which he focuses and on which they focus. That is not the message on which the media focuses. (Alberts 1996)

Rev. Dr. Charles Steele, President and CEO of the Southern Christian Leadership Conference(SCLC)

Eric Ahad Muhammad: Give us a quick synopsis of the condition of the SCLC when you met with Minister Farrakhan; how did Minister Farrakhan and the union of the SCLC come about?

Rev. Dr. Charles Steele Jr.: Minister Farrakhan is a great leader and I always respected that. You can't get a great leader and put him in a corner or put a label on them and forget about them. So, it was my national travel as well as international travel where I had my real meeting with Minister Farrakhan; it was in Libreville, Gabon West Central Africa. He was there and it was an honor for him to be there with Dr. Joseph Lowery and Mrs. Coretta Scott King just to name a few that's related to SCLC. The Reverend Jessie Jackson was there and many others.

I saw at that particular time in Africa. I had to go all the way to Africa to see the real vision of what God wanted SCLC and myself as an individual to do. I saw the coming together of those great leaders but it wasn't in this country. It was on the continent of Africa where I was exposed to and experienced this particular activity; it was an opportunity for me to see the workings of this. I developed even a closer relationship with Minister Farrakhan.

So SCLC called upon me to come to the helm of the organization 2004. When I got here, it was devastation. We ran into many problems that I didn't realize existed, even though I was on the board. I was a state senator at the time. I resigned my state senate seat and came to SCLC and realized that it's one thing being on the board of SCLC. But it's another thing when you're sitting in the chair of the organization that was co-founded by Dr. Martin Luther King. It is to be in the same seat that he sat in. My point is that the utilities had been disconnected and the phone was also disconnected. We couldn't meet payroll! The headline in the Atlanta Journal constitution said, **SCLC has collapsed, it's dead. The only thing that can save SCLC is God himself!**

So I began to realize that we were in trouble. I began to question God and ask Him. Why did you let me leave the State of Alabama to come over to Atlanta, Georgia in such a predicament as this? God you know I want to do your work? Please help me to find a way. And the first thing that I realized in praying to God is that he showed me something. You see God himself can send you your thoughts.

God himself can give you a vision. If you just know how to pray to him and be serious at what you ask for. God told me that you got to get a relationship with other people outside of SCLC. You can't sit around moaning and groaning and think that you're going to be helped. You can't keep doing the same type of planning and working the same strategy that SCLC has been doing for the last umpteen years. You must go out and get your own strategy and I will help you do it.

And I just saw the physical being and face of Minister Louis Farrakhan. I didn't have that type of relationship where I felt comfortable enough to just call upon him by telephone or through some other methods. I felt that if he would receive me after I called him seeking permission to come the palace to meet with him, then I could tell him what my plans are for SCLC. Then I felt that if I can get a connection face to face, eyeball to eyeball it would allow him to feel my spirit.

And so I called the Minister. I called Minister Louis Farrakhan and I didn't tell what the subject matter was. I just said, "Minister, this is Charles Steele Jr. President and CEO of the Southern Christian Leadership Conference. As you know Minister I've just taken over the helm of SCLC.

I want to come to the palace to Chicago to just converse with you for an hour or two." And he said, "No problem my brother. Brother Steele when do you want to come?" I said, "What about tomorrow?" He said "Great, come on up tomorrow let's talk." And after talking with us for about two hours or so, along with Reverend Albert E. Love who was my special assistant at the time who accompanied me, I looked at the Minister, I said, "Minister let me just be honest with you. I'm broke. SCLC is broke. We don't have no money. But if you just help me and loan me a few dollars. In terms of my plight of SCLC. I promise you that I will multiply it and I will pay you back."

And the Minister looked at me and he said "My brother, you got my attention." He said, "Just one thing that I want you to realize. I'm going to give you the money that you asked for because I know you mean well and you are going to do what is right to uplift the organization." He said, "You must realize you can't pay me back. You just go and be successful with Dr. King's organization and make it work for our people and I will be proud and I will commend the fact that you had enough motivation to come all the way to Chicago and to share with me your vision and your strategy. I encourage you to continue and this is what I will do to help you. But. I repeat you can't pay me back."

And from that day forward, I did a holy dance within myself going back on that airplane. And I just couldn't wait to get back to Atlanta to close my door. And I believe strongly in my private prayer to God. I just shed tears and I just thanked Him and thanked Him. And after that, I can honestly say after we got that enhancement financially from Minister Farrakhan, which was a blessing in its own right, the SCLC took off and the rest is history.

We were able to build a brand new building that we are so proud of, of the mere fact that God enable us to raise the money to buy it, to pay it off debt free. We were able to keep our payroll in its existence and we were able to take SCLC to another level and that's internationally. **And again, this would not have been done had it not been for Minister Farrakhan and others. But he was the first one; he was the first one to write the check. Because we had no money; we had no encouragement. We had no financial resource that we could go to. The bank wouldn't loan us no money. We didn't have any individuals that would volunteer to help us at the magnitude that we needed.**

To lift us up financially, God has blessed us to multiply the contribution that Minister Farrakhan gave us. And within three and a half years we built a brand new building and raised a total of twenty million dollars.

Eric Ahad Muhammad: You spoke at the Day of Atonement to the Statement Minister Farrakhan made to the regard after he had loaned you the money something would take place?

Rev. Dr. Charles Steele: Oh Yes. He said, "I believe in what you're doing. You are the man for the job and you're going to run into difficulties." He said, "But I know that you can make it work." And then he said "You don't have to pay me back." I never imagined that anyone would loan you a substantial amount of money without seeking repayment. And to me it was a substantial amount of money. I'm not going to say publicly how much it was.

Eric Ahad Muhammad: No Sir, don't do that.

Rev. Dr. Charles Steele Jr.: To me it was something that God himself just opened up from Heaven and dropped down on us a blessing through the Minister.

I know in his heart, that he would not have given us the money had he not had the vision seeing me as the leader and the rest of us who were supporting me as an organization. He wouldn't have given me the money had he not been faithful enough and had vision enough to believe in my strategy and my commitment and my hard work that we could take it another level. He is such a great leader that he had confidence. And he saw something that I hadn't seen. He saw the opportunity that God had laid on me and that I was the one to lead it.

And to build the building, I told him about the building. I said, "But I'm broke. But I want to build the building." I told him about how we didn't have any money in the bank, and how we couldn't meet payroll. But he, through his wise individual relationship spiritually with himself said that I'm going to make an investment in Dr. King's organization through this man called Charles Steele Jr. because he never would have done it had he not known and had the vision that I could multiply and build the building. And ultimately bring about the kind of service that we got, as well as the financial raising of twenty millions dollars.

Eric Ahad Muhammad: Now, you also spoke to what he said watch how much money you raise after I give you this gift.

Rev. Dr. Charles Steele Jr.: Oh yeah.

He said that I was going to be successful. He said, that by him doing what he did you know, lets you know that he saw something. And I felt something. I felt that I had his backing. In terms of, him recognizing and respecting me as a leader. Hearing from Minister Farrakhan that I could do it! He said, "You're the one Brother! And you can do it. Watch it happen!

It's the second coming of the SCLC. It's the Second coming, and he saw it. And I felt, and he told me we were going to make it. He told me that it was going to happen!

Eric Ahad Muhammad: On that note you've had many Black organizations that have fallen over the last years of our struggle with regards to the freedom, justice and equality. Now you have risen again from the ashes the Nation of Islam and the SCLC. Tell me about your vision for their unity going forward?

Rev. Dr. Charles Steele Jr: You are always going to have to find common ground, and that is what I like about Minister Louis Farrakhan. And that's with any organization and any individual. As I mentioned to you earlier.

Every day of my life I have to find common ground with my wife. By the mere fact that Minister Farrakhan came to Birmingham. You know he came to take a tour with us along with Hank Sanders and his Attorney Rose Sanders. They worked with me along with others in getting the Minister to come; to do a tour of Alabama with us. Where Alabama was the battle ground, as you know, historically for all of the great movements of the civil rights era. In terms of Montgomery, had it not been a Montgomery, it would not have been a Birmingham. Had there not been a Birmingham, there never would have been a Selma. And on and on and on.

So we know that there is common ground. You see people are always try to find things to divide you; but I ask what can you find to unite us. And all any organization has to do is to find common ground for betterment of the upward mobility and the progression to help our people. Just think about it, we have an opportunity to bring most African Americans together with the SCLC and the Nation Of Islam. (Jr. 2013)

Young Thug, Hip-Hop Artist

I want to give a huge, huge apology to the Minister Louis Farrakhan for not keeping my word. I am so sorry I caught up on tour. I missed the March. I won't ever miss another thing you ever in your life do. I promise you that. (Thug 2015)

The Game, Hip-Hop Artist

I watched him on The Breakfast Club—the whole interview—and the way that he speaks and empowers our youth, I think that commands attention. It really got mine. I loved the approach that he took talking about this newer generation. With media and the government, what they're doing is labeling our youth as this and that, but they have us in these situations where we can't better ourselves, so we're forced to deal with what it is they're throwing at us. But the way that the Minister is approaching it is a solid way. It is opening a lot of doors. The way that he's attacking it—we're going to see in the next coming months. People are just gaining awareness and a lot of doors are going to open. A lot of people are going to be ready to ride.

I think that he's one of the last powerful real true leaders that we have and that people should take as many pictures and open their ears as much as they can before he decides to sit it down. I think it's remarkable and I think when you talk about figures like the Honorable Elijah Muhammad and you talk about Dr. Martin Luther King Jr., and you talk about Brother Malcolm and just really amazing Black historical leaders, I feel like Minister Farrakhan is the last of that era, and it doesn't need to be taken lightly. (A. Muhammad, Rapper The Game says: 'A lot of people are going to be ready to ride' with Farrakhan - #JusticeOrElse 2015)

Dominique Zonyee, Writer-The Boombox

Admit it, you look to your favorite artists for guidance at times. If you are going through a break up there's a song for that. If you need to be inspired and uplifted, there is the perfect tune for that. And if you just want to get ratchet and twerk it out, there's a soundtrack for the moment. But just as much as you use music as a source of inspiration, rappers and singers need seek words of wisdom as well. Minister Louis Farrakhan is their go-to guy. (Zonyee 2015)

2 Chainz, Hip-Hop Artist

"It was a dope experience, I'm happy to be in the presence of The Minister. Big things on the way for the community," (Hollywood 2015)

Sway, Journalist Radio Host

Coming up in Oakland, we face a lot of challenges, and sometimes you look for inspiration from different places. So I can't tell you how many times just by listening to your words, or listening to you speak, especially even now having worked on MTV for 15 years and being in radio for 20 years, and being considered, humbly, a voice of this generation or hip hop culture—you know, sometimes you feel challenged, and you need those things to kind of strengthen you, and I'll look at a speech you made or something you said, and it's always something I could take away from it that'll keep me smiling and make me feel strong the next day. So, I always wanted to thank you for that. (H. M. Farrakhan 2015)

Damon Dash, Hip-Hop Mogul & Entrepreneur

"Had to get some advice from the super OG @louisfarrakhan ...now I know I'm fighting the right fight...finally some guidance from a real fighter trust me when he talks I sit quiet and listen #honorablepeoplesticktogether #honorup ...won't ever stop" (Dash 2015)

Ice Cube, Hip-Hop Artist, Actor & Entrepreneur

I met him before I physically met him. This guy named Drew from Public Enemy used to give us tapes of the Minister. So one Saviours' Day I flew in to Chicago to watch him speak and he invited me back to the Palace to eat. We ate kicked it and had a good time. ...it's a philosophy tailor-made for the Black man and Black woman. I am not a member of the Nation of Islam. I'm not a Muslim, but his program no matter if you're a Christian, Baptist or whatever is tailor-made for us to survive in North America and be successful. If his whole program was followed to the tee by the whole 40 million Black people in America we wouldn't have no problems. We wouldn't have no drug problem, no problems with teenage mothers or shoot-outs. His teaching is self-love. Everything we got from America is self-hate. So once you start loving yourself you can respect anybody that looks like you or comes from your family. If not your immediate family, the family of who you are. Once you teach that love all the problems seem to go away. (Cube 1993)

Corey Holcomb, Comedian

Minister Farrakhan saved my life. After listening to what he had to say I realized I wasn't alone mentally in this world. So I always give him his props. (Holcomb, www.youtube.com 2016)

I done heard all this shit about Farrakhan…what he did this and what he ain't and all this. But that is one man who I always see speak up for his people. I've never seen him caught up. I done seen entire panels, where it was 3, 4 or 5 motherfuckers set up to try and debate him and he make them all look stupid.

I don't claim no religion. I'm wise enough to watch how somebody conducts themselves; watch how they always have the information; always prepared; that's that brother Farrakhan man. I remember when I didn't even know anyone who thought like that when I was young; that's why I say he saved my life. Because I was like damn, here goes a man that got information for us. I could never prove it, but I always felt it. And when I saw him, I was like goddamn I'm not the only motherfucker out here who see this shit. (Holcomb, www.youtube.com 2015)

T.I., Hip-Hop Artist, Actor & Entrepreneur

Happy Birthday to one of the most honorable, influential men in American History. We owe you so much. Thank you for being a fearless leader of multiple generations, spreading truth to the masses at any & all costs. I'm honored to have met and shared a meal and conversations with you during the most trying time of my life. Enjoy your day sir. You deserve it. The Honorable Minister Louis Farrakhan: We appreciate all you have done. ("troubleman31" 2016)

Harry Lennix, Actor

Roland Martin caught up with Harry Lennix, one of the stars of NBC's hit drama *The Blacklist,* after Minister Louis Farrakhan's address at the Justice or Else rally.

When asked his thoughts on this weekend's rally, Lennix told Martin Min. Farrakhan's speech was "practical, passionate — it had spirituality to it."

"I think it was indicative of the mood" present at the historic rally, said Lennix.

He added that Farrakhan's address reflected the "people's need to be heard" and "gave great solutions" those in attendance could implement once they return to their respective neighborhoods. (Now 2015)

Lil' Herb, Hip-Hop Artist

Farrakhan…the Minister, he is phenomenal, he's awesome. All the "plays" he put together is awesome. He could have enemies that have shed blood against each other or did something to other people in the same room talking about what's going on. So anything the Minister put together I'm gonna be all for it; and pretty much anybody in Chicago is who's trying to do something positive. So the Minister put it all together, because the Minister know his stamp could make it what it need to be. So all the artists: me, King Louie, Katy Got Bands, and Common; they gonna jump on it quick for the Minister. Not to say they wouldn't do it for anybody else. But the Minister got that stamp that makes it national and global. Anything with his name on it is global.

I met up with him a few months ago in Chicago at the castle. He had me come up there and it was a lot of powerful people, me, King Louie, Joey Capone…a lot of people who got a lot of influence on Chicago and can make a difference. The Minister speaks on a lot of what's going on, not just Chicago, but the whole world. So anything the Minister put his stamp on is going to go…powerful-the positivity.

Me I'm younger; I'm only 19. A lot of people my age are more of a renegade; ain't nobody listening to nobody. But when it comes out of the Minister's voice, its power, so you go to tune into it. And it makes you feel a certain type of way about everything. Certain stuff he puts his finger on and talk about, it makes you feel a certain type a way about it. (VladTV 2015)

Phaedra Parks, Actress-Reality TV Star

You saw that I had the opportunity to take some of the ladies to the Million Man March [Justice Or Else gathering]. Some of the footage you didn't get to see was a very powerful conversation with the Honorable Minister Louis Farrakhan, that lasted for several hours. We didn't get to show that on our show. He has been a great mentor to me and a great support system for me and my boys. (Parks 2015)

Rick Ross, Hip-Hop Artist & Entrepreneur

"Wise words from a Great mind. Minister Farrakhan blessed me w/ peaceful words today." (Ross, Before Its News 2013)

Cora Masters Barry, Former First Lady of Washington, D.C.

"It's always inspirational and educational hearing the Minister. It's always life changing too. I think it brought all of us together, the Nation of Islam and Christians in a way that's never been done before and it's prophetic that this meeting was here at this church. It was planned way before the South Carolina massacre happened. God knew before we knew that this was where we needed to be." (J. M. Muhammad 2015)

Rev. Dr. Jamal H. Bryant, Pastor & Activist

"I'm so appreciative to be able to mark in history that I lived in the same chasm of time of one of the greatest leaders of our people. Never in the history of this nation have one million people ever gathered, except at your call. I'm appreciative that God preserved your life over these twenty years so another generation will be able to in fact have the reverberations of greatness. I'm thankful that he sustained your health and has kept you strong for such an hour as this." (A. Muhammad, FinalCall.com 2015)

Rev. Elisha B. Morris

Minister Louis Farrakhan just put the Bible on the top of the WORD NETWORK like no preacher, pastor, reverend has done in over a dozen years. He stood up for the word of God and Jesus and then called on us to come together and restore order as Christians and Muslims. Get the DVD!!! He said what a few of us have been saying, we are not sheep we are soldiers in the army and we fight for He whom died for us or we really aren't for HIM! (Morris 2015)

Scarface, Hip-Hop Artist

I fully support the Minister as you should. Let's make it a 20-million-man march in October. (Scarface 2015)

Gloria Naylor, Scholar & Award Winning Novelist

…there are a lot of issues that I've thought about since the Million Man March. I don't know, I was very moved by what I saw, as were many people. And maybe it was just a little bit different for me because we had just lost my father. That would have been his idea of the impossible, you know. Having a kid who went to Yale was for him the equivalent of the fact that men could walk on the moon. And he had lived long enough to see both happen. And the Million Man March would have been his third miracle, to have watched that many men come together. Because he followed Malcolm X for many years, and then Louis Farrakhan. And there's a lot of sane talk coming from those guys. And we're asked to emphasize the insane stuff they do, but for me nine-tenths of the weight is on the prescription they have for my people, and I think it's a darn good one. I believe we should try self-determination. We tried integration, and that didn't work. And at some point people have got to start realizing that. It has not worked. Integration hasn't worked. So, where do we go from here? But we never get into that conversation…" (Montgomery 2004)

Birdman, Hip-Hop Artist & Entrepreneur

I do listen to Minister Farrakhan a lot. He is my mentor, somebody that I really, really look up to. If I don't call him, he will call me just to check on me. I'm not really a talkative person, but I just really listen to him and take his encouragement and he makes me want to do more in life. He told me "You're a genius. You know how to take nothing and turn it into something." …He came to my house and he blessed my house. We got on my yacht. It was like a moment for me I'm going to take to my grave. It was like a moment for life for me. I had my kids there, my brother was there. I really cherished that moment. He came to my house 2 days in a row. He's someone that I have the utmost respect for,

for what he did for us as Black people, what he stands for and what he lives for. (Birdman 2016)

Bill Cosby, Comedian & Actor

I'm a Christian. But Muslims are misunderstood. Intentionally misunderstood. We should all be more like them. They make sense, especially with their children. There is no other group like the Black Muslims, who put so much effort into teaching children the right things, they don't smoke, they don't drink or overindulge in alcohol, they protect their women, they command respect. And what do these other people do? They complain about them, they criticize them. We'd be a better world if we emulated them. We don't have to become black Muslims, but we can embrace the things that work. We need people, not just in the church but in the community, who are not afraid to speak up because they want to hear a child's laughter — not a child's blood-curdling scream because a bullet hit them. We want them playing outside. (Brown 2013)

Abraham Foxman, Former Director of ADL of B'nai B'rith

"The only leadership that now exists in that community"—the "African American community"—"is Louis Farrakhan. Farrakhan can assemble 20,000 people several times a year,…" (Shalev 2013)

Former Governor of Pennsylvania and Mayor of Philadelphia, Ed Rendell

"I would like to thank the Nation of Islam here in Philadelphia. To thank you for what you stand for and what you stand for all the good it does to so many people in Philadelphia. And if there is anybody out here…who doesn't know, this is a faith that has as its principles, the family. This is a faith that doesn't just talk about family values, it lives family values. This is a faith where men respect their women and children and they manifest that faith by staying in the home with them. This is a faith that doesn't just talk about being against drugs but is out there every single day and night fighting against drugs. This is a faith that just doesn't talk about the value of education, it imbues in their children and schools that education is the way to opportunity." (H. M. Farrakhan 1997)

Actor and Celebrity Bruce Willis

Like a character in one of his movies, Bruce Willis came out blazing with both barrels in a George magazine interview, calling Bob Dole a ``nitwit,'' pronouncing Louis Farrakhan ``a hero of mine'' and declaring that organized religions are ``dying forms.'' The ``Die Hard'' star told the political magazine edited by John F. Kennedy Jr. that if he were black, ``I'd be with Farrakhan, too.''

``A lot of people feel Louis Farrakhan stands for a lot of negative things,'' Willis said of the Nation of Islam leader. ``But he is raising his voice against inequality. Anyone who stands up against injustice is a hero of mine.'' Willis also said he switched from Democrat to Republican in 1992 and supported President Bush for re-election because he felt Bill Clinton's campaign was too divisive. But he sat out the 1996 election between Dole and President Clinton because he considered the Republican ``a nitwit.''

Willis also criticized organized religions, which he called ``dying forms.'' ``Modern religion is the end trail of modern mythology,'' he said. ``But there are people who interpret the Bible literally. Literally! I choose not to believe that's the way. And that's what makes America cool, you know?'' (Associated Press 1998)

Rapper Chuck D

"Farrakhan scares people, at least white people. But a lot of people who attack him have never even heard the man. They just take quotes that the media throws out at them. Farrakhan is a man I believe in and a lot of black people believe in because he lays everything out logically." (Hilburn 1988)

Rapper Nas

FC: Now, of course, the song that's being talked about, the song "Louis Farrakhan." Take us into your thinking when you laid down the lyrics to that.

NAS: Louis Farrakhan has made me cry. You know, what do you say about that, you know what I'm saying? When you see a man who put his life on the line for something—be he right or wrong—you admire him. But to me, Farrakhan is all the way right! I'm not sitting here going line for line, detail for detail, everything he says and all of that. It's a whole body of work that he's laid—he's laid his life down for his people. No matter if you like it or not. Anybody like that I admire. And, you know, anybody in this position, they would kill off. He was smart enough to say "I have an army who believe in what I'm saying, that this is the Truth." That "I would die for everyone, every soldier in that army." They believe that and they know that's true. So, you know, how could I not acknowledge that's that; that's what I acknowledge in my life, then, it's going to bleed into the music. It's not even on purpose. It just happened. It's just my thoughts. "Some revolutionaries get old, although I'm told..." you know?

It's like everybody's scared to speak out about what's in their heart, just because they're scared of who is going to come down on them. They're scared they're going to get "blacklisted." They're going to get all their endorsements taken away from them. They're scared that they can't feed their families. I understand that, but I admire those people who know that, and still go and do what they have to do, you know what I mean? If I had enough money, I'd buy him a Rolls Royce tomorrow! You know what I'm saying? Like, that's just how I feel about him!

He is a serious piece of history, you know, coming from Elijah Muhammad; coming from Malcolm X, coming from—that part of history is so special because it's what America is scared to talk about. They're scared to talk about that. And, if they would talk about it, it would help a lot of people. I know a lot of White cats that listen to Farrakhan! I went to a Coldplay concert, and his introduction was Farrakhan's speech! So, I was blown away! I'm sitting next to Gwyneth Paltrow—we're rocking to a Farrakhan speech! So, it made me go: "Damn! If he—why didn't I use that in my music? I've been wanting to!" So I'm just trying to show the love back now. (A. Muhammad, Hip Hop Lives: FCN Interview with Nas 2008)

5 term Memphis Mayor Willie Herenton

Among the Memphis notables present during the events held by the Nation of Islam were County Commissioners Sidney Chism and Henri Brooks, State Rep. G.A. Hardaway, state Sen. Reginald Tate and City Councilman Joe Brown. On Sunday, Mayor Pro Tem Myron Lowery brought symbolic gifts and called the Memphis gathering a historic occasion for the city. Lowery said everyone needed to hear the message of self-reliance and "we need to take the message back to others." Former mayor Dr. Willie W. Herenton was a prominent figure at the leadership conference and at the Sunday event. Farrakhan said Herenton had earned the support he should receive in his bid to become the Ninth District representative and noted that as mayor, Herenton had the courage to present him with the key to the city. (Ajanaku 2009)

On Sunday, Herenton said it was easy to extend the key to Farrakhan, whom he described as worthy, a man who speaks the truth and who is anointed and committed to improving the human condition.

In comments to the crowd before the speech, [Memphis Mayor Willie] Herenton recalled presenting [Nation of Islam leader Louis] Farrakhan with a key to the city despite the controversy it caused.

"It was easy for me as a mayor to present a key ... to a man who is worthy, to a man who speaks truth, to a man who possesses wisdom, to a man who is courageous in thought and in action," said Herenton, who was the first elected black mayor of Memphis. "To an anointed man." (Schelzig 2009)

Chicago Tribune Editorial Page Editor, Don Wycliff

All his hatreds aside, one thing is clear about Farrakhan: He loves black people. He loves them so much that he has made himself hated by virtually every other group in this nation to prove his love for blacks. He loves them so much that he will criticize them as no white person and dam few black people could. Indeed, he boasted about that in his overlong (but far more coherent than most critics gave it credit for being) speech at the Million Man March. "I point out the evils of black people like no other leader does," Farrakhan declared, "but my people don't call me anti-black, because they know I must love them in order to point out what's wrong so we can get it right to come back into the favor of God. One other thing also is certain: Farrakhan, a Muslim, employs Christian and Judaic religious themes more effectively than almost any other prominent contemporary preacher. He did it to powerful effect in his Million Man March address, and in the process summoned up memories of that old religious tradition of which Dr. King was the greatest exemplar. (Wycliff 1995)

Trumpet Magazine Editor Rhonda McKinney Jones

"Because of the Minister's influence in the African American community, *Trumpet News magazine* honors him this winter at its Sounds of the Shore gala with an Empowerment Award. It seemed a fitting tribute for a storied life well lived. And as our brief interview drew to a close and he thanked me for taking the time to talk to him, I could not help but think the Minister, the man with whom I had been so casually speaking, truly epitomized greatness." (Media Matters for America 2008)

Rev. Jeremiah A. Wright

"When Minister Farrakhan speaks, Black America listens," says the Rev. Dr. Jeremiah A. Wright, likening the Minister's influence to the E. F. Hutton commercials of old. "Everybody may not agree with him, but they listen ... His depth on analysis when it comes to the racial ills of this nation is astounding and eye opening He brings a perspective that is helpful and honest.

"Minister Farrakhan will be remembered as one of the 20th and 21st century giants of the African American religious experience," continues Wright. "His integrity and honesty have secured him a place in history as one of the nation's most powerful critics. His love for Africa and African American people has made him an unforgettable force, a catalyst for change and a religious leader who is sincere about his faith and his purpose." (Media Matters for America 2008)

Former economic adviser to Pres. Ronald Reagan and Wall Street Guru, Jude Wanniski

"I believe Minister Farrakhan is the most important Muslim leader in the world, who can best represent the concerns of the Islamic world to our government. I have spent countless hours with him…I told him this morning that no one had yet come forward with proof that he ever said, 'Judaism is a gutter religion,' or 'dirty religion,' as I have an outstanding offer of $1000 to anyone who can." (The American Prospect 2002)

ACLC President Archbishop George A. Stallings

Speaking to fellow pastors following Minister Farrakhan's message, ACLC-USA's national co-president Archbishop George Augustus Stallings, remarked that he noticed many taking "copious notes," probably in preparation for Sunday morning sermons. Archbishop Stallings said Min. Farrakhan had a "Triple A rating" meaning "anointed, appointed and approved" and was "a prophetic voice for our time and age."

"I wish that we as Christian ministers would know the Qur'an the way the Minister knows the scriptures. I wish that we as Christian ministers would get out of our Eurocentric, hegemonic superiority attitude, embracing a religion that is a stolen legacy, rather than celebrating its Afrocentric roots," said Archbishop Stallings.

"I wish that some of us would seek to purify our Christianity. We cannot purify our Christianity until we study the Qur'an. I know that's a shocking statement to some of you Christian folks, but you and I cannot appreciate the true heritage of Christianity until we know the Qur'an, until we know Muhammad (PBUH) until we can articulate the principles of the Islamic faith the way the Hon. Louis Farrakhan articulated the principles of the Christian faith, and not only the Christian faith but also the Jewish faith," Archbishop Stallings added. (A. Muhammad, Farrakhan to spiritual leaders: 'God has never done His greatest work in politics' 2009)

Archbishop George Augustus Stallings, Jr., national president of the American Clergy Leadership Conference, said he admires Minister Farrakhan because he leads by example, and is a man of principle, at a time when many spiritual leaders sacrifice principle for popularity.

"The sterling quality that I appreciate most about the Honorable Minister Louis Farrakhan is that he is uncompromising when it comes to spiritual principles and he does not base his message on what will tickle the ear or what is popular to receive an applause," Archbishop Stallings told *The Final Call.* "What is more important to him is principle rather than power. It is service rather than being served. And it is his ability to challenge all of us to be the watchmen and the watchwomen that we accepted the call to be when we were ordained and yet maybe have fallen by the wayside." (A. Muhammad, Farrakhan delivers a warning and offers a healing for spiritual leaders and humanity 2011)

Torah Jewish Group Neturei Karta

In an historic Feb. 28 announcement, the rabbis told the world of their support for Min. Farrakhan and the Nation of Islam during a press conference after the Saviours' Day weekend celebration.

"We've had hours and hours of conversations with Minister Farrakhan, "said Rabbi David Weiss, "Minister Farrakhan is a strong-willed person. The Jews misconstrued his statements. They (Zionists) changed Judaism with their new style. This is Zionism. Judaism is not like this."

Rabbi Weiss led a delegation of rabbis that were invited to Saviours' Day by Min. Farrakhan as part of their ongoing dialogue and reconciliation. The rabbis spoke throughout the weekend and addressed the capacity crowd at the United Center on Feb. 27.

"Zionism is a transformation from godliness to materialism," explained Rabbi Weiss. "Know the difference between Zionism and Judaism. We are diametrically opposed. We apologize for those who attacked Minister Farrakhan. Those who attacked represent the façade of Judaism."

This example of peace and reconciliation has not been received by all as good news for the faithful. On the contrary, so-called mainstream Jewish groups have attacked this bond as insincere.

In news reports Michael Siegel, president of the Chicago Board of Rabbis, said that "the Jewish community is fairly well-organized and there are bodies equipped to have a conversation. (Farrakhan) knows their phone numbers and the fact that he chose to go elsewhere shows the lack of sincerity" in his outreach.

But the rabbis pointed out that Min. Farrakhan has made outreach for dialogue with his attackers.

Their own relationship with the Nation began last summer when they approached the Muslims seeking help in securing the release of several Jewish rabbis held in Iran for alleged spying.

That led to additional meetings to foster a better relationship. "This Jewish community is an excellent example of how Black and Jewish relations can be," said Nation of Islam Chief of Staff Leonard F. Muhammad.

Before the 1984 elections there was hardly a mumbling word about Min. Farrakhan and Jews. The waters were parted with the great divide when Min. Farrakhan defended Rev. Jackson against Jews seeking to "ruin" his campaign. Those Jews labeled the Minister a new "Hitler."

Although Min. Farrakhan condemned Hitler as being wicked for his deeds, somewhere and somehow that message got deleted from the media reports and all that was played over and over in the press was that Min. Farrakhan called Hitler great.

The next media distortion was the misinterpretation of the following quote: "Now, that nation of Israel never has had any peace in 40 years, and she will never have any peace because there can never be any peace structured on injustice, thievery, lying and deceit and using the name of God to shield your dirty religion under His holy and righteous name."

Again, the media had a field day with that and soon all that was reported was that Min. Farrakhan called Judaism a "gutter religion."

In their new pamphlet, "Exile and Redemption: The Torah Approach, An Introductory Exploration of Zionism, Jewish-Gentile Relations and the Recent Dialogue with the Nation of Islam by a Friend of Neturei Karta, " that remark is explained by Jews themselves.

"The media widely reported that the Minister had referred to Judaism as a 'gutter religion.' This error (or distortion) was deeply troubling to the Nation of Islam. The reason was that in Minister Farrakhan's vocabulary the phrase 'dirty religion' has a particular meaning. It referred to adherents of a faith who sinned against the tenets of that faith. The 'dirty religion' is the distorted faith which emerges from its manipulation by hypocrites or sinners.... The use of 'dirty religion' in the Minister's lexicon could have been discovered by any researcher interested in generating light instead of heat," the statement reads. (N. I. Muhammad 2000)

Former U.S. Representative and HUD Secretary Jack Kemp

"But Kemp also said he so admired the Million Man March organized by Farrakhan last year, and the speech Farrakhan delivered at the event, that he wished he had been able to take part. "That Million Man March was a celebration of responsible fatherhood, individual initiative, of not asking the government to do everything for you, and getting an opportunity to be the man that God meant you to be," Kemp, 61 said. "I would have liked to have been invited to speak." Kemp, a former U.S. Secretary of Housing and Urban Development and one of the few nationally recognized Republicans to consistently focus on the problems faced by minorities and the poor, acknowledged the risk he was taking in praising Farrakhan's emphasis on black self-reliance and family values." (Rezendes 1996)

Former EEOC Chairman and U.S. Supreme Court Justice Clarence Thomas

President Bush's nominee for the Supreme Court, Judge Clarence Thomas, expressed admiration for the Rev. Louis Farrakhan in speeches eight years ago. But Judge Thomas said today that he never shared any of the clergyman's anti-Semitic views. The content of the speeches was disclosed today by The Dallas Times Herald. After leaders of Jewish organizations and civil rights advocates expressed concern about Mr. Thomas's remarks, he issued a statement saying he was not an anti-Semite.

Mr. Farrakhan, the Black Muslim leader, became notorious in 1984 when he spoke of Judaism as "a dirty religion" and described Hitler as "wickedly great." Leaders of Jewish organizations said Mr. Farrakhan had been making anti-Semitic statements at least since 1972.In two speeches prepared for his use in 1983, Mr. Thomas, then chairman of the Equal Employment Opportunity Commission, described Mr. Farrakhan as "a man I have admired for more than a decade." The speeches were for a meeting of the Capital Press Club here on Sept. 19, 1983, and for a meeting of the national Association of Black M.B.A.'s in Atlanta on Oct. 6, 1983. Mr. Thomas quoted Mr. Farrakhan on the need for self-help among blacks, without mentioning any of the minister's views of Judaism. (Pear 1991)

Hip-Hop Mogul and Entrepreneur Russell Simmons

Minister Louis Farrakhan: My Second Father

"When we think of Minister Louis Farrakhan, we often think about the man who helped guide Muhammad Ali or the man who came up together in the Nation of Islam with Malcolm X. Do we ever think he's the man who helped hundreds of thousands (or even millions) of black people to love themselves? Well, we should.

When I grew up in Hollis, Queens there was a rehab, a mosque and a "Steak n' Take" on my corner, all of which were run by the Nation of Islam. There was also a heroin epidemic on that corner that was killing off our teenagers and young adults. Our parents would tell us that when we grow up we should make a choice to either join the army or "be a Muslim or something." The Nation of Islam secured our housing projects, promoted dignity and transformed men with criminal pasts. Those men would then, in turn, raise refined, educated black children. Hard to dispute this. It took guys off the street and created a powerful, non-violent movement. The Nation of Islam has never been associated with any form of violence and always been about uplifting our communities and making a better future for black people. If you ask anyone from my generation, from any ghetto in this country, I promise you they have roughly the same experiences regarding the Nation's presence in their communities.

Certainly some of their preachers were fiery, especially in their pointing out the evils of white supremacy. They said some things in a way that was hard for most whites and some blacks to digest. For example, "THE WHITE MAN IS THE DEVIL." We have to remember the climate of the country during this time. It was an all-out war and the Nation was not about to back-down. The Nation of Islam, which was started by Elijah Muhammad and a white man named, Master Fard Muhammad, always pointed out that one day we would all live in harmony. Although this still isn't quite true, their message under the leadership of Minister Louis Farrakhan has evolved to fit the time.

It is true that some blacks are still not "free" and stuck in a slave mentality, due to the lingering effects of 400+ years of slavery. It is the recognition of this condition that the Nation continues its important work in ghettos across America, giving steady doses of spirituality or sense of higher self to many men and women who need it.

This past week, it was my honor to host the Honorable Minister Louis Farrakhan at my apartment in NYC. He was joined by his sons Louis Jr., Mustapha and Joshua Farrakhan, along with their personal chef and at least 75 security personnel. It was quite a scene to see how they set up shop at my apartment. This was a week where I didn't miss my 6 am prayer because I could hear them already awake and ready to start the day off right. This was a week where the word "Allah" was on the tip of everyone's tongue. And was a very special time when I got to hang with my "second dad" and my other brothers. We reminisced about the three marches where more than three million people marched on Washington. We talked about how we brought Snoop, Ice Cube and other LA rappers together with members of the east coast rap community and how he

74

helped mediate the beef between 50 Cent and Ja Rule and countless other instances where he was there to help hip hop. And of course we talked about his keynote address at the hip hop summit that created the Hip Hop Summit Action network. We even mentioned a subject that the Minister doesn't care to discuss, his legacy. He has talked about the oneness of god for years, about the sameness of all religion and all people. He has given his followers spiritual roadmaps to happiness on Earth his whole life. I want future generations to know him as I do, so I am working to have his thoughts on this subject made into a book. I believe that his memoirs are going to be one of the most interesting and inspiring autobiographies ever written.

So that is my goal.

If America can know his heart, it will inspire millions of Americans for generations to come. It will happen with or without me, but I just thought writing this would be a good karmic expression for me, and a chance to reflect on a very special few days in my life. (Simmons 2009)

Rapper 50 Cent

I never met my father, right. But if I had the opportunity to pick a father, ah, man   I'd probably pick...who would I pick man?...I'd pick Minister Farrakhan...I would. Minister Farrakhan would be a cool father; like 'Minister Farrakhan my pops nigga, don't play with me I'll pop off.' (G-Unit Radio 19 2013)

R&B Vocalist Stephanie Mills

"He's a great man, I think he's misunderstood in a lot of ways, but I think he's a great man. And I am happy that he's been able to endure." (Black Entertainment Television 2003)

Rev. Jesse L. Jackson Sr.

"Average people follow a path; leaders of significance carve a trail where there was no path, to that extent the Minister is a trailblazer...No one speaks to them more powerfully and more consistently than Minister Louis Farrakhan...His being alive is a miracle unto itself, he just refuses to surrender; his spirit, his body, his religion, he keeps on fighting back." (Black Entertainment Television 2003)

Professor Michael Eric Dyson

"And despite the outer perimeters of controversy that attach to Minister Farrakhan, I think Black people always understood that this was a man who loved Black people, who engaged Black people where they lived, and long before rap singers where talking about keeping it real, Minister Farrakhan was speaking truth to power... His ability to tell what's on his mind that most Black people love him for, because we have so many leaders who kowtow and genuflect before the shrine of popularity, who don't want to speak their mind because they think it might hurt their bottom line...For the first time in African American history; a non-Christian leader is a significant, if not the significant leader within Black America" (Black Entertainment Television 2003)

Elma Lewis, friend of the Minister's mother

"He was the jewel of the neighborhood really, in the church and school, wherever he went; he had a real talent for lighting up the world." (Black Entertainment Television 2003)

Pastor of St. Sabina Church and Community Activist Father Michael Pfleger

"He has—first of all; he has not called Judaism a gutter religion of blood suckers. That is not what he has said because I have heard that talk. I stick up for Louis Farrakhan because he is another person that the media has chosen to define how they want to do it. And they demonize how they want to demonize somebody. I know the man, Louis Farrakhan. He is a great man. I have great respect for him; he has done an awful lot for people and this country, black, white, and brown. He's a friend of mine." (O'Reilly 2008)

Journalist Gregory Kane

What I'm about to say will no doubt get me in trouble with the Jewish community. Protesters will have to stand in line. They can queue up behind my friends in the Nation of Islam, where perhaps they will come to a meeting of the minds on at least one issue.

Because the truth is there is much about Farrakhan and the Nation of Islam that is praiseworthy. Comparisons to Hitler and Mussolini for making the trains run on time don't begin to describe the nature of the Nation of Islam's work. Carlos Muhammad of Baltimore's Mosque No. 6 pointed to one NOI member who, before he joined, was a crack addict.

Reaching out to redeem drug addicts and others filled with hopelessness has been part of the NOI's mission for years. If Louis Farrakhan sends his ministers out into the streets to help save such people, he deserves praise, not condemnation. Funny, isn't it, how those of us who have viciously vilified the man over the years are now shamefully silent about the allegation of the San Jose Mercury News that it was indeed the CIA that backed a group that introduced crack to Los Angeles, triggering an epidemic that spread across the nation. We excoriate the man fighting to end it and say not one negative comment about the ones who may have helped start it.

Earlier this year, Farrakhan told Mike Wallace of the television show "60 Minutes" that America was the most corrupt society on earth. If the CIA/crack story is true, it turns out that Farrakhan was on the mark. Don't you loathe him when he's right?

We loathe him when he's right and wrong, and in spite of the clearly good things his organization has done in the impoverished areas of urban black America. But if we apply moral absolutism in the case of Louis Farrakhan, let's be fair and apply it to everybody.

Because the CIA may have helped flood America's streets with crack, let's conclude that America's government is evil and incapable of being reformed.

Because former Mossad agent Victor Ostrovsky charged that the Israeli intelligence agency recruited three Palestinians to assassinate former President George Bush; executed the would-be assassins when the plot failed; did indeed assassinate British media magnate Robert Maxwell; and used Palestinians and blacks in Soweto, South Africa, as guinea pigs in biological and chemical warfare experiments, the government of Israel must be inherently evil.

We won't do that, of course. We'd much prefer to bask in the rays of our own self-righteousness, not even acknowledging that next to those good ol' boys in the Mossad, the Nation of Islam leader looks downright saintly. Louis Farrakhan, we charge, is anti-Semitic, bigoted, intolerant and intransigent. But it looks like his most vocal critics may be guilty of some intolerance and intransigence of our own. (Kane 1996)

Haki R. Madhubuti

That Minister Farrakhan had the vision, organization, money, independence and spiritual strength to stand up against gangsta odds and say, "let's meet in Washington," and to reach out to the Black church, Black fraternal organizations, Black professional organizations, Black women organizations, Black Nationalists and Pan-Africans, Black college students and Black street people all across the country was definitely an act of humility, spiritual growth, inclusion and political insight. (Karenga and Madhubuti 1996, 68)

Dr. Cornel West

Needless to say, Minister Louis Farrakhan was brilliant, gracious and open as was his wife, Khadijah...Since this substantive meeting I have been trashed by many (some former friends and acquaintances) and eschewed by others. And in the eyes of some in the Jewish world, I've met and collaborated with the new Hitler. This is sheer nonsense- and part of the problem. When Black people sit and talk with their white adversaries, they are praised. When Martin Luther King preached that he loved such white supremacists as Bull Connor, the white media showered him with approval and admiration. When Black people trash and denounce other Black leaders-demonized by the white media-they are praised. But when Black people who disagree in public decide to meet in private-all of us are trashed and denounced. When Martin Luther King preached that he loved Elijah Muhammad-and met with him in private-the white media denounced him. The double standards and differential treatment-the core of white supremacy-are evident.

My support of the Million Man March and dialogue with Minister Louis Farrakhan is based on neither blood nor race. As a radical democrat and, most importantly, Christian, my support and dialogue are based on spiritual, moral and political grounds. Spiritual because I view each and every one of us as, human beings made in the image of God capable of growth, development and maturity. Hence, I give up on no one of us-we are all in process, in need of one another. Morally, because though I believe patriarchal, homophobic and anti-Jewish sentiments are wretched sins, we all must be pushed to minimize the evils in all of us. None of us are pure and pristine, free of sin and evil. Yet we grow, develop and mature owing to loving criticism, not hateful castigation. Politically, I am convinced that white supremacy is the major dam holding back the progressive energies in the American body politic. If we can target white supremacy, then the other crucial issues of poverty, mal-distribution of wealth, corporate power, patriarchy, homophobia and ecological abuse will be brought into daylight. Why so? Because race matters so much in American society. (Karenga and Madhubuti 1996)

Alice Walker

I can't imagine becoming Muslim...I did not think Farrakhan was proselytizing...I was moved by his apparent humility; and underneath all the trappings of Islam, which I personally find frightening, I glimpsed a man of humor, a persuasive teacher and someone unafraid to speak truth to power, a virtue that makes it easier to be patient as he struggles to subdue his flaws. (Karenga and Madhubuti 1996, 42)

Selwyn Seyfu Hinds

Farrakhan's self-help doctrine hardly resembles hollow right-wing platitudes. The right's practice of telling folks to pull themselves up is coupled with vicious attacks on the structures that lend them a modicum of support, while Farrakhan's is fleshed out by tangible outreach into the meanest streets and souls of besieged Black America. In this way, of this afternoon, Farrakhan has reached me. (Karenga and Madhubuti 1996, 64)

Ron Daniels

Minister Louis Farrakhan more than any other leader in this period has captured the imagination of Black America precisely because of his steadfast denunciation of racism and white supremacy and his persistent call for moral and spiritual renewal, self-reliance and self-determination. Though Minister Farrakhan has remarkable appeal across classes and constituencies within the Black America, his appeal among the poor and disadvantaged is unrivaled. Hence, the enormous response to the Million Man March/Day of Atonement among people who have not been attracted to or participated in any mass action in their lifetime. When Farrakhan made the call for the Million Man March/Day of Atonement, the masses responded.

Obviously, anyone who can issue a call for a Million Man March/Day of Atonement and get massive response becomes a leader to be reckoned with within Black America. Minister Farrakhan, therefore, emerges as the pre-eminent African American leader in this period. (Karenga and Madhubuti 1996, 108)

Dr. Charshee McIntyre and Dr. Barbara Sizemore

Dr. Charshee McIntyre cited Dr. Barbara Sizemore, the eminent educator and currently Dean at DePaul University in Chicago, as another associate who strongly endorses the march. "She told me that the Nation of Islam is the best group in the country for the development of Black men, for instilling unity and camaraderie, and I agree," McIntyre said. "And as women become more educated you'll notice that they are rising to prominence within the Nation, and that to me is a natural progression." (Karenga and Madhubuti 1996, 114)

Dr. Geneva Smitherman

Quiet as it's kept, Farrakhan is respected by millions of African American, on all socio-economic levels, for his courage in standing up to an oppressive system and his penchant for calling white folk out. Truly "unbought and unbossed," he often says the things that many Blacks feel but don't have the freedom to express. According to a poll reported in Time, 59% of Blacks believe Farrakhan is a good role model for Black youth and that he speaks the truth. Since the March, some Black folk have started saying things like: "Now, I tell you what the problem is with her son, even though it's gon hurt, cause I'm like Farrakhan, uhma tell the truth." (Karenga and Madhubuti 1996, 104)

Journalist and Publisher of Emerge Magazine George Curry

Despite all the criticism enveloping Farrakhan, the Million Man March was a stunning success. There was a sense of love and brotherhood that cannot be adequately conveyed to those who chose to stay away. Man after man said, "Pass the love," as they gently pounded one another's fists. They even passed money to total strangers. Now the challenge is to take that love and trust, and spread it among our respective communities. (Karenga and Madhubuti 1996, 128)

Journalist and Activist Kevin Powell

"God knows, when I heard Farrakhan, I had never heard a black man talk like that. It blew my mind, absolutely blew my mind, It was intoxicating, as intoxicating as crack was for a lot of people in our community in the '80s. (Cheney 2005)"

Musician and Composer James Mtume

Well first and foremost, I think he's the only person or personality that the hip hop community respects...I've seen his symphonic work and I think personally that's one of the things that really separates him from many of the other so-called leaders. I personally believe that true leadership has to be connected to some artistic sensibility and he more than anyone else demonstrates that. (Black Entertainment Television 2003)

Actor Bernie Casey

What he primarily proselytizes, I think all Black Americans agree with, which is to be stand up men, responsible men, men that are dependable that take care of their families, that respect their wives and children, that try to get gainful employment, to be a help to the community; all those things. How could you possibly object to that? (Black Entertainment Television 2003)

College Friend Clarence "Jeep" Jones

Some don't have the courage to say the things they believe even though in our hearts we think it; I know I think some of the things that he said. Would I have the courage to say them, I 'm not sure.-Clarence "Jeep" Jones. (Black Entertainment Television 2003)

Brother Wayne Grice

When he would give us (his staff) something to do or share his vision, he was always open to our natural and real reaction and we were free enough, he gave us freedom to say what was really on our mind. (Black Entertainment Television 2003)

President Bill Clinton

Former President Bill Clinton said that he supports the efforts of African American leaders who are organizing the Millions More March, a national gathering of Blacks scheduled to take place in October in Washington, D.C, a decade after the Million Man March was convened.

In a rare interview at his Harlem office with the Amsterdam News earlier this week, Clinton said that the gathering--publicly announced last Monday by Minister Louis Farrakhan, Rev. Al Sharpton, and Rev. Jesse L. Jackson--could train a positive spotlight on critical issues impacting African Americans.

"I think this is a very positive idea," said Clinton, who spoke to the Amsterdam News on his first full day back in his office since his second operation due to complications following his quadruple bypass surgery last September. "I think the country's focus understandably has strayed a little over the last few years," Clinton said, adding that while America should focus on homeland security, it must also solve the racial and economic disparity that still exists.

Clinton, who remains extremely popular among African Americans, said that another march, followed by aggressive organizing efforts, could help to curtail some of the challenges in the Black community, which range from high unemployment and alarming prison rates.

"Jesse [Jackson] and Mr. [Louis] Farrakhan and Rev. [Al] Sharpton probably have internal domestic political differences, but they've agreed on this and I think it's a good thing," said Clinton. "I like the idea of a march, but I think it would also be good at the march for them to say, 'We want to call your attention to this problem and here's something else you can do. And that it's fine to be concerned about [homeland] security, but we also have to keep trying to make America strong and better here at home. And we can't neglect the quality of our jobs, the quality of our education, the quality of our environment.'"

The event, scheduled to take place in October, is expected to draw millions of African Americans to the nation's capital for the three days to participate in a Day of Absence from work and school on Friday, Oct 14, followed by a march on Oct. 15, and religious services the next day.

Clinton said that he supported the Million Man March a decade ago, adding that the gathering was a powerful symbolic expression.

"They were basically standing up for the dignity of family and asking African American men and fathers to be more responsible," Clinton said. "It was totally non-violent and got a big participation and it also showed frankly, a face to a part of America that is not as sympathetic to the problems that African Americans in the cities and the poor rural areas have ... that hey, there's all these people and they are advocating a responsible agenda and not just asking for something, and they're saying, 'This is our responsibility; this is what we're supposed to do.' I personally thought it was quite positive." (Watson 2005)

U.S. Representative James Traficant

James Traficant (D-Ohio) praised the march, in a one-minute speech. "I attended the Million Man March," he said, "I thought it was the right thing to do." He said that "the message was powerful. The themes were responsible: self-responsibility, economic independence, morality, love, parenthood. Those are good messages for all America." He concluded that "there is reality here. The Pope and Billy Graham are great human beings, but the Pope and Billy Graham and all the religious leaders of the world will not solve the race problem in America. It is going to; in fact, require the help of all people. Congress should join in and commend that march. It was good for the country." (Osgood 1995)

LaWanna Mayfield

The following is an excerpt of an interview with LaWanna Mayfield conducted by Matt Comer. Ms. Mayfield is a Charlotte, NC city councilperson who appeared at a leadership meeting held by the Honorable Minister Louis Farrakhan during the Holy Day of Atonement observance in October 2012. Ms. Mayfield was pressured by media outlets within the city of Charlotte to renounce the Minister. She refused and stood resolutely by her decision to attend the meeting.

What do you say to people who want you to publicly denounce Farrakhan?
[The] same thing I said at the beginning. It's God's place to judge people. The great thing about the United States is everyone has an opinion, and I represent an extremely diverse community. It is not my place to place judgment on anyone. I'm not God, and I don't intend to be.

Would you consider denouncing Farrakhan based on his anti-LGBT and anti-Semitic remarks?
It is your responsibility as an individual, as an adult and as a young adult to not listen to everything one person says. We need to be individual thinkers, so I'm going to look at the good people have done and I'm going to look at where we can build something together as opposed to focusing on our differences. At the end of the day, there are things I do not agree with, but I also recognize, as an African-American female, a lot has been done for the African-American community by the Muslim community under the leadership of Minister Farrakhan.

84

Is there a tipping point where Farrakhan's beliefs are harmful versus helpful?

I am African American first before I am anything else. Every room I walk into, before you identify my sexuality, before you know I'm an elected official, before you know where I went to school, what you see is an African-American female. The day I was born, my ethnicity was stated on my birth certificate. The day I die, that's what's going to be on my birth certificate. It is not going to say whether or not I was heterosexual, lesbian, bi or transsexual. I'm going to continue to be as respectful to as many people as I possibly can be, but I'm not going to shy away from who I am as an African-American female.

I am not going to discount the work Minister Farrakhan has done any more than I would discount the work I have done in the Latino, Asian Pacific and other diverse communities. I'm not going to let anyone bully me into taking a stance I don't personally believe in.

How would you explain your position to an LGBT person in your community?

Very few people have asked me. When MeckPAC was called to denounce me, they did not. When [the national Gay & Lesbian] Victory Fund was called to denounce me, they did not. I am doing exactly what I said I would do and represent everyone, not get side-tracked because one or two people feel like I should take a stance without having had any real conversation about the totality of an individual.

The Southern Poverty Law Center calls the Nation a hate group.

Are we saying Muslims are hateful? How many Muslims follow the leadership of Minister Farrakhan? I'm not concerned with anything other than what I was there in attendance for; to participate in an African-American leadership discussion.

Do you think Southern Poverty Law Center's hate-group designation is inaccurate?

For me, the hate group designation has as much merit as those of us in the community who think all Muslims are terrorists. It's that type of intolerance that encourages "us versus them," as opposed to encouraging communities to work together. (Comer 2012)

Jeffrey Steinberg

The largest peaceful demonstration in American history, the "Million Man March" which gathered at the foot of the U. S. Capitol on Monday, Aug. 16, has changed politics in the United States and effectively reflected the growing disgust of the American public with the Conservative Revolution of House Speaker Newt Gingrich and his allies. The rally was built around a call for a national "Day of Atonement" issued by Minister Louis Farrakhan, the head of the Nation of Islam, who called last year for 1 million black men to come to Washington, D.C. (Steinberg 1995)

Kweisi Mfume

"We want the word to go forward today to friend and foe alike that the Congressional Black Caucus, after having entered into a sacred covenant with the NAACP [National Association

for the Advancement of Colored People) to work for real and meaningful change, will enter into that same covenant with the Nation of Islam," said CBC Chairman Rep. Kweisi Mfume (D-Md.). The Nation of Islam in Washington, D.C. has gained a well-deserved reputation for their effectiveness in cleaning up housing complexes overrun by the drug trade, generally recognized as the number-one threat to the black community, and has also played a prominent role in the fight against AID S. In a declaration of unity that brought a standing ovation from the 3,500 people in attendance at the meeting at the Washington Convention Center, Mfume said, "No longer will we allow people to divide us." CBC membership increased 50% in the last election.-by William Jones (W. Jones 1993)

Andrew Young

Atlanta Mayor Andrew Young, U.S. ambassador to the United Nations under Jimmy Carter, interviewed by the Baltimore Jewish Times on Aug. 30, said he agrees with "nine tenths" of what Nation of Islam leader Louis Farrakhan says. Farrakhan, who has made frequent anti-Semitic remarks, is on the receiving end of millions from Libyan dictator Muammar Qaddafi, and has also characterized himself as an admirer of Adolf Hitler. Young calls Farrakhan a "legitimate player in the mainstream of black ideas" and says his POWER plan is "wonderful . . . because it would employ lots of people." Young insisted that he "has never heard him say anything against the Jews." Asked how he would feel if the situation were reversed, and the Ku Klux Klan were advocating race hatred against blacks, Young replied, "I have always said that the Ku Klux Klan is made up of poor white people who are part of the mainstream of America's social and political life, and they need to be helped, not hated." (Executive Intelligence Review 1985)

Debra Hanania-Freeman

Farrakhan used the opportunity to release a statement entitled "A Torchlight For America," whose text was excerpted from his forthcoming book of the same title, to be released sometime in May. Farrakhan's remarks examined the status of the nation's health care system, welfare reform, taxation, prison reform, the national debt, and the economy. Although the speech was packed with facts and statistics, and was bitingly accurate in its critique of the state of the U. S. economy, what was most striking about the presentation was not Minister Farrakhan's acumen as an economist, but his personal vision of God, his good humor, and the kind of passionate defense of African Americans that could only be delivered by one who has fully internalized his own responsibility to provide leadership for his people....Hearing Farrakhan in person for the first time was clearly startling to many of those gathered who had only read news accounts of him circulated by his enemies. But Farrakhan's wit, vitality, and most importantly, his humanity, were irrepressible. Farrakhan is, without question, a far different man than the sound-bite target that the Anti-Defamation League (ADL) of B'nai B'rith has constructed. Indeed, he thanked Lyndon LaRouche's associates for their work and insights exposing the ADL, saying; he was shocked when he saw the ADL's "Farrakhan dossier" portraying him and those associated with him as criminals. Clearly, Farrakhan came to Washington to deliver a message and to offer his help to a troubled nation. He is a national asset whose voice should be heard. (Freeman 1993)

Fredrick Allen

Frederick Allen, columnist for the Atlanta Journal/Constitution, titled his Thanksgiving Day column, "Farrakhan's Real Message Has Validity." "Where other leaders invariably make blacks feel helpless, [Nation of Islam leader Louis] Farrakhan offers hope. ...anti-Semitism is not the source of his appeal, and for this we can be thankful," Allen wrote. (Allen 1985)

Professor Derrick Bell

Anything out of the accepted is seen as a problem, by an awful lot of us. When Lewis Farrakhan speaks to his audience he upsets a hell of a lot of white people, you see. But while he is speaking to the needs and the hopes and what have you, of the people to whom he is speaking, and that's just going to happen. I see Lewis Farrakhan as a great hero for the people. I don't agree with everything he says, and some of his tactics, but hell, I don't agree with everything anybody says. (MacNeil Lehr News Hour 2012)

Smart and super articulate, Minister Farrakhan is perhaps the best living example of a black man ready, willing and able to 'tell it like it is' regarding who is responsible for racism in this country .... Every black person important enough to be interviewed is asked to condemn Minister Farrakhan--or any other truly outspoken black leader. (Bell 1993)

Journalist Clarence Page

Clarence Page, one of the best-known and most admired African American commentators, described his experience in Washington as therapeutic. "Since black men, particularly young black males, are the most feared and loathed creatures on urban streets today, we need self-esteem more than most." To recognize that it was Farrakhan who called the march and who pulled it off is not to condone Farrakhan's rhetoric. As Page notes, "Those who refuse to acknowledge the ability of blacks to support the march without supporting Farrakhan refuse to allow blacks the right to be diverse or the ability to be complicated.... I wish a black leader who was less incendiary than Louis Farrakhan had issued the call for black men to come out to the Million Man

March. But they didn't and he did. He stuck his neck out and it paid off. It was his day. Give it to him. (Wall 1995)

Poet and Writer Nikki Giovanni

I BELIEVE that old virus, racism, is still running rampant in our community, but I think we may have found an antidote in the Million Man March. I think one of the most important movements of this decade took place on October 16, 1995 in Washington, DC. That hundreds of thousands (though I believe a million plus) Black men came together to commune, to atone, to simply be close to each other and absorb some love and some support from each other was a great, historic event.

I am not expecting either Minister Farrakhan or the million men to create any miracles. We all, men and women, are just people trying our best to make sense of our lives. But I feel that by standing up, a great shaking of the earth occurred. There was no grandstanding. There were no putdowns of folk who were scared to go. There was a positive feeling that men needed to do something to affirm their existence.

As a Black woman, as a Christian, as a citizen of Planet Earth, I simply believe we all have to not only acknowledge but rejoice that the men are moving. If Black women alone could save this planet, then it would have been done. We need our friend, our partner, our son to stand with us. Before they can stand at our side they needed to take measure of each other.

This is a wonderful calling that Louis Farrakhan caused. I am sure everyone noted that Bill Clinton had not stood up to any Republican demand until after the March when he finally found his backbone.

I am very happy for the men. They will need to continue to touch base with each other, to cooperate with each other, to love and care for each other in the future. They may or may not have another march. I believe the one that they had will be sustaining. I know, if I may quote my own poetry, "... Walking down the street is the same old danger... But a brand new pleasure." (Giovanni 1996)

Snoop Dogg (Lion) Rapper/Actor

And it was exactly around the time that I (seek) the information from Minister Farrakhan, because we never had a leader, but we could always depend on Minister Louis Farrakhan because he understood us. And he spoke my language; he never talked bad about us. He always encouraged us. So we always respected him. And, when it got bad, I reached out to him. And he accepted me with warm arms and he had me come out to his house. … The Minister has always been there for the hip-hop community. I want to tell yall 'bout a story, that takes too much time but, it was about 10 years ago, when the rapper Notorious Biggie got killed in Los Angeles. I put a call out to Minister Farrakhan and we put a gathering where all of the rappers came together and we ended all of our beefs and we all had peace and it was love, and we been living that way ever since then. And that's all I've been on, peace, love and positivity – anybody that know me. When I went to go see Minister Farrakhan over 11 years ago; he gave me my mission to go do that. And I've been on it. I've been organizing and bringing the rappers together being the main advocate for peace. Just doing my thang and never really knowing why, but just doing it. So now it's like it came to a catapult, with like where this is why you're doing this. This is the reason why. It's always been in you, now let it out. (Lion 2013)

Boxing Heavyweight Champion Mike Tyson

Larry King – Uh, what do you think that is going out there in the world with the Farracans (Farrakhans) and the like?

Mike Tyson – I, personally as a person man, you know what I mean, people differ with me; I absolutely love Farrakhan. I don't know the gentleman by the name Kolod (Khallid) Muhammad. But Farrakhan as a person, I love Farrakhan. And it's very easy for a person to judge someone of what they say, but if you're a wise man, a real man would never have ill feelings (of) the speaker but to take (in) heed of what he says if what he says is true. You know what I mean? You must correct yourself, and if it's not true, you must prevent it from happening.

Larry King – But if he's wrong you should correct him?

Mike Tyson – If the man's wrong, then what he says has no significance.

(Larry King/CNN 2013)

Journalist and Writer Fahizah Alim

"In the NOI, black Americans see a group of proud and fearless black men who follow Minister Farrakhan. Black men who will go into drug and gang infested public housing complexes and confront the lawless. And they see an economic plan to revitalize black families and black communities that have been abandoned by government and corporate entities.

I know Farrakhan's real world impact on people. For example, when I started attending the University of California, Berkley, I also started taking the birth control pill. I think it was included in the registration packet. I mention the birth control pill because at the time, it was the drug of choice for most single young women. Many who were still in high school and not yet sexually active were prescribed the potent drugs, allegedly to "regulate their cycles."

Moreover, marijuana, "drop out," and "free love" were the buzzwords of my generation. The Beatles, Jimi Hendrix, Sly and the Family Stone, our Pied Pipers of modernity, lured us into a dark and swirling hole of hedonism. And Farrakhan, espousing the teachings of Elijah Muhammad, brought me out of the tailspin. Until that point, I had been taking birth control pills to keep from getting pregnant. **But after listening to Louis Farrakhan speak about how potent a drug must be to be capable of shutting down one of nature's powerful biological functions-that of reproducing itself-I stopped.**

It took me another 2 years to ovulate or produce eggs again. And some years later, the pharmaceutical companies revealed that we had been guinea pigs and the pills prescribed to some young women were about 10 times more potent than they should have been.

"You are poisoning yourself," Farrakhan has said. "Why kill the fruit of your womb and prevent maybe another great Black Leader from being born? Hasn't Pharaoh killed enough of our children?" **I am glad I heard him, I stopped**

91

taking the pill. And now I am the proud mother of 4 children: a daughter and 3 sons."

In major cities across the country, Minister Farrakhan is trying to build businesses, open schools, and teach black people how to pool their resources to build something for themselves...But, most important, he loves black people. [He] loves them more than he loves white people. And that is a rare black person to find. Most "black leaders" want to appease white folks. They need to have their intellect, their humanity, their worthiness validated by white people-the same people brought up to despise them. But not Farrakhan. That is his appeal.

As an NOI lieutenant during the 1970s, my task was teaching and training the women who joined the organization. I witnessed young chemically addicted female prostitutes come out of the drug culture and become good, loving mothers and homemakers. I saw former alcoholics and hustlers, wayward men and cheats become honest, dependable, and hard-working family men. I saw radical anarchists become community builders and schoolteachers. I even saw men involved in homosexual activity become satisfied husbands and fathers. This was done by a belief system and program that told them that their humanity did not originate in slavery or the jungles of Africa.

For me the Nation of Islam was a womb in which I was allowed to flourish and grow, to a point. It served as a womb that sheltered me and allowed me to develop and gain a knowledge of myself absent the presence of white supremacy. In America, blacks need a healthy framework by which we can shape ourselves...I am proud of my experience in the Nation of Islam and glad for the personal evolution it provided me. (Alexander 1998, 161-167)

Fahizah Alim is an award winning columnist for the Sacramento Bee and a former member of the Nation of Islam. The above quote is taken from the book Farrakhan Factor by Amy Alexander

Dr. Aminah McCloud

Now, in the last decade of the twentieth century, while the overall number of traditional black Muslims living in America continues to swell, the realities of the Muslim condition in the world community and the tensions between the ummah and the domestic realm remain constant.

Minister Farrakhan is trying to bridge these two worlds-and link his at-home concerns with the greater ummah. When Farrakhan visits leaders in Iran or Libya, an uniformed observer might see only that the Minister is willfully consorting with America's enemies, rather than recognizing the visit as an expression of his commitment to ummah...

In the same way that the five-times-daily prayers erase one set of class and gender issues, the notion of ummah obscures nation-state borders. This detail is critical in beginning to place some of Farrakhan's thoughts and actions within a larger Islamic context. For instance, by his continual condemnation of neocolonialism on the African continent and in the Caribbean, Louis Farrakhan demonstrates an understanding of the notion of ummah, however unorthodox his methods of expressing this understanding. (Alexander 1998, 175-177)

Dr. Aminah B. McCloud is an associate professor of religious studies at DePaul University. Excerpt from The Farrakhan Factor by Amy Alexander

Imam Warithudeen Mohammed

I introduce the man that left me. He said I got to go out, there are too many going astray, I hate to see them going back to what we pulled them out of with your father's teachings. So I'm going back. Did I ever tell you don't do that? Did I ever tell you don't do that? No, I didn't tell him not to do that. So he went out and he became another leader, new leader of the Nation of Islam, and he has done a marvelous job. Stay with him until you all get to the Promised Land. We embrace him and we are going with Minister Farrakhan all the way to the Promised Land. (Mohammed, Saviours' Day Jumuah Los Angeles 2002)

Imam Warithudeen Mohammed during February 15, 2002 Friday Jumuah Prayer Service during the Saviours' Day Weekend in Los Angeles

93

Dear Muslim brothers and sisters, it is not difficult for Minister Farrakhan and Wallace D. Mohammed to embrace each other. That's easy for us. When I first met him in the early '50s, I liked him on first sight, and I became his friend and his brother. And I have not stopped being his friend and his brother. Maybe he has not understood the way that I have been his friend and his brother at certain times, but I have always been his friend and his brother. For me this is too big a cause for our personal problems and differences. Allah-u Akbar.

We are to support each other in all good things. When the brother Muslim stands upon the Qur'an, the last of the revealed books and the complete book for all times and all societies, and when he stands upon faith in Muhammad as God's last prophet and Messenger to all the worlds, mercy to all the worlds, we are to support him in that.

As I said, it's easy for me to embrace Minister Farrakhan. Our families are together. We are really one family. Our friendship has not died, and it will not die. And the little problem, the small problem, that we've had along the way, struggling to present ourselves as God willed that we present ourselves, it's not bigger than the word of God, the Qur'an, and (it's) not bigger than Muhammad, the model for all human beings, for all people of faith. It's very small.

So we see, we think, what have we done to bring about this togetherness? What have we done to bring about this closeness that we have this minute? What have we done to free our hearts so we can hug each other and kiss each other, as I did kiss my brother? What have we done to bring that about? Nothing but tried to find the way in the path of Islam, and Allah did the rest. Allah did the rest.

I want to say that Minister Farrakhan is a great leader. I've watched him over the years, since the passing away of my father and our fallen leader, the Honorable Elijah Muhammad. I've watched him and I have done a little mathematics, a little calculation, and I've come up with progress for the Nation of Islam under the leadership of Minister Farrakhan. Whatever has troubled us in the past, I think we can bury it now and never look back at that grave. And never look back at that grave. (Mohammed, Saviours Day Jumuah 2000)

Imam Warithudeen Mohammed, excerpt from comments delivered by Imam W. Deen Mohammed during Jumu'ah prayer service held Feb. 25, at the McCormick Center as part of the Nation of Islam's Saviours' Day 2000 celebration in Chicago, published in The Final Call Newspaper

Imam Siraj Wahhaj

"Minister Farrakhan holds the key to the development of (Islam) in this country—so we're going to talk about where we go from here, let us now continue the process so that we can move even further on toward the development of Islam in America because the attack is against Islam and they don't ask you the question (are you) Sunni or Shiite, (are) you with the Nation (of Islam) or what? No. We have to recognize that the enemies of Islam are united against us," said Imam Siraj Wahhaj. (A. Muhammad, Life and ministry of Imam W. Deen Mohammed remembered 2008)

Imam Siraj Wahhaj, Amir of Muslim Alliance of North America during the memorial service held for Imam Warithuddin Mohammed. Quote excerpted from in The Final Call Newspaper September 21, 2008 article by Ashahed Muhammad

Henry Louis Gates and Dr. C. Eric Lincoln

Certainly the Farrakhan I met was a model of civility and courtesy. I was reminded of C. Eric Lincoln's account of the last couple of visits he paid to Farrakhan at his home: "Louis insisted on getting down on his hands and knees on the floor to take my shoes off. You know, I'm overweight, and it's a difficult task to get shoes and socks off. And so Louis said, 'I will do that.' And I said, "No, no.' And Louis said, 'No, I want to do it.' He took my shoes off and rubbed my feet to get the blood circulating." I met someone who was eager, even hungry, for conversation; someone of great intelligence who seemed intellectually lonely... In the end, however, it isn't Farrakhan but Farrakhan's following that demands explanation. We might start by admitting the moral authority that Black Nationalism commands even among those blacks who ostensibly disapprove of it. In the village where I grew up, there was a Holiness Church, where people spoke in tongues and fell down in religious ecstasy. It was not my church; my family and I shunned the Pentecostal fervor. And yet, on some level we believed it to be the real thing, realer than our own, more temperate Episcopal services. It was the place to go if you really needed something-if you go desperately sick, say-because the Holy Ghost lived there. (There are Reform Jews who admit to a similar attitude toward their Hasidic brethren.) In this same vein, the assimilated black American, who lives in Scarsdale and drives a Lexus, responds to Farrakhan and Farrakhanism as a presence at once threatening and exhilarating, dismaying and cathartic. (Alexander 1998, 47)

Henry Louis Gates, Jr. is the Alphonse Fletcher University Professor at Harvard University, as well as director of the W.E.B. Du Bois Institute for African and African American Research. Excerpt from The Farrakhan Factor by Amy Alexander

Professor Ernest Allen Jr.

On the positive side of the balance sheet, Louis Farrakhan often provides an exemplary example of black male leadership. He articulates the aspirations of large numbers of African Americans (including our entrepreneurial strata) and speaks out forcefully against incidents of African American oppression. Generally speaking, his internationalism presents a salutary aspect of his leadership as well, a constant reminder that we, as black Americans, must strive to avoid the trap of parochial thinking and steadfastly conceive of solutions to our social and political problems in global terms. Finally, whatever may have been the limitations of the Million Man March, it has provided a catalyst for untold numbers of black men to involve themselves in their local communities, an achievement that cannot be gainsaid even by Farrakhan's most trenchant critics...One of the long-term salutary roles of the NOI, both old and new, has been its demonstrated capacity to resurrect the "fallen" of the race and restore them to productive lives. (Alexander 1998, 87)

Ernest Allen Jr., is an associate professor in the W.E.B. Dubois Department of Afro-American Studies at the University of Massachusetts at Amherst. Excerpted from The Farrakhan Factor by Amy Alexander

Dr. Michael Eric Dyson

The Nation's singular focus on helping black men get their lives together is driven by its ideology of resistance to white supremacy. The Nation has worked diligently to make proud men out of black prisoners, those in jail or those whose self-image is distorted because they are captives to a worship of the white world. The Nation has always seen black male addictions-as symptoms of a virus of lostness that infects the entire black community. The Nation holds that the lostness of black men leads them to abuse their wives and children; to abuse their bodies with alcohol and bad food; to maim and murder each other; and to embrace, like black revolutionary theorist Frantz Fanon, the breasts of white womanhood in search of the milk of affection and affirmation. Long before the decline of black male life became widely apparent; and long before black males were vilified and glamorized by both the cultural right and the left, the Nation of Islam preached its own brand of salvation for black males. And from the very beginning, the core of the Nation's message has not changed. NOI followers believe that black men can be saved only by being restored as loving leaders in black families where they receive and return adoration and respect. (Alexander 1998, 140)

Dr. Michael Eric Dyson, University Professor of Sociology Georgetown University. Excerpt from The Farrakhan Factor by Amy Alexander

Ron Nixon

No black leader has had more of an impact on the Hip-Hop Generation than Louis Farrakhan. This is increasingly evident in the outward trappings of some young African Americans, the post-Civil Rights Era blacks who came of age after the pitched struggle for integration and who have taken up rap music and black neo-nationalism as their preferred form of cultural expression. Pictures of Farrakhan and the words "Nation of Islam" adorn the postmodern uniforms of black and Latino youth in sparkling suburbs and dying cities alike: On oversized T-shirts, jackets, and clean baseball caps, the silk-screened image of Farrakhan often shares space with those of Marcus Garvey, Malcolm X, and Nelson Mandela. From portable CD players and thumping auto-speakers come the sounds of hip-hop artists, their song lyrics sprinkled with allusions to NOI teachings and tensions between blacks and Jews.

Less conspicuously, black students are the largest consumers of NOI publications, and Farrakhan is undoubtedly the most sought-after speaker on black college campuses. Thousands of black youth joined adults to fill an Atlanta hall in 1992 when the minister came to speak-many more, in fact, than turned out across town at Fulton County Stadium to watch the World Series game that took place the same night...In Farrakhan, many black youths see a symbol of defiance and an alternative to established black leadership.

Some youth use kinship language when speaking of Farrakhan, with words like "brother" and "love" helping them describe their feelings for the minister.

"I love Farrakhan without question or reservation," Jason Broom, a twenty-six year-old African-American in Kansas City, told Newsweek magazine in March 1997. "He's a strong, stand-up black man. I don't practice his religion but I support him. He never turned on us on the street. He's for turning us to men." (Alexander 1998, 184-185)

Ron Nixon is a staff writer at the Roanoke (Virginia) Times. Excerpt from The Farrakhan Factor by Amy Alexander

Robert Michael Franklin

But what is Farrakhan's role in the political realm today? First, he is a prosecuting attorney on behalf of this nation's poor and oppressed minorities. He understands his role to be one of forcefully pointing out discrepancies between American political rhetoric and the reality of black American life. His eloquence and analytic gifts, extraordinary memory, and refined debating skills uniquely qualify him to represent the cause of the unemployable masses which most civil rights organizations and churches have not consistently advanced. Farrakhan speaks to black audiences in a manner that resembles old southern preachers who preach for two or three hours without notes, modulating their presentations between impassioned intensity and humorous, mischievous conversation. One has to sit in his presence to appreciate the quality of his dramatic performance. Many young blacks have been motivated (some would say seduced) by Farrakhan's charisma. Unemployed young people have banded with him, and he has given them hope. Many cannot read or write and are therefore ineligible for the job opportunities which Rev. Jackson and other civil rights leaders generate through protest and bargaining. Farrakhan demonstrates to such young people that after they have been rejected by the wider society they have a chance to become self-respecting persons within their own community.

He has gone into prisons and helped to reform numbers of America's most troublesome population. He has preached family stability and male-female mutual respect in a way that makes him sound more like Jerry Falwell than Malcolm X. But the black underclass has embraced his conservative ethical teachings and his Dale Carnegie-style lessons on personal hygiene, dress, manners, and salesmanship...

Second, Farrakhan is a prosecuting attorney for the Islamic faith and Afro-American Muslims. No other non-Christian leader in black America has so forcefully indicted the Christian tradition for its tacit and explicit racism, classism and hypocrisy, and still managed to command large audiences in the most prestigious churches across the nation. Farrakhan knows the Christian tradition intimately from his years as an altar boy in the Episcopal Church. Indeed, I think that he is drenched with the Anglicanism of his formative years. He believes that all things should be done decently and in order, that religion is a matter of rational understanding and that religious authorities, hierarchy, and traditions should be respected-all motifs which are emphasized in most quarters of the Episcopal community. Farrakhan also reminds us that Islam is not a parochial Arab tradition but a world-wide religion that creates a global community of Muslims who worship Allah. (Franklin 2001)

SalimMuwakkil

He is a remarkably gifted man. With his eloquence, his physical grace, and his flair for the dramatic, he is, by far, Black America's finest orator. His considerable intelligence and organizing abilities combine in a rare synthesis of leadership that has placed him near the top of several black public opinion polls. He's addressed millions of people in the last few years and was the only one capable of pulling off the enormously successful Million Man March. His popularity among African-Americans is even more unlikely. Although the Nation's message is as conservative and as unsensual as that of the most rigid Christian fundamentalist sect, he manages to attract the interest of the most testosterone-saturated segment of African-American community-young men. Listen to some rap records these days, and you're likely to be startled by a stern Farrakhan sermon floating incongruously over a deep bass groove.

Farrakhan seems pretty much unparalleled in his ability to corral the raging energies of this hip-hop generation. One of the ironies of gangsta rap is that pioneering purveyors of the genre also are attracted strongly to Farrakhan's Nation of Islam (many, in fact, are members). The Nation traditionally has attracted the outlaw element among African-Americans. Keep in mind the gangsta pedigree of Malcolm ("Detroit Red") Little who later became Malcolm X. One of the major reasons Farrakhan's group is accorded such street-level respect is its historical connection to the black "underclass."

Although Farrakhan's fiery oratory is heavy with race-man swagger and challenge, he also urges self-discipline, family reverence, ethnic solidarity, hard work, honesty, civility, and all the other virtues held dear by Judeo-Christian civilization. The Nation's rehabilitative success among people utterly forsaken and abandoned by the rest of society recently has prompted mainstream black organizations to look more favorable in Farrakhan's direction. (Alexander 1998, 207)

SalimMuwakkil, Chicago writer and editor of In These Times. He is a former editor of Muhammad Speaks. Excerpt from The Farrakhan Factor by Amy Alexander

Gwendolyn Brooks

Farrakhan. We don't have tea. I have met the Avidly Assaulted One once. About a quarter century ago, a woman poet, then a Muslim, brought him to meet my husband and myself. He was impressively relaxed. He brought no guards, no guns. We were impressed by his warm eyes, his kind patience, flexible dignity. He listened to our ideas. He listened to every word we said. He waited for us to finish our sentences. He never interrupted. (Today, interruption is an Art.) He did not feel the need to pastor. At least, he did not pastor. He did not ask us to join anything. This man I have not seen since. He is, however, a member of the Black Family. He is a Family Picture. I look at the picture. I don't want to forget that this individual has saved a lot of sick-souled, gasping, bare-footed Blacks no one else cared to save. He has fed them, medicated them, detoxicated them, schooled them: thus making many of our lives, homes, and little children a SMIDGEN safer. (Alexander 1998, 270-271)

Gwendolyn Brooks is a Pulitzer Prize winning poet in Chicago. Excerpt from The Farrakhan Factor by Amy Alexander

Professor Derrick Bell

Unlike those conservatives, black and white, who only preach self-help to the poor as a crowd-pleasing abstraction, Farrakhan's formulas emphasize the Nation of Islam's experience in educating black children, rehabilitating black prisoners, ridding black communities of drug dealers, and rebuilding respect for self-the essential prerequisite for individuals determined to maintain the struggle against the racism that burdens our lives and , unless curbed, will destroy this country." (M. L. Farrakhan 1993)

Henry Louis Gates Jr.

Talk story about Minister Louis Farrakhan's sermon at the Million Man March. Henry Louis Gates, Jr., asks five masters of black sacred oratory to give a strictly professional assessment of a colleague's delivery. THE REVEREND WYATT T. WALKER (Canaan Baptist Church, Harlem): Even though I have my quarrels with Louis Farrakhan, I would say that on a scale of ten he was about a twelve, oratorically speaking. THE REVEREND JAMES A. FORBES (Riverside Church, Harlem): As a piece of communication, it was an extraordinary moment. In terms of style, especially in his public condemnation of the President and whites, and so forth, there was a balance of courtesy and critique that I liked. (Gates 1995, 33)

Daniel K. Tabor, City Councilman

The appeal of Farrakhan's POWER (People Organized Working for Economic Rebirth) program for blacks has nothing to do with anti-Semitism. Jews are not the issue; the appeal is in its call for the economic development of the black community, and Farrakhan's program offers sound steps for that development. It should be endorsed and supported by the Urban League, National Association for the Advancement of Colored People, the Black Agenda (a coalition of black organizations working for economic development) and by all black elected officials, not because it is Farrakhan's program but because it will work for us. Black people have tried to be everything to everyone else. It is time for us to be pro-black for ourselves. (Tabor 1985)

Robert A. Jordan

If any speech from last Saturday's Washington march grows in greatness - as did Dr. Martin Luther King Jr.'s of 20 years ago - it will not be the one delivered by Rev. Jesse Jackson. Jackson was expected to be the most inspiring speaker at this year's march because of his oratorical skills and popular appeal among blacks and many whites. As a result, most of the news media, particularly television, focused on Jackson and his final words - "March on. Dream on. March on. Dream on. Our time has come." But as for highlighting the best, most inspiring speaker that day, the media - and television in particular - focused on the wrong man. Although he drew a standing ovation from many of his fans, Jackson was hardly awe-inspiring, and his speech is unlikely to be cast as one of the more memorable of our time. Many marchers felt, perhaps because of high expectations, that his performance was disappointing. One of the best speeches, according to reporters and marchers, was delivered by NAACP Executive Director Benjamin Hooks, who focused his early remarks on politics - "Reagan no more in '84" - and later, assuming his role as a Baptist preacher, ended his speech with the religious fervor that reaches such audiences, as King did so well 20 years ago. However, many who listened to the 40 speakers said the most inspiring speech was given by a lesser-known figure, Louis Farrakhan, organizer of the new Nation of Islam, a Black Muslim religious group. In fact, Farrakhan, who followed Jackson on the speaker's rostrum, was not even mentioned by the news media in the next day's reports. One reason is that they already had their minds made up that Jackson, currently the most popular activist in America, was going to be the focal point for that news event no matter how poorly he performed. Yet it was Farrakhan, one marcher said, who gave him "goose bumps" when he spoke. And it was a black postal worker and a black private business consultant who said that Farrakhan "said some very good things." For example, he told the diverse religious, racial and ethnic groups that "we cannot tolerate any longer these artificial barriers that divide us as a people." Twenty years ago, or even 10, no self-respecting Muslim would have made such a speech. At that time, they were preaching black separatism. But in recent years they have begun to include whites in their membership, and have worked to improve relations with Christian organizations. Farrakhan, whose eloquence has been heard mostly by black Muslims, said in a clear, ringing voice that "this government must say that they will overcome this desire to tell others how to live abroad while neglecting Americans at home." But he added that whether America overcomes this problem or not "we the poor, we the oppressed, we the blacks, we the Hispanics, we the disinherited, we the rejected and the despised, we will overcome and then together we will be able to say in the words of Dr. Martin Luther King - free at last, free at last, thank God Almighty we have united and made freedom a reality at last." Some reporters as well as marchers did not even hear Farrakhan's speech, partly because they left after hearing Jackson, and partly because Farrakhan did not have the name recognition of Jackson, Hooks, or others at the march. His moving speech may not come close in rank to King's great speech. Not many do. But it should not have been ignored. Ironically, King's "I Have A Dream" speech of 20 years ago was almost totally ignored - except in the New York Times - in press accounts the following day. The speech, which King largely ad libbed after he felt the spiritual mood of the crowd, did not become famous until years later. However, perhaps because Farrakhan's Muslim organization does not give him the status of blacks such as King, Jackson or Hooks, his speech may not grow with the passage of time. But it certainly did not deserve to be a victim of the media's pre-occupation with the charismatic Jackson. (Jordan 1983)

Black Entertainment Television

"An overwhelming percentage of our users agreed that Minister Farrakhan made the most positive impact on the Black community over the past year and chose him as the person most worthy to receive the honor of BET.com's 2005 Person of the Year," said Retha Hill, BET.com's vice president for Content.

They agreed that he has done what no other African American leader has: "mobilize hundreds of thousands of Blacks around the issues of atonement and empowerment, and to convince the masses of our people that we must be the primary catalysts and engines for positive change in our communities," she said.

"I am greatly honored and extremely humbled that the BET.com users have chosen me as the 2005 Person of the Year, especially since the nominees for such an honor are some of the greatest members of the Black community in the world; Ms. Oprah Winfrey, Senator Barack Obama, the father of BET Robert L. Johnson and the suffering victims of Hurricane Katrina of New Orleans," Minister Farrakhan told BET.com.

"Honor is never deserved until after the work and mission is completed. The work of the liberation of our people, and the poor and oppressed around the globe is a long, difficult, protracted struggle.

"So, I accept this great honor as encouragement to work as hard as I can in the twilight years of my life to facilitate the success of this ongoing struggle."

Minister Farrakhan said his next move is to continue the work of building the Millions More Movement, which he said will utilize the skill and talent of our people to lift us up.

The minister told BET.com that the Millions More Movement faced many obstacles, but with faith in God, hard work, and the unity of those whose desire it was to create the movement, "we have overcome many obstacles and still are overcoming obstacles in the pathway of our success."

In 1995, Farrakhan became the chief organizer --and a leader -- of a large rally of African-American men in Washington, D.C. Known as the Million Man March, the event was designed to encourage Black men to take personal responsibility for improving conditions in Black America. The crowd was estimated to be up to a million people or more. (Staff 2005)

Wyclef Jean

The reason why I believe it is important for the Honorable Minister Louis Farrakhan to come to Haiti, because the Honorable Minister Louis Farrakhan is one of the most powerful people in the world. I want Haitian people to know their powers. We know that the Honorable Minister Farrakhan has Jamaican roots. In the history we read about Boukman, the Honorable Minister Louis Farrakhan is speaking in the spirit of Boukman. I studied him in the United States. I remember one time when he got all of us in a room, Wyclef, Jay Z and told us guys "the real power it to unite." Today the message I bring to all the Haitian people is that unity produces power. A lot of people when they hear Wyclef speaking, they don't realize I am speaking from the knowledge of my father. The Honorable Minister Louis Farrakhan has been my teacher for a long time. I want to tell you something that is important about this man that is sitting next to me (Minister Farrakhan). I think about 7 to 8 years ago, this man told me about 7 or 8 years ago that I was going to be a presidential candidate and at that time I didn't know what he was talking about. I didn't know I was going to lose (laughter). I want to tell everyone who is listening in to Radio Caraibes, there is no question this wonderful man (Minister Farrakhan) cannot answer, so I thank the listeners of Radio Caraibes for having him here. (FCNN 2011)

Erykah Badu

Louis Farrakhan is a Superhero, that's a beautiful brave being (Badu 2013)

Mary J. Blige

Thank you Minister Farrakhan for spending time with us and sharing your words of wisdom with us. We love you so much (Blige 2013)

Journalist Ellen Hume

Mr. Jackson has disavowed Mr. Farrakhan's words. But he has refused to go further and denounce the man or renounce his political support. The candidate insists that he can't "muzzle" the Muslim leader; Mr. Jackson adds, "Minister

Farrakhan has a very high batting average for fighting for good." That view may have cost Mr. Jackson white votes, but it may also have intensified his support in the black community. "We are convinced that the white establishment is trying to divide us," says Lu Palmer, a black political activist in Chicago. "We were concerned how we were going to keep things going for Jackson. The media gave it to us by jumping on Farrakhan." Whatever the case, Mr. Farrakhan -- unknown to the white community a few months ago -- apparently has influence in black America far beyond his estimated 10,000 hard-core religious followers. Moreover, Jackson campaign officials say that Mr. Farrakhan, who has ties to Arab leaders, played a crucial role in Mr. Jackson's success in freeing U.S. flier Robert Goodman from Syria...After replacing Malcolm X as head of the coveted Black Muslim Harlem Temple No. 7, Mr. Farrakhan met Jesse Jackson for the first time in 1972. Mr. Jackson, as a civil-rights leader, called a press conference to support the Muslims after a police incident at the temple. It was a rare moment of friendship between the separatist Muslims and the civil-rights movement they had scorned; Louis Farrakhan never forgot it. "We are not close associates or what one would call buddies. But we mutually admire each other," Mr. Farrakhan says. When he learned that Mr. Jackson was running for president, he broke Muslim tradition and registered to vote, sending a signal that prompted many black nationalists around the country to follow suit and register in order to vote for Mr. Jackson. Thomas N. Todd, a Chicago lawyer who is one of Mr. Jackson's closest associates, says regarding Mr. Jackson's showing so far, "My personal opinion is that we wouldn't have been able to do what we did in Philadelphia, Chicago, New York and the South without Minister Farrakhan." He adds that Mr. Farrakhan was a "substantial part of the success" of Mr. Jackson's Syria mission to free Lt. Goodman, although he got little publicity at the time. "To assume Minister Farrakhan is on some lunatic fringe, away from the mainstream, is not true," Mr. Todd emphasizes. "His influence extends far beyond the Nation of Islam, to black professionals, educators and others who agree with Farrakhan's position on some of the social ills and how we got there." Mr. Farrakhan's following isn't nearly as large as the Jackson support in black Christian churches, others stress. "There's no comparison," says the Rev. Charles Stith, a black Methodist minister in Boston. "You're comparing apples and peanuts." Yet it was Mr. Farrakhan's highly disciplined followers who helped the Jackson campaign get off the ground. They were the candidate's original bodyguards before the U.S. Secret Service stepped in; they contribute money collected in baskets at their religious meetings and they continue to stage the huge Jackson rallies in key cities like Philadelphia, New York and Chicago. Mr. Farrakhan is a "leader, like Benjamin Hooks, John Jacob, Vernon Jordan and the others," concludes Dorothy Leavell, the publisher of the New Crusader, a black newspaper in Chicago. (Mr. Hooks is the executive director of the National Association for the Advancement of Colored People, Mr. Jacobs is the president of the national Urban League and Mr. Jordan is a former president of that group.) At another time and place, Mr. Jackson and Mr. Farrakhan might have been rivals. "He is probably the only other person, in terms of charisma, who could challenge Jesse," says Boston's Mr. Stith. "He's powerful. (Hume 1984)

Harry L. Thomas, Sr.

On Oct. 24, I did indeed present a resolution to Minister Louis Farrakhan. In its introductory clause, that resolution reads: "To recognize the Nation of Islam for their commitment and dedication to the 'War on Drugs.' "As that clause states, the Nation of Islam was honored for its fight against drugs. The resolution addressed not what Mr. Farrakhan stands for or has said, but what he, as leader of the Nation of Islam, has done. While others talked about a solution to the drug activity in Mayfair Mansions, the Nation of Islam acted and achieved outstanding success in the face of ostensibly insurmountable odds. The resolution praises the Nation for their "commitment and dedication," no more, no less. Should I, or the D.C. Council, be condemned or second-guessed for acknowledging the success of the Nation for recapturing our neighborhoods from the drug dealers? The article also observed that, because of Minister Farrakhan's "racially inflammatory remarks . . . black politicians are uncertain whether to openly support him or openly denounce him." I cannot speak for other black politicians, but as for Harry Thomas, I unequivocally support the minister and the Nation of Islam for their efforts to stem the tide of drugs in our neighborhoods. My feelings in this regard are so unflinching that I would, for once, even give unequivocal support to The Washington Post should it decide to man the front lines in the fight against drugs. In that instance, to say that my "unequivocal support" for The Post for its drug-fighting efforts translates into my support of The Post in general would be a gross misstatement of fact. Further, if The Post undertook such a drug-fighting effort, but does not represent my views in general, are my only two choices to "openly support" it or "openly denounce" it? Finally, my support of the Nation of Islam and its leader, Minister Farrakhan, will continue for as long as their effective leadership in helping rid the black community of the scourge of drugs continues. That support, however, will extend to any others who choose to assist in that fight. (ThomasJr. 1989)

William Raspberry

Farrakhan says what so many black people believe but have learned not to say in public: for instance, that Jews wield tremendous influence in the news and entertainment media. That doesn't mean that most blacks accept Farrakhan's notion of a small Jewish cabal that meets in Hollywood or in a Park Avenue apartment to decide which ideas and trends are to be foisted off on the public. But few of us doubt the disproportionate influence of Jews-for good or ill- on what we see on television or in the movies. Nor do blacks doubt the disproportionate influence of Jews on American foreign policy, particularly with regard to political and economic support of Israel. But we also know that to say these things is to be accused of anti-Semitism. That's why blacks can cheer when Farrakhan says them, even in gross overstatement. (Raspberry 1990)

Matthew Pulver

Lord only knows what sort of paranoiac frenzy Glenn Beck would spiral into were he to discover this recent trend in hip-hop: Rappers are increasingly seeking the wisdom and counsel of Minister Louis Farrakhan, leader of the Nation of Islam. And not just the Muslim rappers you'd expect, like Lupe Fiasco or Mos Def; since the beginning of the year, superstar rappers like Kanye West, Young Jeezy and Killer Mike have all met with Farrakhan.

I can see Glenn Beck flying between multiple chalkboards, manically scrawling the connections proving the imminent danger of some coming caliphate. How had we not seen it all along?! ISIS HAS INFILTRATED THE MINDS OF OUR YOUTH THROUGH THEIR HIPPITY HOPPITY!

Beck would be wrong, as usual, to make the ominous links, but the trend does signify something of a shift in attitudes. Black Islam occupies a particular place in the civil rights struggle: Malcolm X's "by any means" militancy versus Dr. King's conciliatory nonviolence. The turn toward black Islam might indicate disappointment and an impatience with the lack of progress made during the Obama years.

Kanye West met with Farrakhan in January, bringing wife Kim Kardashian and baby North. The minister and rapper had "a beautiful meeting," said Farrakhan. The two spoke on the state of rap music in this turbulent time in race relations, and Farrakhan was glad to see rappers "becoming conscious now," lending their voice to battling injustice. Kanye mentioned the meeting, or perhaps another, on the first single off his upcoming album, referring to Farrakhan as his "sensei."

Jay Z publicly celebrates black Islam, despite controversially flirting with agnosticism. On his last album, Hov begins the song "Heaven" with a line whose reference likely eluded most listeners: "Arm, Leg, Leg, Arm, Head," a cryptic naming of Allah used by Five Percenters, an offshoot of the Nation of Islam. Hov has also been seen rocking a chain with a Five Percenter medallion.

Killer Mike, one-half of the critically acclaimed Run the Jewels, met with Farrakhan in January, as well. Like Jay Z, Killer Mike is openly skeptical of organized religion, making each rapper's acceptance of black Islam particularly stand out.

Even Young Jeezy met with Farrakhan earlier this month. Jeezy–unlike Hov, Mike and Yeezy–does not often tend toward political or "conscious" rap. Jeezy is more of a trap rapper than the others, but he calls Farrakhan his "mentor" and posted a proud photo on Instagram of his meeting with the minister.

Farrakhan is back. He's fostered relationships with a number of premier rappers, and seeing something of a power vacuum in black leadership, the controversial cleric is moving in to align a more radical approach to racism. He's rallying black Americans to be ready for an eventual eruption in the face of police violence in communities of color. "You've got to prepare your people for what is coming down!" he screams as he recounts the uprising in Ferguson, Missouri, and what he sees as the failure of black leaders to appropriately respond–to actually change a system under which virtually every black man feels threatened. He indicts Obama and former Attorney General Eric Holder, as well as inveterate civil rights activist Jesse Jackson. Black preachers are called out for being "pacifiers for the white man's tyranny."

Farrakhan's Nation of Islam was credited by protesters on the ground in Baltimore with establishing a gang truce in the city to unify black Baltimore against the police. The NOI and its well-dressed Fruit of Islam were on the ground in Ferguson, as well, in a leadership role. (Pulver 2015)

George Curry

It's time to give Minister Louis Farrakhan credit. When he issues a call for people to join him in the nation's capital, Blacks show up. At least a million showed up for the Million Man March 20 years ago and at least two-thirds as many showed up for Saturday's Justice or Else assembly on the National Mall.

Without a doubt, Farrakhan-led events in Washington, D.C. attract more people than marches called jointly by all of the other civil rights leaders. And whenever Minister Louis Farrakhan is involved in a major event, there is always a controversy about numbers. In his speech at the Million Man March, people were fascinated by his fascination with numerology.

In the aftermath of that event, the U.S Park Service made the ridiculous estimate that 400,000 people attended. But Boston University's Center for Remote Sensing placed the figure between 655,000 to 1.1 million – more than twice as large as the 1963 March on Washington.

Farrakhan manages to be a magnet while withstanding withering attacks. Consider a few recent headlines:

* "Nation of Islam's leader Louis Farrakhan: White People 'deserve to die.'"

* "Nation of Islam's Louis Farrakhan: 'We need to put the American flag down.'"

* "Cancelled: Charleston Wants No Part of Farrakhan's 'Justice or Else' Movement."

How is it that the most reviled Black man in America consistently attracts waves of people?

African Americans trust Minister Farrakhan. Even if strongly disagreeing with some of his views and the well-known antipathy between the Nation of Islam (NOI) leader and Jews, Blacks know that he won't ever sell them out for personal gain or any other reason. (Curry 2015)

Salim Muwakkil

Nation of Islam leader Farrakhan and hip-hop go way back. The minister believes that hip-hop artists have a profound impact on African-American life and culture. The respect is mutual; Farrakhan's voice has been popping up on rap records since the genre's earliest years and rappers ranging the spectrum (from "conscious" to "gangsta") often speak his praises on record and off…. In 1997, Farrakhan gathered a group of hip-hop artists and activists in Chicago to call a truce in the destructive beef that likely took the lives of Wallace, Shakur and countless others. He said at the time that hip-hop often got a bad rap for reflecting what society would prefer to hide, but that artists also had a responsibility to be balanced in their portrayals.

Farrakhan's recognition of hip-hop's cultural validity was unique among old school black leaders, most of whom dismissed the genre as a faddish and vulgar aberration. Many analysts blame those clashing verdicts about the music's value for a growing generational divide within black America.

At a hip-hop summit two years ago in New York City, Farrakhan urged performers and record executives to be more responsible for the effect of their words. He said hip-hop artists were black America's new leadership. "One rap song from you is worth more than 1,000 of my speeches," he told the crowd. "Will you accept your responsibility as a leader?" (Muwakkil 2003)

111

Nathan McCall

I suspect that, for some white Americans, complaints about Farrakhan are a smoke screen to conceal their blanket contempt for any black man who attempts to lift us up. White America may now pledge allegiance to the memory of Martin Luther King but black America has not forgotten that King, who preached love, peace and every other noble virtue that we claim to embrace, was intensely disliked and opposed by many whites when he was alive. His plan for a march on Washington 32 years ago was also described as divisive, unnecessary, potentially violent. I have even less patience with so-called black church and political leaders nationwide who have criticized the Million Man March. With all that black men have been going through in recent years, there's been no broad-scale effort -- symbolic or otherwise -- by national black politicians and clergy to inspire us. If there were more black leaders out there with courage and imagination, we'd have done something like this long ago. Everywhere I've gone in recent months, from barber shops in Prince George's County, to college campuses in Kentucky, the irrelevance of this traditional leadership has been clear. Black men -- the regular brothers whose voices are seldom captured on TV or in print -- say they don't need to consult so-called black leaders to determine whether or not to attend the march. (McCall 1995)

Clifton E. Marsh

Minister Louis Farrakhan was one of Jackson's early supporters in running for the presidency. Early in 1983 Minister Louis Farrakhan "wrote Jackson a letter urging him to seek the country's top office and offering his support." Prior to Rev. Jackson being considered a serious candidate, he received no Secret Service protection. Minister Louis Farrakhan directed his "Fruit of Islam" to protect Rev. Jackson on the campaign trail. In each city in which Jackson arrived to speak, he was greeted, escorted, and protected by disciplined cadres of bow tie-wearing black men. When candidate Jackson was finally given Secret Service protection by the U.S. government, the agents would complain that they "couldn't get close to him for the crowd of Muslims around him."

Minister Louis Farrakhan played a significant and vital role in enabling Jesse Jackson to secure the release of navy Lt. Robert Goodman. Minister Louis

Farrakhan accompanied Rev. Jackson to Syria. Surely, this would be a test for the ideas of the Honorable Elijah Muhammad. The so-called contrast between Orthodox Islam and the Nation of Islam could derail negotiations, put Lieutenant Goodman's life in further danger, and embarrass the United States and the entire African American community. The charismatic Minister Louis Farrakhan impressed Syria's heads of state, Imams, Muslim scholars, and true believers with his knowledge with his knowledge of Islam and ability to speak perfect Arabic. He led the Jumuah prayer service with all the grace and eloquence of Bilal himself. So much for those who said the international community of Islam would not accept the ideology of the Lost-Found Nation of Islam in America. (Marsh 2000)

Dr. Boyce Watkins

"Minister Farrakhan fascinates many Black people because he represents a type of freedom and truth that they can only dream about. Even those who disavow him in public rely on him behind closed doors because he has the courage and capacity to confront obstacles that leave most Black Americans in fear. He doesn't bend, fold or change his tune due to corporate or political pressure, and he doesn't spend his time tap dancing for White people. He also has a degree of ownership of his own being that is nothing short of extraordinary. The truth is that he has negotiated a relationship with White America in which they may not love him, but they do fear him and respect him. It is mutual respect from White America that Black people are lacking today, largely due to our inability to secure economic, psychological and social self-sufficiency. We get these things from Minister Louis Farrakhan. When I met Minister Farrakhan, I felt like I was talking to my own father. As a Black man who has worked to teach myself to be strong and free, it's difficult to find older Black men who understand my path and journey and can show me how to pursue that path more effectively. My three hours with the Minister in private conversation, my meetings with him in Arizona and our event in Chicago were all life-changing for me and in each case; I knew I had the rare opportunity to be a part of history." (S. Muhammad 2013)

Alabama State Senator Hank Sanders

(The following letter is Senator Sanders response to complaints by the Birmingham Jewish Federation over the appearance of Minister Farrakhan in the state of Alabama, specifically to lend his support influence and popularity to the civil rights leaders' efforts to maintain the right to vote for Black people in the state of Alabama)

Dear Mr. Friedman,

Thank you for your letter expressing concerns about Minister Louis Farrakhan's coming to Alabama to stand with us in fighting to save our voting rights in general and Section 5 in particular. I respond in this open letter because of the extensive communications around this issue.

We are fighting for a basic constitutional right -- the right to vote. It is the right that protects all other rights. The right to vote is so important to us, our children and our children's children. I personally know the terrible sting of not being able to vote. It affects every part of our being, including our sense of worth. The right to vote is extremely critical.

Minister Louis Farrakhan is coming to Alabama at our invitation. We welcome everyone who will stand with us to protect this basic right -- the right to vote, which is under great attack.

You and other Jewish people have and have had the right to vote. It is not under attack. You have not suffered the loss of the right to vote provided by Fifteenth Amendment to U.S. Constitution as we have. You were not prevented from voting for nearly 100 years as our people were. It is a terrible thing that I hope Jewish Americans never have to suffer.

We are fighting to protect a constitutional right -- the right to vote. You are fighting to keep a person out of Alabama because of his exercising his constitutional right to freedom of speech. The words you attribute to him are offensive, but it is his constitutional right to speak. (Additionally, he has denied many of the allegations.) I do not fault you for objecting to offensive language.

You have not publicly stood with us once to protect our constitutional right to vote during the series of events we have held in Alabama, Washington DC and throughout the Southeast, events that commenced in February and continue today. Now you ask us to reject someone who believes in our fight for the constitutional right to vote and is coming to stand side by side and fight. This does not make sense to me.

When US Supreme Court Justice Antonin Scalia made disparaging remarks about Section 5, calling it a "racial preferment" and comparing racial minorities to "child abusers," I did not hear you standing against these racist remarks.

We cannot fault you for whomever you stand with or have stand with you in your struggle. By the same token, we cannot allow you to determine who stands with us in our struggle.

All of us fall short. I know I fall short all the time. While Minister Farrakhan has said things that are offensive (many of which he has denied), he has also lifted many from societal degradation. Should that not count for something? Should we not value people for what they do as well as what they say? I applaud him for the good things he has done.

Finally, if all the people in Alabama who have uttered racist words were removed from Alabama, we would have a greatly depopulated state. I think the same standards ought to apply to all of us, including Minister Louis Farrakhan.

Again, I appreciate your expressing your concerns to me, but the right to vote is too important not to fight for it with all available resources. Please consider this letter in the spirit in which it is intended -- one of forgiveness and inclusion.

Sincerely, Hank Sanders (Sanders 2013)

Tuskegee Alabama Mayor Johnny Ford

"I'm here to say that not only is he(Minister Farrakhan) welcome, with the power invested in me by the people of Tuskegee, Alabama, I hereby proclaim this night as 'Minister Louis Farrakhan Night' in the City of Tuskegee. Not only do I present to him the key to the City of Tuskegee, I'm proud to say that he is honorary mayor of Tuskegee for life!" (A. Muhammad, Farrakhan tells students: You are chosen to build a world! 2013)

To a great extent, in other words, Farrakhan now *is* the black leadership—the cutting edge, the storm center, the presence against which others are measured. 1985. (National Review 1985)

Frank Paul Jones

Before I discuss Minister **Farrakhan's** speech, I'm gon'na describe what I witnessed. I went there with an idea that Minister **Farrakhan** was an egocentric preacher of hatred. (This is how white media influenced me.) I was wrong. What I witnessed was a very humble man, who has been character assassinated by white media, for speaking the truth as he understood it, and at the time expressed himself as he felt it was necessary.

I witnessed a man who is apprehensive, yet he is willing to risk death for the sake of truth. As he stood inside a bullet-proof case, he cried out to all people including white society and Jews, for help. In that moment, in my eyes, he was not a man of hate, but a man of love; a man of God. He became the unspoken voice for tens of thousands of Black people, holding hands in prayer, who were referring to each other as "my brother" and "my sister" and it was an event full of love. (F. P. Jones 1996)

Prof. Andre C. Willis

The best of the legacy of Farrakhan is twofold. First, he has demonstrated a deep understanding of and shown an unswerving courage to publicly detail the lived reality of anti-black racism. There is simply no Black person in the world that has — over so many years — been as consistent, as unrestricted, and as forthright in defending the humanity of Black people throughout the world against its attackers. This is partially due to the power of black institutions: Minister Farrakhan does not rely on white financial support. It is also due to a sense of discipline and commitment inscribed in his practice as a man of faith. Demonized by some and ostracized by many, Farrakhan's story has been one of "staying the course" for racial uplift.

Second, Farrakhan's captivating speaking style and scriptural knowledge have made him, undoubtedly, one of the great religious orators of our time. His entrancing public speeches, which never lose track of race, are crafted at the intersection of the religious and the political. Farrakhan, in the style of the eighteenth century "Great Awakening" speakers, unapologetically deploys the sacred texts of Christianity and Islam in his public witness. Yet these "religious" speeches are deeply politicized and they rely on different religious traditions. Thus, they stand in a class all by themselves. Further, his visual appeal, stylized voice and phrasing, as well as his effective use of silence are incomparable. When Biblical and Qur'anic scholars begin to attend to the body of his work, this aspect of his legacy will stand even taller. (Willis 2012)

President Ibrahim B. Syed, Ph. D.,

I asked Sheikh Ahmed Tijani as to how he came to know about me. He did not answer me specifically. Later on I came to know a mutual friend recommended my name. I accepted the invitation to attend and speak in several sessions, such as the two plenary sessions on "The Oneness of Allah and the Oneness of His Community", and two workshops on "Islamic Science and Technology", "Islamic Health", and one workshop on "Modern Methods of Propagation for the New Century" and I was assigned the job of a Moderator on a session on "Islamic Science, Technology and Communication Systems for the New Century." Other interesting and timely workshops that were conducted were "The Need to Return to Moral Excellence", "Islamic Education in the New Century", "Islamic Family Life. Courtship and Preparation for Marriage. Strengthening Family and Home Life", "Islamic Law in the New Century", "Islamic Economics and Banking in the New Century", "Conflict Resolution Among Muslims", "The Role of Women in Islam", "The Place of Architecture, Art, and Culture in Islam", "Advancement of Muslims Socially, Politically, and Economically in Western Society, and in other Countries" and Plenary Sessions on "Inter-Faith Dialogue." I accepted the invitation for two reasons, one to share my humble knowledge and secondly to observe first-hand the activities of the controversial organization "The Nation of Islam."

This International Islamic Conference is one of the best I have ever attended in North America or anywhere in the world. It was well organized and executed. Many scholars came from many parts of the world, such as Canada, Mexico, Panama, Trinidad, Sri Lanka, Great Britain, Philippines, Dagestan (Russia), South Africa, Nigeria, Morocco, Gambia, Uganda, Senegal, Ghana, Greek Cyprus, Egypt, Jordon, Palestine, Lebanon, Yemen, United Arab Emirates, and of course from many cities in USA.

The attenders were kept busy from morning till late in the night. I attended the Jumuah prayers at the Mosque Maryam, where we also prayed Maghrib and Isha prayers. The Zuhr and Asr prayers were conducted at the Hilton Inn and Towers. I saw the Hon. Minister Louis Farrakhan praying with us like an Orthodox Muslim or mainstream Muslim. The Muslims in the Community of the Nation of Islam both men and women behaved extremely well and were well dressed. I was impressed with them, as they are a good role model for other Muslims.

The Nation of Islam identifies itself as Islamic. Members call God "Allah," they call themselves Muslims, they teach and worship in mosques, they appeal to the prophet Muhammad (peace be upon him), they recite the Muslim creed, and they view the Qur'an as inspired Scripture. The chief leaders of the NOI (Elijah Muhammad, Malcolm X, and Minister Farrakhan) have all made pilgrimages to Mecca, and at the present time NOI members are instructed to fast during the Muslim month of Ramadan and to consult the *hadith* or traditions ascribed to Prophet Muhammad (pbuh) to determine proper conduct and doctrine. Thus, for broad purposes of classification, it seems reasonable to place the NOI somewhere within the Islamic camp.

I did not witness any controversial thing during my five days of association with them. The final session ended at the McCormick Place where Col. Muammar Qaddafi, the Libyan Leader spoke to the participants by satellite T.V. Also this session was televised all over the Muslim World. The finale of the International Conference was when Imam Farrakhan spoke to the audience for almost two years with his remarkable ability to spellbind and charm the audience. At the end of the session Mr. Jerry Thomas of the Chicago Tribune interviewed me, as others appeared to be reluctant to the interview. In my interview with reference to the Nation of Islam, I told what I witnessed . . . . "They were first identified as black Muslims. That barrier has been removed. They are now just Muslims, like any other Muslims in the world."

On that final day evening, I received a dinner invitation at the home (Palace or official residence) of the Leader of the Nation of Islam along with all the foreign delegates and a few American delegates. Imam Farrakhan was a gracious host and everyone enjoyed the delicious dishes and a sumptuous dinner. That memorable night was concluded with an individual photo session with the Imam or the Leader of the Nation of Islam…

Muslims who still have doubts and upset should have a dialogue with the Nation of Islam. Alhamdulillah, Muslims are doing very well in Inter-Faith dialogues with Christians and Jews. Why not we have dialogues with the Nation of Islam? I personally believe we must interact with the Nation of Islam with Hikmah (wisdom) and Sabr (patience) in the model of our Rasoolallah (SAS). I completely agree with the sentiments expressed by the popular and well-known Muslim journalist, Mom "Moon" Khan, that "it is time for healing, a time for moving ahead, understanding each other and respecting each other. It is not the time of dividing people and isolating people in a community and putting other communities ahead of each other."…

Muslims of North America will derive immense benefits and rewards by uniting with the Nation of Islam and by welcoming them as our brothers and sisters in Islam. It is highly gratifying to know that the Nation of Islam and the Ministry of Imam Wartih Deen Mohammed have united to advance the cause of Islam and the Muslims in North America. May Allah (SWT) guide us and show us the right path and bring us from darkness unto light. Ameen! (Syed n.d.)

International Islamic Conference

Imam Ahmed Rufai: "As Salaam Alaikum, Brothers and Sisters.
On behalf of the Muslim World, we have the Grand Sheikh of Cypress, Sheikh Muhammad Sobhi Bello; The Grand Sheik of Egypt and Vice President of Al-Azhar University, Sheikh Abu Al Azayem; and The Grand Sheikh of Yemin Sheikh Abu Ghazela and our Sheikh of Ghana and Nigeria Sheikh Abdul Razzaq

Tahir Muhyideen, and Sheikh Yusuf Shibly who want to show their admiration for the leadership of our brother The Honorable Minister Louis Farrakhan by recognizing him as an Imam of the Muslim World.

Translator for Sheikh Mohammed Sobhi Bello of Cyprus: "In the Name of Allah (swt), the Most Merciful, the Most Beneficent, blessed are you and blessed is this conference. In the symbol of the leadership and the knowledge of the Qur'an, we signify that, symbolize that by putting this cap on the head of our leader, Brother Louis Farrakhan because the scholars and the knowledgeable are the people who are the inheritors of the Prophets of Allah (swt). And to signify that we have put that on his head in order to show our appreciation and to show that he is knowledgeable and will lead the Islamic Nation, inshallah, with his inspiration." (H. M. Farrakhan, International Islamic Conference 1997)

Professor Mattias Gardell

His long lectures are composed much like orchestral numbers. He starts by displaying a theme, and then varies the expressions, moving his audience to tears and laughter, serious consideration and explosive anger, before reaching the grand finale in which he dramatically drives his points through. Farrakhan combines a number of diverse roles during each sermon, such as the strong warrior, the trickster, the stern father, the heart warmer, the stand-up comedian, the encyclopedic scholar and the Doomsday prophet. As is common in the black church, a kind of dialogue is established as the preaching evokes responses from the audience, with the worshipers shouting cries of approval such as "That's right," "Tell it like it is," "Go on, Minister, go on," and "Teach, Brother teach."
There is no doubt that Farrakhan's oratorical brilliance contributes heavily to his rising popularity and explains, in part, the crowds that jam auditoriums when he speaks. Farrakhan is able to attract larger audiences than any other black spokesperson: 35,000 people showed up at Madison Square Garden, New York; 17,000 in Los Angeles; 26,000 in Detroit; 19,000 and then 15,000 in Atlanta; 15,000 in Chicago; 21,000 at Jacob Javits Center in New York, and 10,000 in Baltimore. (Gardell 1996)
—Mattias Gardell, Professor of Theology Uppsala University, Sweden; In The Name of Elijah Muhammad, Louis Farrakhan and The Nation of Islam

Socialist Economist and Professor Dr. Michael D. Yates

Cedric Muhammad: Earlier this year you met with the Honorable Minister Louis Farrakhan and were presented with an introduction to the Economic Blueprint of the Honorable Elijah Muhammad. What were your impressions of both the Minister and that Program?

Michael D. Yates, PhD.: I was impressed with Minister Farrakhan's energy and considerable knowledge about the many economic issues we discussed. His concern and love for those in need was evident. Minister Farrakhan also proved a gracious and generous host in his home, where we enjoyed a fine meal and good conversation. He and his family went out of their way to make everyone feel welcome. It was certainly a day to remember and reflect upon.

In terms of the Economic Blueprint, I found it worth developing further. Much of it is applicable today. Its most fundamental principle is that we must control resources if we are to address our economic and social difficulties. And we must be part of a project larger than ourselves, one motivated by ideals of human solidarity and not just by self-interest.

Concretely, the Blueprint asks us to stop spending money foolishly and to save for both future growth and emergencies. This seems like excellent advice in a society built upon mindless consumption. Next, the Blueprint wants our savings to be pooled for community investment, in what we might call a development bank. Large sums of money could be raised from the small savings of millions of people. Then the bank could use the funds to benefit the community. Land could be purchased and agricultural enterprises begun. Distribution mechanisms could be established to get the food into the homes of those in need, and stores could be set up for food sales.

The Blueprint has been partially realized, first by the Honorable Elijah Muhammad and then by Minister Farrakhan, notably through the purchase of farmland and the growing of organic food. At our meeting, we discussed the possibility of building on this. Perhaps cooperative businesses could be started, such as urban farming and housing, both of which could include the training of those in need of meaningful work.

Minister Farrakhan made an important point. Although the blueprint focused on community self-help, the larger society, as embodied in the government,

121

owed something to the people who built the nation. So, we must demand that our national government ensure the economic security of its people. As the Nation of Islam's ten-point platform of 1963 demanded (and that of the original Black Panther Party reiterated), we must insist on full employment, decent housing, good education, an end to police brutality in our communities, an end to an unjust criminal justice system, and access to land, housing, clothing, and justice. (C. Muhammad 2013)

Dr. Michael D. Yates, an expert on labor and economics and the Associate Editor of Monthly Review (http://monthlyreview.org) one of the most influential Socialist publications in the world. In addition to providing instruction at the University of Pittsburgh, Johnstown, MDY has taught working people for many years throughout America.

Holy People of The World: A Cross-Cultural Encyclopedia (Misbahudeen Ahmed Rufai)

Louis Farrakhan follows in the footsteps of Elijah Muhammad, leader of the Nation of Islam (NOI) from 1934 to 1975, to whom he refers as the "man who taught me what I know" (Haskins 1996). Born Louis Eugene Walcott on May 11, 1933, in Roxbury, Massachusetts, Minister Farrakhan and his late brother, Alvin, were raised by his mother, a native of Saint Kitts. He never knew his father, a Jamaican native.

To his followers, Farrakhan is God's instrument for a "New World Order of Peace and Righteousness on the foundation of Truth and Justice; to put down tyrants and to change the world into a Heaven on Earth" (ibid.). Elijah Muhammad is the Moses, while Farrakhan is the Aaron who will lead black America to the Promised Land. His ministers often introduce him as "our divine leader and guide." In 1997, Muslim scholars and spiritual leaders from Africa, Asia, Australia, the Middle East, and the Americas, converging in Chicago, turbaned and acknowledged him as an imam of the Muslim world. Farrakhan's mission is expressed by the title of the Nation of Islam's official newspaper, *The Final Call*. The paper's logo is a trumpet, which signifies the end of time and the beginning of God's judgment. This mission is best articulated in *Farrakhan, The Traveler,* one of the longest-running columns since the paper's inception in 1979. The columnist, Jabril Muhammad, describes Farrakhan as the fulfillment of Jesus' predictions of the signs of the end of this world and of his return, hailing him as the long-awaited *Mahdi* (messiah) of Islam. In 1993, Minister Farrakhan published his first book, *A Torchlight for America,* to provide a guide to the nation's spiritual abyss. (Jestice 2004)

Time Magazine

In a historic cover for Time Magazine's February 28, 1994 edition, Time did a survey of Black America's view of Minister Farrakhan. They found that 73% of Black people were familiar with The Minister and that 66.7% held a favorable view of him. The survey was conducted via a telephone poll. Poll respondents were asked several questions about Minister Farrakhan and the following results were compiled.

Someone who says things the country should hear.......... 70%

An effective leader......... ....67%

Speaks the truth 63%

Good for the black community.......62%

A role model for black youth.........53%

Someone you personally admire 40%

A bigot and a racist....................34%

(Asked of 364 African Americans familiar with Farrakhan. Sampling error is plus or minus 5%.) (Henry III, et al. 1994)

President Nelson Mandela

Our meeting was able to cover those things that we considered to be fundamental. And there was no issue that arose on which there was disagreement. He has explained his position. His view are identical with the principles that I put forward. (The Final Call 1996)

USA Today

One year after the Million Man March turned the Mall in Washington, D.C., into a flowing sea of black humanity, one year after the marchers returned home with high hopes and renewed energy, the question remains: Was there a lasting effect?

Was the march called by Nation of Islam leader Louis Farrakhan only a fleeting, goose bump-raising moment for black Americans? Or was it the beginning of a lasting national movement, like the one that grew out of Martin Luther King's 1963 March on Washington? Will the Million Man March one day be viewed as such a pivotal event that people who weren't there will say they were?

Interviews with dozens of marchers suggest that many of the men who marched on Oct. 16, 1995, took to heart the messages of black self-reliance and responsibility, and that they channeled those messages into action.

Men like Jacob Wheeler III, of Los Angeles, who went home and started Summit 2000. The coalition of 16 organizations had the goal of helping 1 million more black families across the country own their own homes.

Wheeler left the March feeling as if "it was all kind of a dream." But, he says, "By the end of January we decided this was a dream that could become reality."

And reality, he says, can be measured. ...

- Up to 15,000 new applicants wanting to adopt black children.

Leonard Dunston, president of the National Association of Black Social Workers, says his group was flooded with 2,500 phone calls just two hours after its toll-free number was announced at the march. Another 12,500 inquiries have come in since. Dunston says more than 300 children have found homes as a direct result of the Million Man March.

But with more than 40,000 black children available for adoption, "it's still a drop in the bucket," says Maureen Hogan, national executive director of Adopt A Special Kid/America, a private adoption agency....

- Increased interest among black men in serving their communities.

Anecdotal evidence suggests this may be the march's most tangible legacy.

In Philadelphia, 19 men joined the Big Brother program during a November 1995 recruiting drive as a direct result of the march.

"Many of them were still on that high of 'you got to do something for the community,' " says Cheryl Dennis, head of recruitment for the Big Brother/

Big Sister Association of Philadelphia.

The Memphis Big Brother organization estimates that 33 of the 100 people picked up in last year's recruitment drive came as a direct result of the march.

In Denver, 100 black men went door-to-door in a neighborhood after a 3-year-old was killed in a drive-by shooting, seeking information. In a neighborhood not known for cooperating with police, their efforts helped lead to an arrest.

In Atlanta, the local organizing committee held a drive to encourage people to open accounts at black-owned banks. Timothy McDonald, leader of the committee, said the drive resulted in $3 million being transferred into Atlanta's black-owned banks. The committee also ran a Saturday school during the summer that helped 75 students with reading, writing, math, geography and English literature.

Although assessing the success of the Million Man March on a national level yields no clear answers, it is clear that something did happen.

At the very least, black men had one sun-drenched day to shine and show the best of themselves. And the communities from which they came had hope that problems that had besieged them for decades might finally be addressed.

The memory of thousands of positive black men gathered in Washington is so powerful that it still overwhelms Masai Minters, 45, director of student supports services at the University of California Los Angeles.

"It was a winning day for those men who have experienced a lot of losing days," Minters says.

"I still feel it today." (Fields and Puente 1996)

Journalist Vince Beiser

Whatever else, Louis Farrakhan may be, let no one say he is not a gracious host – even to a Jewish journalist. Before beginning our interview at his palatial residence in an affluent, integrated South Chicago neighborhood, the leader of the Nation of Islam makes sure that my photographer and I are comfortable in our high-backed chairs at his long dining-room table, well supplied with pineapple juice and coffee, and apologizes for having made us wait, even though we actually arrived early. The house feels peaceful, the quiet disturbed only occasionally by the muffled crackles of the walkie-talkies carried by the neatly dressed security men passing by outside. Soft light flows in from a skylight over the adjacent atrium, in the center of which a fountain surrounded by lush green plants burbles serenely. The carpets are deep and soft, the floors marble, the chandeliers crystal. The mosque-like mansion is home to Farrakhan, 64, and is also the NOI's symbolic headquarters - their black equivalent of the White House, he has called it.

"I want you to feel at home, and ask any questions you feel your readers would be interested in," says Farrakhan, his voice as honey-smooth as a Motown Singer. One reason he has become perhaps the nation's most important African-American leader is immediately obvious: The man practically glows with charisma and charm. The Honorable Minister is dressed casually today, having swapped his usual dark suit and bow tie for an off-white pants and tunic ensemble set off by a couple of hefty gold rings and a gold necklace. Farrakhan, who always has so much to say about Jews, has agreed to speak to them directly through an interview with a Jewish publication, one of only a handful of times he has done so and the first since the Million Man March he convened in Washington in 1995 catapulted him to the forefront of black political leadership. (Beiser 1997)

Julius Lester

The appearance of Louis Farrakhan at Madison Square Garden on October 7 demonstrated, without doubt that he is now America's preeminent black leader. Benjamin Hooks of the NAACP could not have filled the Garden. There would not have been people standing against the walls on every level of the arena to hear John Jacob of the National Urban League. Jesse Jackson might just have filled the Garden. But Farrakhan filled not only the 20,000-plus seats; he also drew another 3,000 to 5,000 people to watch the whole event on closed circuit television in the Felt Forum next door.

If people get the leader they deserve, then something dire has happened in Black America. No people should make the journey from Martin Luther King Jr. to Louis Farrakhan in fewer than 20 years. Most of these were not members of Farrakhan's Nation of Islam, and never will be. Nonetheless, they came there to applaud, cheer, yell, and shout. What they came to voice approval of was apparent from the start. (Lester 1985)

TUSKEGEE-MACON COUNTY NAACP BRANCH
PO Box 618
Tuskegee Institute, AL 36087

~Unanimously Adopted Resolution~

*"In Support of Tuskegee University
(Administration, Staff & Students)
And Endorsement of Invitation
To The Honorable
Minister Louis Farrakhan"*

WHEREAS, In *1881, over 131 years ago, Tuskegee (Institute) University was founded by Dr. Booker T. Washington. It has thrived and survived as one of the top rated Historically Black Colleges/Universities (HBCU) in the country;* and

WHEREAS, *Tuskegee University (TU) has also become one of the nation's most outstanding institutions in the Academy of Higher Education;* and

WHEREAS, *The mission and goals of the Institution have been sustained, developed, and advanced by its progressive leadership of six (6) Presidents;* and

WHEREAS, *Throughout its history, speakers of renowned statue and leadership positions have graced the campus with messages of spiritual, intellectual, social and political magnitude and persuasion;* and

WHEREAS, *Both the academic climate and exposure opportunities for the enrolled students prepare them to be investigative and responsive to a speaker's message with an open mind of intellectual discernment; and*

WHEREAS, *Dr. Gilbert L. Rochon, currently serving as President of Tuskegee University, has vowed to "Bring the World to Tuskegee and Tuskegee to the World;" and*

WHEREAS, *Recently, an invitation was extended to Minister Louis Farrakhan to visit and speak at Tuskegee. His visit would be part of an ongoing series of addresses at HBCU campuses. This invitation, initiated by the Tuskegee University Muslim Student Association and the Black Belt Deliberative Dialogue Group, was sanctioned and endorsed by the Administration of the University; and*

WHEREAS, *Concern has been expressed in the press, by a member of the TU Board of Trustees, regarding Minister Farrakhan's visit, scheduled for March 21-22, 2013. It is especially disheartening that the Board Member stated: "We shouldn't endorse him anymore than we endorse the Ku Klux Klan. They are two organizations of a similar breed;" and*

WHEREAS, *TU Alumni across the country are concerned about the negative news blast that the Trustee has interjected into this scheduled visit on the campus of Alma Mater.*

NOW, THEREFORE, BE IT RESOLVED, *That the Tuskegee-Macon County NAACP Branch, an active affiliate of the Oldest Civil Rights Organization in the Nation, recognizes and supports diversity and cross-cultural exposure for the TU Family, particularly its students.*

BE IT FURTHER RESOLVED, *That the NAACP Branch commends the groups for their vision when extending an invitation to Honorable Minister Louis Farrakhan. We urge the community to support the visit with our presence and participation in the sessions.*

BE IT FURTHER RESOLVED, That *Tuskegee-Macon County NAACP Branch welcomes Minister Farrakhan upon this, a return visit to Tuskegee (Institute) University. He is the Father of a proud Tuskegee Graduate. He is also a former speaker at the University.*
We further endorse the recent letter of support that was transmitted by the Black Belt Deliberative Dialogue Group to the President of Tuskegee University

FINALLY, BE IT RESOLVED, *That the NAACP Branch shall deliver a copy of this Resolution to the Tuskegee University Board of Trustees, seeking the Board's support for the visit of Minister Farrakhan. A copy shall also be delivered to: Tuskegee University-Office of the President; The Student Government Association of TU; The Tuskegee National Alumni Association-Board of Directors; The Press; Alabama State Conference of NAACP; and the National Office of NAACP, Benjamin Todd Jealous, President/CEO.*
Unanimously Adopted On This Date:
March 19, 2013

Barbara Howard
Barbara Howard
NAACP Branch President

Elaine C. Harrington
Dr. Elaine C. Harrington
NAACP Branch Program Coordinator
&
Drafter of Resolution

This impressive list of laudatory comments regarding Minister Farrakhan's value is extremely compelling. It is a witness bearer to his function as an instrument that Allah (God) is using to reach the masses with the truth. These are testimonies from government officials, Black people, White people, professionals, entertainers, spiritual teachers, politicians, leaders, journalists and more. We therefore conclude that Minister Farrakhan is unique, peerless, extraordinary and divine

ARTICLES

The "armaments of argumentation" are assembled and employed in the effort to vindicate the Honorable Minister Louis Farrakhan against the various charges and false accusations of his enemies and critics. To defend Minister Farrakhan we examine and explore Biblical and Qur'anic scriptures; Black history; Science; and all appropriate sources of empirical truth.

Stop the Mischief Making!:

Setting the Record Straight on the Nation of Islam & the Police

"Unless the LORD protects a city, guarding it with sentries will do no good." -Psalms 127:1

Several on-line bloggers, conservative talk-show hosts and media outlets have begun a wicked, mischievous campaign to paint a picture in the minds of the American people that the Nation of Islam and its illustrious and honorable Minister Louis Farrakhan are radicalizing young Black men and turning them into "cop killers."

Reports have even circulated that former prosecutor Larry Klayman has filed a class action lawsuit that names Minister Farrakhan along with President Obama, Rev. Al Sharpton and former Attorney General Eric Holder. In his complaint he maintains that the aforementioned prominent Black men have used their large platforms to incite a race war and are ultimately to blame for the shooting deaths of police officers in Dallas, Texas and Baton Rouge, Louisiana.

As I have watched the news stories-one after another-exposing the reality of Black life in America, particularly the deaths coming from the hands/guns of "bad apple" police officers, I have been horrified. It has been equally disturbing to witness news reports of police officers who had nothing to do with the murders of Alton Sterling, Philando Castile et.al. lose their life via vigilante lone-wolf assassins.

All of what has and is taking place, is making the condition of the American Black man and woman the leading issue of our time. It harkens to my memory something that I once read from the Most Honorable Elijah Muhammad. The November 22, 1963 edition of the Muhammad Speaks newspaper records the following from Messenger-Muhammad.

"You have not realized how precious you are in the sight of God today. You don't realize that you are the real problem of the civilized world. You don't realize that without the solving of the so-called Negro problem today there will be nothing done. It is your problem today that the whole world fears. It is your problem that troubles America."

The violence, police brutality, protests and civil unrest in 2016 is reminiscent of the 1960s. And in 1968 the Most Honorable Elijah Muhammad published a series of 4 articles devoted to outlining in the plainest and simplest terms just what the proper relationship between the Black community and the police should be.

In providing guidance and divine wisdom to the police officer, especially Black officers, Mr. Muhammad directs the officer toward policing in the most respectful and noble way. Consider a few excerpts from his magnificent 4 article series:

"If the Black policeman arrest his Black brother who has broken the law that he is out here to enforce, he should not provoke his prisoner to say something or to do something just for the sake of beating him under arrest and shooting him after having already arrested the man, or before he arrest him, for nothing but for the sake of his office, as the officer of law over his Black bother.

It is an injustice and is out of the due process of law to arrest a man and handcuff him and then take him to jail, beating him while he is under arrest and then inside of the jail, going in his cell, beating him up."

"Tell the judge the truth, officer, on your Black brother and do not think of telling other than the truth and do not think of striking your Brother when you have him helpless in your custody."

"If he curses you or swears at you, he cannot harm you. He is behind bars. The judge will deal with him. You will tell the judge how you were treated by the lawbreaker, but just remember now you have him under control. He has submitted to your arrest, what do you care about him talking? He cannot harm you."

"BLACK POLICE officers, we do not want you to break the law to show sympathy for us, but we want you to remember the justice of the law in dealing with us. And, Black people will be your friends and obey you and there will not be any hiding behind homes and in the streets to do

bodily harm to his Black officers. You are our people, officer, and not our aggressive officer; therefore, when we look and see you we expect you to bring about peace and not increased trouble. That is destroying our peace."

"If he shoots at you, certainly you should shoot him, try and conquer him. If he runs from you in the streets, do not aim at his body and head; aim at his legs. If you are trying to shoot him, shoot him in the leg, not the head. If you do this, you are trying to murder him. Officers practice target shooting and they can stop a person without killing them."

The Most Honorable Elijah Muhammad then turns his attention to instructing the Black community on how we should relate to those who police our communities. And since, in times past it was only Black officers who were assigned to Black neighborhoods, the Black community is here encouraged to embrace the Black police officers as "brethren" and to view them as valued assets to the community. Consider these excerpts:

"We, of the Black community must treat Black Officers in such a way that they would not dare think of doing injustice to us. Once in their power, we should respect the Black Officer with all sincerity, because he is supposed to be our peace officer and not our aggressive officer."

"Respect the officer. Approach him with a smile and not so with a sour cursing face and murder in our eyes for him, as he is our protector against foreign trouble."

"A good police officer is loved. Let us love our Black Brother. He is our Brother. And, let us help him by having as little trouble in our community as possible."

"Obey our Black Officer. Love him as yourself, for we all are brothers. And let us show the world that we can control our Black community as white communities are controlled by white officers."

With these statements coming from the leader of the Nation of Islam, it becomes crystal clear that, the Nation of Islam has no policy of antagonism or hatred for police. And this is

the Nation's position, despite a long record of suffering harassment, sabotage and even NOI members being killed by rogue elements within the police department.

Last August, the Honorable Minister Louis Farrakhan visited the city of Memphis to promote the 20th anniversary of the Million Man March and the commencement of the Justice or Else movement. During a moment of reflection, the Minister praised the Memphis Police Department for their professional and extensive protective detail that they provided for his safety during his stay in Memphis. The Minister's stay in Memphis was the occasion

for a photo taken by social media professional Jesse Muhammad. The viral photo is a beautiful scene of local police officers standing hand in hand with one another and with Minister Farrakhan during a moment of prayer.

(Minister Farrakhan prays with members of Memphis Police Department, Photo: Jesse Muhammad)

The officers were Black, white, old, young, Muslim and Christian. Such a photo is indicative of how the Nation of Islam has always considered itself as an ally of all who want a society that is orderly, peaceful and free of violence and crime.

Over the long history of the Nation of Islam in America, which is now 86 years, many police officials have lauded the Nation for its crime reducing presence in the many cities where it is established. A sampling of such complimentary testimonies includes:

"The Muslims have done more to rehabilitate narcotics addicts than any corrective agency in the country."- *NY State Senator Basil Patterson from Harlem at the National Society of Afro-American Society of Policemen's tribute to the Nation of Islam (July 5, 1969)*

"They stand out; they're conspicuously trying to do something positive, and that's different in many parts of the community. They have been unfairly harassed in the past." *-Edward L. Kerr, Police Director of Newark, New Jersey (January 1974)*

"Religious philosophies such as the Muslims' can go a long way toward reducing crime even in the most adverse circumstances." *– Sherriff Richard J. Elrod of Cook County (January 1974)*

"Compton has become an example relative to the Muslims in that overall attitude of respect. I for one am glad that the Muslims moved into Compton." *-Officer Saul Lankster (November 1974)*

"That's one of the reasons I've always respected Mr. Muhammad even before now that they've gained a measure of respectability. When everybody else was trying to condemn Him. I had some pretty close friends who belonged to the Nation. They kept themselves clean, they worked and they looked out for themselves. You have to admire the man for the way those people conduct themselves." *-Chicago Deputy Police Superintendent Mitchell Ware (November 1974)*

"As a large group of people, the Muslims tend to be law abiding and seem to have a rehabilitating influence in the community." -*Thomas W. Chochee, Police Chief Compton California (February 1974)*

"One thing I can say-where ever Muslims go, crime goes down. We policemen are always happy to have them in a community; it makes our job that much easier." -*Chicago Deputy Police Superintendent Sam Nolan (January 1974)*

During the rebuilding of the Nation of Islam under the guidance of the

THE MUSLIMS TO
THE RESCUE

Community patrol chases drug dealers out of Washington's Mayfair Mansions

THERE used to be a saying that if you lived in the Mayfair Mansions apartments it was the next best thing to being in heaven. Forty years ago this community was the showcase neighborhood for emerging Black Washington, D.C., professionals. But in the '60s and '70s, when the upwardly mobile began integrating other areas around the city, the neighborhood changed. Mayfair Mansions and neighboring Paradise Manor underwent such a metamorphosis several years ago that this once tranquil community quickly became one of the worst drug and crime-infested areas in the city.

But something happened almost overnight. Without a penny of federal or city money, Mayfair Mansions and Paradise Manor were transformed

again — into drug and crime-free zones.

"Credit the Muslims," says Arthur Reynolds Sr., managing general partner of Kenilworth Associates, Ltd., the owners of Mayfair Mansions. "They have done a tremendous job."

When a Nation of Islam group under the national leadership of Minister Louis Farrakhan opened Muhammad's Mosque No. 4 several blocks from the housing units, they saw the area as a ripe spot for community development. The problem was that the community of some 7,000 residents was virtually held hostage by drug trafficking.

Ruth Holmes, a Mayfair Mansions resident for 35 years, says the community had become "a 24-hour drug block party. They were like zombies walking

136

EBONY • August, 1989

Continued on Page 138

(Members of NOI Security in Ebony Magazine Article, August 1989)

Honorable Minister Louis Farrakhan, the Nation of Islam developed a community security force affectionately known as the *"Dopebusters."* From the Nation of Islam Research Group article entitled *How Farrakhan Solved The*

Crime and Drug Problem we see the Dopebusters described in the following description:

> "In 1988, the Black men of the elite Fruit of Islam, under the training and guidance of Minister Farrakhan, formed into units and began to conduct security patrols in some of the most drug-infested public housing developments. Armed with only a deep love for their own people and a determination to improve their condition, they became known as the "Dope Busters." The Muslims in Washington DC marched unarmed into a veritable drug gang war at the Kenilworth Parkside and Mayfair Mansions housing projects and a remarkable thing happened. The Muslims closed open-air drug markets and brought peace and quiet to those neighborhoods. It was a condition that had never been seen in that area since those projects were built."

And just like the Most Honorable Elijah Muhammad, Minister Farrakhan has students and followers that have achieved wide acclaim for their work and success. A sample of some of glowing commendations bestowed upon the Dopebusters includes the following:

"I am currently a lieutenant in the Metropolitan Police Department, assigned to the 7th District as the Commander of the Special Emphasis Unit and Support Coordinator of all vice, detective and tactical operations. I have been employed with the Department for 26 years in a sundry of assignments. It is most noteworthy that the areas of the city which they[Dopebusters] have contracted to provide security have shown drastic reductions in crime. This, within itself, speaks to the basic tenets of community empowerment policing. Some of the communities in which I personally know that crime has been reduced by their presence are the Clifton Terrace Apartments, the Mayfair Mansion Apartment Complex, the Paradise Gardens Apartment Complex, the Atlantic Street Apartment Dwellings and the surrounding areas. I have had the occasion to observe some of their security training and to participate in the training as a volunteer instructor. I have found them to be professional, courteous and committed to the delivery of service to the communities in which they patrol and provide security." -*President DC Black Police Caucus, Lowell Duckett*

"The founders [of the Dopebusters] formed the company after volunteering their services during that period to secure the Paradise/Mayfair community of over 1200 apartments, which had become the largest open-air drug market in the Mid-Atlantic States in the mid-1980s. At the time no security firms were willing to work in the neighborhood; in fact the police came into the neighborhood only in force because of the very dangerous conditions. The volunteers patrolled the two complexes, confronted dangerous individuals, and testified in court about the activities of accused felons; all at great personal risk. Their leadership allowed the police to become more effective and encouraged the residents of the neighborhood to work for a safer community. Both Paradise at Parkside and Mayfair Mansions are now healthy, vibrant and safe communities' thanks in good part to the efforts of the [Dopebusters]." -Deputy Assistant Secretary for Enforcement and Investigations Office of Fair Housing and Equal Opportunity U.S. Department of Housing and Urban Development, Ms. Susan Forward

WEST

Crime drop follows Nation of Islam patrols

LOS ANGELES — Crime has dropped dramatically at 15 Los Angeles housing projects since the arrival of security guards affiliated with Louis Farrakhan's Nation of Islam, the city attorney says.

The unarmed guards in gray business suits and red bow ties have been on the job for eight weeks. Tenants say the guards drive away drug dealers.

"We can see the difference," Mara Perez, who lives in the city's seaside Venice area, said in Sunday's Los Angeles Times. "The building seems to be quiet."

Since the guards began work Nov. 1, trouble has decreased from an average of 32 arrests and reports of crimes a month to eight a month, the city attorney reported.

"In terms of bottom line results, they are doing such a good job and the living environment in public housing developments has so markedly improved that I would be reluctant to remove NOI security from those developments."-Baltimore, MD Kurt L. Schmoke

"Crime at Westview Terrace has fallen drastically since the Black Muslims moved in."-New Castle, PA Police Chief Louis Piscitella

We pray that what we have shared here of the facts of the Nation of Islam's history, record and true relationship with police will inoculate the mind of the reader against the flood of propaganda and slander aimed at de-magnetizing the Honorable Minister Louis Farrakhan and the Nation of Islam. For we believe that this is the ultimate aim of this present manifestation of a long-standing commitment by those in the most powerful positions within America to maintain the status quo of "White supremacy/Black inferiority" and its more contemporary goal of "White existence/Black extinction." To do this, they have determined they must get rid of the Nation of Islam. And negative propaganda (i.e. lies) about the Nation must be implanted into the minds of an unsuspecting public as a prelude to an onslaught against the Nation of Islam and the Honorable Minister Louis Farrakhan. If they can be successful in turning the public against the Nation, the public will be made to feel that any and all actions made to "neutralize" the Nation and the Hon. Min. Louis Farrakhan is justified.

The Nation of Islam could be Chicago's savior

By Armstrong Williams

[NOTE: Mr. Williams is a longtime critic of Minister Farrakhan and we share this article of his to show the impact of the Minister to out work the criticism of his critics. We disagree with Mr. Williams implications that there is any bigotry or extremism associated with the Minister's message. We agree with him that cities like Chicago and others should form partnerships with the Minister for the good of all its citizens]

On the evening of Sept. 28, a family of six was gunned down as they returned to their home, killing a grandmother and a pregnant mother and wounding three others, including an 11-month-old baby. The weekend marks the second in a row when more than 50 people have been shot on the streets of Chicago.

Mayor Rahm Emanuel and the Democratic leadership in Chicago continue to run around in a daze, denying the obvious and blaming the problem on gun laws to deflect from the real issues. The crux of the issue is that in Chicago, entire communities have completely disintegrated from within. Effective leadership at the local community level is sorely lacking, as are present fathers and strong family structures. The vicious cycle shows no sign of abating, as gangs of fatherless children and young adults raised by the prison system are left to fend for themselves and form their own fractured and violent facsimile of a social structure.

The situation in Chicago is so desperately broken that alternative solutions bear considering. One of the few sources of strong leadership in many of these communities is the Nation of Islam.

The religious organization has long endured controversy over allegations that it is a virulently anti-Semitic and extremist black-nationalist group. The inflammatory rhetoric of some of its leaders — including its current leader, Louis Farrakhan — lend credence to such claims. These extremist elements should be sternly and unequivocally condemned. On the other hand, more moderate Muslims have made it a point of standing up for their communities.

David Muhammad, a retired mechanic who lives on the West Side of Chicago, was featured in the CBS News "48 Hours" documentary "The War In Chicago" for his work in documenting drug dealing in his neighborhood. For more than a year, he recorded live video of an open-air drug market that had set up shop in front of a Baptist church, and posted the videos to YouTube. The radical strategy garnered Muhammad scores of death threats from local drug dealers, but the spotlight ultimately proved more than they could endure and they eventually moved on.

Some might be perplexed as to why a Muslim would risk his life protecting Christian worshippers, but for Muhammad, the answer was simple. "In Islam, we're taught to protect all institutions of God. So it was like a slap in my face for them to deal drugs right out of the door of the church."

Security firms affiliated with the Nation of Islam began informally patrolling communities beset by violence in the late 1980s, and proved quite effective in several cities — including Washington, D.C., Baltimore and Chicago. The basis of their presence was to establish respect among the community and serve as a presence teaching young men how to carry themselves with dignity. A largely unarmed force, they were able to achieve consistent and dramatic reductions in violent crime in the neighborhoods they patrolled. Ultimately, security firms affiliated with the Nation of Islam entered partnerships with the U.S. Department of Housing and Urban Development (HUD) to guard HUD-operated government housing projects in several cities.

Although few complained about the effectiveness of the Nation of Islam in reducing violence and crime, its relationship with HUD created a political firestorm that resulted in most of its government contracts being rescinded. Most notably, in 1995 HUD abruptly canceled the security contract of a firm affiliated with the Nation of Islam to secure Baltimore public housing buildings, citing bidding irregularities and other violations that were widely viewed as a smoke screen for a political battle raging in Congress over the group's anti-Jewish rhetoric.

Tenants of the city's seven high-rise public housing projects complained bitterly. Wells Fargo Security, a competing firm that was eventually granted the security contract, drew the ire of residents who complained that crime, vandalism and violence had skyrocketed within a mere two months of the takeover. Within two years, Wells Fargo's contracts were also canceled and the firm was chased out of town amid a rapidly disintegrating quality of life in the city's housing projects.

The fact is, the Nation of Islam brings to the table things that other private security firms and the police don't: Credibility within the community. It is one of the few community-based organizations that actually recruit in the prisons and also offer transitional services to ex-offenders. One of the problems cited by HUD with regard to the group's Baltimore contracts was that it had hired ex-offenders as guards. But this was actually a strength. The Nation of Islam had in fact cleaned up ex-offenders, taking them off the streets, getting them off drugs and instilling them with discipline before redeploying them in neighborhoods where they were known and now respected.

All the king's horses and all the king's men have given it their best, and yet violence in Chicago remains an ongoing tragedy that has shown no signs of abatement. It is time Chicago takes the next practical step in partnering with moderate members of community-based organizations with proven track records of curbing violence and crime. While we should condemn bigotry and extremism in all forms, this should not deter us from engaging with more moderate members of the Muslim community to develop constructive, community-based solutions to address the acute problems Chicago is facing. Certainly there is some middle ground to be found in a city that is being torn to shreds in the absence of sane leadership and mutual cooperation.

"Epic Fail": Fraser's Facebook Folly over Farrakhan

George C. Fraser's moment of candor in social media,
a clear misstep, an unfortunate error

It was very disappointing to read professional networking guru, George C. Fraser's baseless and ill-informed comments about the Honorable Minister Louis Farrakhan via Mr. Fraser's Facebook page.

It was disappointing because I have always had great respect for Mr. Fraser's work to raise the business acumen and overall economic position of the Black community. But despite my respect for him as an otherwise positive brother and champion for a noble cause, I can't allow his comments about Minister Farrakhan to go unanswered.

Mr. Fraser took issue with the fact that Minister Farrakhan boldly and forthrightly spoke the truth that many in the Black community feel, but may be afraid to say publicly. That truth is **that President Barak Obama, despite being the first Black president of America, has a legacy that will involve the worsening of conditions within the Black community under his administration.** The Minister's analysis that was recently delivered from the hallowed pulpit of Union Temple Church in Washington, D.C. was actually quite measured, balanced and optimistic especially when compared to many of the Barber shop, water cooler and pillow talk conversations about President Obama that take place every day.

Popular Black scholars and academics like professors Dr. Michael Eric Dyson and Dr. Julienne Malveaux have also borne witness to President Obama's lack of a positive legacy where the Black community is concerned. According to professor Dyson, President Obama's lack of a positive legacy in the Black community is a direct result of that fact that *"He didn't see race as [the] broader American issue that it is."*

Dr. Malveaux told TV One Reporter Roland Martin:

> "President Obama "didn't push us forward, but he didn't move us backward – he missed an opportunity... He has targeted certain communities, but he's never targeted the African-American

146

community... I would have liked to have seen the kind of passion when he talked about transgender issues that he had to talk about African-American issues – he never said to any school, 'I will withhold your civil rights money if you discriminate... He (President Barack Obama) simply has not been a champion of African-Americans in the same way that he's been a champion of others."

The Final Call Newspaper recorded the Minister's words on President Obama's legacy as the following:

"I just want to tell you Mr. President. You're from Chicago, and so am I. I go out in the street with the people. I visited the worst neighborhoods. I talked to the gangs. While I was out there talking to them, they said: 'You know Farrakhan, the president ain't never come. Could you get him to come and look after us?'

"There's your legacy Mr. President. It's in the street with your suffering people, Mr. President, and if you can't go and see about them, then don't worry about your legacy, if you didn't earn your legacy with us.

"We put you there. You fought the rights of gay people. You fought for the rights of this people and that people. You fight for Israel. Your people are suffering and dying in the streets, and you failed to do what should have been done,"

"But it's never too late. Come on back to the 'hood, and start organizing like you did, and with your influence all over the world, let's make a new and better people, and from us, if it's Allah's will, we can build a new and better America,".

There is nothing in the Minister's words about President Obama's legacy that is factually inaccurate. **It is all true and emphatically true!**

Mr. Fraser exclaimed in a Facebook rant that he was tired of people sharing the video clip of the Minister making these statements. And he preceded to spew surprisingly harsh comments about Minister Farrakhan. He even mentioned in a disdainful way Rev. Jesse L. Jackson, Sr. Mr. Fraser literally claimed that Minister Farrakhan was not doing anything about the crime problem in the city of Chicago. And he sought to characterize the Minister as petty, immature and non-productive.

Dear Mr. Fraser, as a constitutional law professor President Obama would tell you that crime reduction and providing a safe environment for the citizens of any nation rests not on the shoulders of individual citizens and groups; but is a function of and the responsibility of the government.

In an article written for the Duke Law Journal, author Steven J. Heyman describes the right to protection and safety as **"the first duty of government."** Heyman's article brilliantly discusses the origins of the duty of protection as it goes back to 18th Century English Constitutional Theory, wherein the citizen was expected to pledge his allegiance to his government and in exchange enjoy the protection of the government. This relationship was considered reciprocal; "*obedience in exchange for protection.*"

Heyman goes onto describe the government's first duty by citing the *Commentaries on the Laws of England* published by *Sir William Blackstone* between 1765 and 1769. From Blackstone's work Heyman concludes *"The state's duty of protection requires not only the enactment of laws by the legislature, but also their **enforcement by the executive (the president)** and the courts. Under the English constitution, the executive power was vested in the king. The function of the king as supreme executive was "to protect the community, and each individual therein, from every degree of injurious violence, by executing those laws which the people themselves... have consented to."*

Heyman's conclusion further drives home the point that the first and most critical duty of government as conceived in America and her mother country Great Britain is the protection of the individual citizen from crime, loss of life and property.

The right of protection was thus a well-established concept in antebellum legal thought. In addition to the right of self-defense, it included civil remedies and criminal protection, as well as the process of requiring security for the peace. By the middle of the nineteenth century, the concept of protection had developed to include the state's responsibility to take reasonable measures to prevent violence, such as the creation of a police force to so that the protection of the life and property of its citizens could be secured.

Dear Mr. Fraser, crime in the Black community whether it be Chicago or your home town of Cleveland, Ohio is largely the result of generations upon generations of poverty. According to a Bureau of Justice Statistics Report entitled **Household Poverty and Nonfatal Violent Victimization, 2008–2012**:

> In 2008–2012, persons in poor households had a higher rate of violent victimization involving a weapon (9.6 per 1,000) and a higher rate of violence involving a firearm (3.5 per 1,000) compared to persons above the Federal Poverty Level(FPL). The rate of violence involving a weapon decreased as households moved away from the FPL. For example, persons in high-income households had the lowest rates of weapon (2.8 per 1,000) and firearm (0.8 per 1,000) violence among all poverty levels. At each poverty level, the percentage of violence in which the offender had a weapon was lower than the percentage not involving a weapon. However, for persons in poor households, a greater percentage of violent victimizations involved a weapon (24%) compared to the percentage for persons in high-income households (16%).

Mr. Fraser these facts present an important problem for your critique against Minister Farrakhan. Based upon your fallacious criticism of Minister Farrakhan and Chicago Black leadership, their work should have eradicated crime in Chicago. Yet you are an economist and businessman, yet **your work hasn't closed the wealth gap, nor has it eliminated the conditions of poverty that lie at the root of violent crime in Chicago and throughout America.**

But the truth of the matter Mr. Fraser is that Black men like yourself and others who work to bring about an improvement in the Black community are needed, precisely because of the failure of the government to adequately meet the needs of the Black community. So your work and the work of Minister Farrakhan is not intended or purposed to let the U.S. government "off the hook" in its duty and responsibility to the more than 40 million Blacks in America. This is the reason why we don't have **"white leaders"** because the white communities of

America benefit from those in elected positions, thusly making those officials de facto **"white leaders."** Whether Black or White, elected officials preside within and over systems that have been designed to benefit the whites of this nation, hence the frequently referenced concept of "white privilege". And it is the 8-year presidency of President Barack Obama that proves this point better than any other example.

For he, being the head of the executive branch of government, presided over a season of quite possibly the worst police misconduct and judicial failings ever witnessed this side of Reconstruction. And sir you cannot attribute his failure to Minister Farrakhan or any other Black leader -all of whom work against tremendous opposition, threats and financial constraints.

Dear Mr. Fraser, you act as if Minister Farrakhan has not been one of the foremost defenders and advocates of President Obama over the course of his presidency. Mr. Fraser, sir you were on the stage as a participant of the **State of the Black World Conference** in New Orleans in 2008. You sat behind Minister Farrakhan when he said this to the thousands of conference participants invited by Dr. Ron Daniels:

> "Barack is our blessing. Barack is America's blessing. Barack could be the world's blessing. He's the most popular Black man to ever arise among us, take it or leave it. I've never seen anything like this, have you? This is a phenomenon. It's God's hand there. Then if his hand is there, where's your hand? Where's my hand? Where's our hand?
> If Barack opens up two and a half million jobs, his goal by 2011, over 10 million Americans are al-ready unemployed, according to the latest statistics. Where will you be if he opens up two and a half million jobs, with us dropping out of school, not pre-pared? Can we take advantage of any opportunity that he opens? No. If he produces five million jobs in making a green economy, how many of us will be qualified to take advantage of what that young man can produce.
> Don't knock this man, I'm telling you. He's not you. He's not me. He's not us. God made him special for a special reason and a special mission.
> He was maneuvering through a minefield. Evidently, he maneuvered correctly.

He's gathered around him people we may not like them. What do we know? Good judgment is needed everywhere. Leave him alone. Watch him. Don't be an impediment. Watch him."

Not only did the Minister encourage this august body of elected officials; Black nationalists and activists to look favorably upon President-Elect Obama, but the Minister's Research Team published an E-book defending the president against the flood of racist and bigoted propaganda that Republicans and conservative groups spread throughout the country. The e-book entitled **Barack Obama: Evil Spoken of** sought to catalog the epic and never before seen disrespect of America's president by Americans.

Throughout President Obama's 2 terms Minister Farrakhan has offered to the President encouragement, guidance and stern rebuke and critique when it was warranted. Such are the actions of a mature man; such are the actions of a real brother; such are the actions of a true patriot.

Dear Mr. Fraser, if you want more of Minister Farrakhan's involvement in the reduction of crime in Chicago and other cities throughout America I can't blame you. So do I. But the way to do it is to figure out a way to ensure that Minister Farrakhan's ministry is ear-marked a definite portion of the budget each year that is devoted to policing the city of Chicago.

The 2016 Budget for Police in Chicago is nearly 1.5 billion dollars. And at that spectacular amount, crime and violence continue at a brisk clip within America's 3rd largest city.

Currently the Minister leads a volunteer corps of his devoted and committed male followers into the worst crime infested areas of Chicago. And the work done by the Minister and the FOI (Fruit of Islam) in Chicago is replicated all across the country. But Mr. Fraser, you are a businessman and you know that Minister Farrakhan's volunteer corps cannot be expected to do what the well-funded Chicago police are paid to do.

And yet there is a history of Minister Farrakhan's brothers of the FOI virtually eliminating crime and violence in high crime areas in communities where they establish a presence. And their effective crusade to eliminate crime and violence by presenting themselves as a moral force of men who courageously challenge violence on sight, while simultaneously serving as instructors, ministers, mentors and big-brothers to young men in the 'hood caught the attention of the national media.

During this time period this group of fearless brothers were known as the **Dopebusters.** Their fame spread and a mutually beneficial arrangement was met and the Muslim men were offered federal contracts to provide security on a full-time basis. An extensive history and analysis of the Dopebusters may be found here at the NOI-Research Group website(www.noirg.org). Unfortunately, Mr. Fraser, powerful and influential forces within the Jewish community have falsely labeled Minister Farrakhan an anti-Semite. Their influence and hatred of Minister Farrakhan resulted in Congressional hearings to end the Dopebusters ability to receive federal contracts to secure public housing complexes.

If you want to know what they have and what they continue to achieve by labeling our beloved Minister as such, just read the words of a memorandum entitled the **Legitimation of Louis Farrakhan**, produced by the Anti-Defamation League of B'Nai B'rith (ADL)

In 1994 the ADL drafted a briefing paper called Mainstreaming Anti-Semitism:

> The Legitimation of Louis Farrakhan wherein they lamented that "mainstream" Black leaders and organizations were embracing their own Black brother-the Honorable Minister Louis Farrakhan. Written by Steven Freeman in January of 1994, the document begins by noting that "Minister Louis Farrakhan, leader of the Nation of Islam (NOI) and long a voice of religious intolerance and racial divisiveness in this country, has recently attained a new level of acceptance among certain mainstream Black organizations and leaders. His "legitimation" has been reflected most notably by his participation last summer in the Parliament of the World's Religions, his obtaining federal funds for NOI's anti-AIDS efforts and the security services it

has been providing at several federal housing projects, and his warm reception at the annual legislative meeting of the Congressional Black Caucus (CBC) last fall.... the black community in this country is wrestling with a desperate crisis situation in our inner cities--and when Farrakhan's NOI is arguably filling a void for that community... "

And in an amazing flourish of arrogance and evil they prove they don't give a damn about what is good for and beneficial to the Black community. Yes, after acknowledging Minister Farrakhan's value in filling a void in the Black community, the ADL leadership discuss punishing any and all public figures who partner with or give a platform to the Honorable Minister Louis Farrakhan's "void filling message." In coded language Freeman writes: *"What we can and should do is impose an obligation on those who deal with him, or, as in the case of universities, give him a platform."*

So just like the "Godfather" or any other mafia or gangster boss who says "*I am going to make you an offer you can't refuse,*" the ADL leadership speak to one another in a coded language what is equivalent to a threat against the reputation and livelihood of anyone who will work with Minister Farrakhan.

Dear Mr. Fraser, this is the kind of sabotage and wicked interference that Minister Farrakhan is challenged to make progress in spite of. And by the grace and power of Allah(God), he makes tremendous progress. Add to this the 2007 revelation that the Homeland Security Department had essentially re-instituted J. Edgar Hoover's COINTELPRO program against the Nation of Islam. So in addition to Jewish efforts to sabotage the Minister, one of the mightiest law enforcement agencies in the world had determined to spy on and infiltrate his movement.

Lastly, Mr. Fraser your words of folly against Minister Farrakhan are all the more egregious because during that State of the Black World Conference in 2008, Minister Farrakhan called upon you by name. It was in the closing portion of his message where he was giving guidance to all who follow him that we should not '*act like we know everything*', but that we should work with others, even those who disagree with us. He said 'on this stage are those whom we can't even lace up their shoes.' Pointing in your direction he said, "for economic development here is Mr. George Fraser [that we should work with]."

So before thousands of attendees who had come to receive guidance from the Minister, he endorses your work and directs the people to work with you and to support your initiatives. **In addition to that The Final Call Newspaper, which is published by Minister Farrakhan, has published 16 stories that contain positive mentions of your work and initiatives.** The point of citing this history is to show you Mr. Fraser that Minister Farrakhan has been a big brother to you. He has encouraged you and directed people to you and your products. For you to return the Minister's kindness, respect and brotherhood with insults and baseless criticisms is a great blow to your own integrity.

Mr. Fraser, sir, you owe Minister Farrakhan a sincere public apology. The failure to apologize to Minister Farrakhan may result in the further erosion on your own integrity and threatens to further damage your connection to the millions of young Blacks who have been magnetized around the Minister's message. Mr. Fraser, think about it and do the right thing.

Important Excerpts from the Trotter Report on the Media's Mishandling of the Honorable Minister Louis Farrakhan

Mainstream Media as Guardian of Racial Hierarchy: A Study of the Threat Posed by Minister Louis Farrakhan and the Million Man March

by William E. Alberts

Dr. William E. Alberts is Hospital Chaplain at Boston Medical Center and teaches social science in the Veterans Upward Bound Program at the University of Massachusetts Boston. A Unitarian Universalist minister, he received his Ph.D. from Boston University in the field of psychology and pastoral counseling. He has written numerous essays and articles on religion and racism and politics in Boston which have appeared in newspapers, magazines and journals. His most recent research reports are published by the William Monroe Trotter Institute.

Page v - Rabbi Bruce Kahn important observations of Million Man March

I am White. I am a rabbi. I attended the Million Man March where I stood hour after our in the midst of a sea of excited, highly principled, welcoming Black men. I listened to the speeches and shared in the grandeur of an extraordinary moment in history. Mostly, it was my privilege to bear witness to how important this gathering was to the African Americans who were present.

On that Monday, I was enveloped in an overwhelming sense of joy, pride, responsibility, thoughtfulness, hope and love. Yet, no one seemed to dodge one bit an awareness of what is wrong and what needs repair in Black neighborhoods across America. Speaker after speaker, especially Minister Louis Farrakhan, confronted self-destructive behavior by too many Black males in a hard-hitting, no nonsense, clearly defined and agonizingly descriptive fashion. The people around me did the same. No cover-ups. But there was so much more that made this day unique. It was a day of atonement and affirmation. This was a day for recognizing that most Black men in America care about their families, work hard, have a love of God and country, and possess a strong and positive moral code which embraces confession and atonement. That is not a message that is perceived by the media or transmitted by it.

While I disagree, at times most vigorously and on moral grounds, with several points William Alberts advances in this report, I find his evidence compelling. He reveals media too often determined to make the news and shape the opinions of readers. When it comes to reporting on African Americans in general and Minister Louis Farrakhan and the Nation of Islam, in particular, this weakness is most pronounced. Reporters are driven to take the quotes that will antagonize the reader and do not let go of those words. Convey a negative impression and generate conflict, regardless of how out of line that is with the point and mass of a presentation. There seems to be a mission, conscious or subconscious, to put before the American people as much bad stuff about Blacks as possible. Proportionality is lost. Responsibility for the impact of what is reported is not assumed. The overall shaping of attitudes of viewers and readers of the news is, at best, disregarded. Make the story sizzle. Get people going. Make a splash. These seem to be the goals.

I can say with reasonable assurance that my intense contacts over the years with members of the African-America community, especially clergy, tell me that the White community has no understanding whatsoever of the suffering endured by African Americans over history or now. The role of systems controlled by White America in perpetuating that suffering is something most worthy of in depth and continuous reporting. But doing that takes a different agenda from that which seems to motivate reporting today. That agenda of disservice will prevent us from ever understanding Minister Farrakhan or the Nation of Islam. Yes, the Minister says things that I consider terribly bigoted, hurtful and false. Yes, I believe he has wrong and inadequate information and understanding of Judaism, Zionism and Israel. I am appalled by his defense of a group of middle eastern leaders I consider to be among the most despicable in the world.

But as offensive as such aspects are, I believe through dialogue and shared study we can work out these problems. The war of insults must end. It is a distraction which deflects attention from the real issues at the heart of the Minister's messages before the March, at the March and since the March. We all must learn about, confront and seek to understand every holocaust, including the Black Holocaust. It is different from the Jewish Holocaust. But there is nothing less important about it. The Jewish Holocaust was more concentrated, more recent, and it was an out and out attempt at genocide which murdered close to forty percent of the entire Jewish population in the world. The Black Holocaust was vastly longer, taking vastly more lives, and its residual impact also remains cataclysmic.

It is not possible to measure the anguish of Jews ripped from their homes and families and tortured in the camps. There is no way to measure the anguish of Africans ripped from their homes and families and tortured on slave ships and beyond. What an affront it is to them all to suggest that one group suffered more. When pain and terror and inhumanity and death go beyond levels any of us can comprehend or tolerate, what value is there in trying to crown a winner? There are no winners. There are only victims.

We must know the stories of the victims. We must learn and grasp the meaning of the torment of Africans in America over the centuries. Each group must know enough and feel enough about the other to see life through that group's eyes; life as it has been and as it is now. Instead of doing that we rush to judgment and flail away at each other bolstered by harmful media reports that lead us to faulty conclusions.

I am White. I am a rabbi. Long before the March I began reaching out to try to understand the suffering Minister Farrakhan addresses. Since the March I have exchanged views and information with several of his key associates on the East Coast. I am encouraged by the dialogues. I believe we can advance our knowledge, understanding and empathy so that the rhetoric that echoes across the land will be both empathic and useful, focusing on defining problems and generating solutions to advance trust, peace, justice, equality and opportunity.

There is only one Black American who could have pulled off the Million Man March. Give him the credit he deserves for doing so. It was one of the single most positive events in the social history of our country. The people who were there attended for several reasons, not all of which had to do with Minister Farrakhan. But without him the March would not have been envisioned nor would it have succeeded. It did succeed. If it did nothing more than give a huge boost to the trampled upon ego of the Black American male, it succeeded.

Minister Farrakhan is not the leader of the African-America community. He is one of the leaders within that community. It seems clear to me that despite what

I consider to be the horrifying insults that have issued from the Minister, the people who listen to him do not go chasing down Jews, or gays or Whites or Koreans to beat them and murder them. They do not do that for two reasons: First, he warns them against such violent behavior. Second, these verbal onslaughts do not constitute the main thrust of his message. As unacceptable as they are, they are also tangential. His listeners know that. They are sufferers who know how tough it is to get a fair shake as Black people. They want that to change. They hear in Minister Farrakhan's words inspiration and instruction to begin to bring about that change. That is the message on which he focuses and on which they focus. That is not the message on which the media focuses. William Alberts's study makes that clear.

Rabbi Bruce E Khan, Temple Shalom

Page 5 - Media Consistent False Characterization of the Honorable Minister Louis Farrakhan

The print media's coverage of Minister Farrakhan consistently characterizes him as a "separatist," "anti-white," "anti-Semitic," "sexist," "anti-gay," and "anti-Catholic." Their repeated references to Farrakhan as "anti-white" and "racist," however, usually offer no substantiating rational explanation. Nothing is presented to explain how a Black person with no real political, economic and legal power can be a racist in a White-dominated, racially stratified society that enslaved his African ancestors and maintains an inequitable, White-favored hierarchy that continues to oppress African Americans. Instead, there is the unexplained assumption that racism is primarily an interpersonal problem between individual Black and White persons. To reduce racism to individual personal relationships is to engage in what may be called *the racism of equality.*

Page 8-9 - Newt Gingrich "back-handed compliment"

Even Speaker Newt Gingrich was quoted as saying, "The march ought to be a wake-up call for all America... And, in a wonderful irony, typical of American history, all of us owe Louis Farrakhan a thank you for having told all of us, if the pain level is great enough for him to be a leader, then we all have a lot bigger challenge ahead."

Page 10 - Kerner Commission via Milton Eisenhower Report America Still Separate & Unequal

In his message at the March, Farrakhan himself stated that "the Kerner Commission revisited their findings 25 years later and saw that America was worse today than it was in the time of Martin Luther King Jr. There's still two Americas - one black, one white, separate and unequal." In 1993, on the 25th anniversary of the Kerner Commission report, a new study by the Milton S. Eisenhower Foundation did, in fact, revisit the Commission's findings and echoed the Kerner Commission's warning that "our nation is moving toward two societies, one black, one white - separate and unequal." The new study, called "Cities Losing Race With Time," found that,

> All major cities studied by the Kerner Commission have been desegregating... Credit, housing, and job discrimination on the basis of race have gained new footing. Infant mortality, unemployment and poverty have increased and life expectancy has decreased among the black population since the 1968 report.

Page 25 - Jewish Place Within White Racial Hierarchy

Similar to the mainstream media, these reports do not explain how hating White people for their historic and continuing systemic oppression makes the oppressed "anti-white," and therefore "racist." Here, the focus is on the oppressed's symptom and not on the oppressor's "sin," with an apparently strong emphasis on integration, equal opportunity and responsibility that denies the existence of a White-favored hierarchy. The assumption of these reports - that an oppressed minority with no political, economic or legal power can be "racist" - leads this writer to make assumptions about the position generally occupied by the Jewish community on the White-dominated hierarchy. It would seem that, like White Christians, the whiteness of most Jewish people is also their invisible means into the mainstream of America's hierarchical life. The history of the Jews is filled with suffering and their strong defense against anti-Semitism is very much needed. But their belief that Black people can be "racist" in a White-dominated society is revealing: they, too, enjoy an access to "the promised land" of a White-favored hierarchy that appears to also render them oblivious to the reality of African Americans. The face of their being White (those of European descendants) indicates that their own tragic historic oppression does not qualify them to fully understand the oppression of Black people.

Page 29 - Defense of Minister Farrakhan's quote about Hitler

It can be argued that the description of Hitler is similar to that used by William L. Shirer, author of *The Rise and Fall of the Third Reich,* and honored by Israel before his death a few years ago. Shirer wrote in the Preface, "Adolph Hitler is probably the last of the great adventurer-conquerors in the tradition of Alexander, Caesar and Napoleon…"

Page 30 - ADL admits to purposely distorting Minister Farrakhan's quote about Hitler

In 1984, Boston Globe columnist David Nyhan reported that the Anti-Defamation League (ADL) of B'nai B'rith deleted Farrakhan's words, "Now I'm not proud of Hitler's evil against Jewish people, but that's a matter of record… But don't compare me with your wicked killers." Nyhan wrote that the ADL defended the deletions: "Alan Schwartz, assistant director of research for the ADL, in New York, said in a phone interview… that he omitted the two sentences for reasons of brevity and that he in no way twisted Farrakhan's remarks to make the black Muslim leader seem more pro-Hitler than he is." Nyhan quoted Schwartz at length:

> "I don't think it is misleading at all," he [Schwartz] said. His omissions did not "substantially alter the import and meaning" and "clearly, he was seeking to promote the idea of a positive attitude toward Hitler." Quibbling over the omission of the two sentences is "splitting hairs," he said. "It was a statement, at the bottom line, in praise of Hitler, which is a moral outrage," Schwartz maintained. Schwartz and other ADL officials interviewed about this believe the case is open-and-shut.

Nyhan then articulated the ADL's obvious distortion of Farrakhan's words: "But the fact remains: Farrakhan originally said, 'I'm not proud of Hitler's evil against Jewish people,' and he added, 'Don't compare me with your wicked killers.'" To delete these phrases changes Farrakhan's meaning. However, neither readers in

160

1984 nor during the March were made aware of Farrakhan's rejection of the comparison with and condemnation of Hitler as one of "your wicked killers." The deletion of such a critical context and the reported explaining away of its significance could indicate a tendency (on the part of those who constantly condemn Farrakhan as anti-Semitic) to only report and print the news that fits the agenda or bias of the racial status quo. The omission of such an important context makes suspect other charges against Farrakhan. It also indicates the need of an in-depth study of the "secret relationship" between Jews and Blacks committed to uncovering the whole truth rather than only those facts that fit preconceived views.

Page 52-53 - Media work to distance minister Farrakhan from legacy of Dr. Martin L. King Jr.

The person whom the media turned to especially in its use of Black leaders to undermine Farrakhan's leadership among African Americans was Dr. Martin Luther King, Jr. The media's repeated association of Farrakhan with White supremacists was matched by the constant disassociation of him from Martin Luther King Jr. In a *New York Times* news story called "Black March Stirs Passion and Protests," writer Don Terry appeared to editorialize in comparing the Million Man March with the 1963 March on Washington led by Dr. King:

> Mr. Chavis... said he expected more than 1.2 million black men to attend. If even half that number shows up, the march will more than double the size off the famous 1963 March on Washington, when the Rev. Dr. Martin Luther King Jr. electrified 250,000 men and women of all colors with his "I have a dream" speech, imploring the county to live up to its ideals of fairness. The march [on the other hand,] has been shrouded in other controversies, including charges of sexism.

Washington Post columnist Charles Krauthammer contrasted King's emphasis on "integration" with Farrakhan's on "separatism." He wrote,

> In an ironic and tragic turn of the civil rights revolution, there is today a powerful movement within the black community away from Martin Luther King Jr.'s vision of integration toward a new kind of separatism, self-imposed and adversarial. Its most extreme advocate

is, of course, Louis Farrakhan, who portrays African Americans as an occupied people in an alien land.

In his piece called "Marching Behind a Bigot," *Washington Post* columnist Richard Cohen stated,

> Are we to conclude that in all of black America, 12.5 per cent of the population and about 35 million people, the only person who can command a vast audience and lead a march on Washington is not, as formerly, a humane and enlightened minister [Martin Luther King Jr.], but a gutter Jew-hater cum [sic] racist?"

New York Times columnist Bob Herbert disassociated Farrakhan from King in a piece entitled, "Harmony or Discord?" He wrote,

> On that long-ago August afternoon, Dr. King dreamed that some day children of all races could play together, learn together, and live together. A nation listened as he said, "I have a dream today!"
> Today there will be another gathering in Washington... It will not be an attempt to bring seemingly disparate elements together - to explore for example, the sameness of the rhythms that run through music and the human heart. And unlike the effort by Dr. king and his colleagues in 1963, it will not be an attempt "to transform the jangling discord of our nation" by celebrating, in blatant and brave defiance of all the odds, the ideal of brotherhood.
> Today's gathering is the opposite of that. It is the theme of inclusiveness turned upside down. Whites need not apply, nor women of any hue. Instead of unity, it has promoted divisiveness on many fronts. As of white versus blacks were not conflict enough, Louis Farrakhan has succeeded in pitting black against blacks.

The *Washington Post* carried an exclusive front-page story by David Maraniss the day of the march on two brothers entitled, *Worship and Brotherhood on the Road to Washington: For Chicago Siblings Fond recollections of King's Dream in 63.* The brothers, who Maraniss interviewed, both "cherished" Kings speech. The one brothers "favorite line... was about the children: 'that one day... little black boys and black girls will be able to join hands with little white boys and white girls as sisters and brothers.'" Maraniss continued,

> They came from march organizer Louis Farrakhan's city, but they did not come because of him. For the most part, they said they want nothing to do with him, especially not with his expressions of hate. They came because they wanted to say something about themselves and to be a small part of the long struggle for civil rights in America.

Maraniss pointed out that "the Watkins brothers did not drive to Washington to make a religious statement, nor to express black separatist sentiments. They grew up under de facto segregation in Chicago… but never lost faith in King's dream of a truly integrated society." Maraniss concluded,

> And when they arrived on the mall yesterday and walked toward the Lincoln Memorial, as Bobby was overcome by the echoes of Martin Luther King's voice, James reflected on how things would be if he were still alive. "Would there be a Million Man March?"

Page 55-Jewish woman quoted as having an irrational fear of the unarmed crime fighting NOI

In all fairness, the media did allow certain "voices "in defense or support of the March to be heard. In a piece called *A Chance To Purge The Poison*, *Washington Post* columnist Cortland Milloy wrote, "To criticize Farrakhan while minimizing the conditions that gave rise to him strikes me as especially naiive… The Nation of Islam is not the 'Sons of the Gestapo,' nor some white supremist militia that seems to be blowing up America bit by bit with far less foul press than Louis Farrakhan gets." In another column, Milloy reported a conversation with a Jewish woman at a birthday party: "She said the Nation of Islam reminded her of Nazi Brownshirts, although they are, in fact, a small group of unarmed men who get rid of drug dealers in public housing projects and bring order out of the chaos in America's penal system." Milloy's favorable commentary on the good work of the "unarmed men," however, did not leave him or the *Washington Post* to respond three weeks later when the contract of a security firm in Baltimore run by Nation of Islam members was canceled. This event was only reported by the *Post* as "tremendously disappointing" to Mayor Kurt L Schmoke who called the cancellation "politically motivated," and led Abdul Arif Muhammad, general counsel for the Nation of Islam Security Agency, to accuse the Department of Housing and Urban Development of bowing "to the pressure of the American Jewish League and the American Jewish Congress."

Page 58 - Author Nathan McCall quote about the Million Man March

The *Washington Post*'s censure of one of its own Black writers may indicate the extent to which "all the voices" are, in fact, included in newspapers across the nation. Nathan McCall was criticized in the *Post* and made to appear devious for writing an upbeat column on Farrakhan and the March without informing readers that Farrakhan had been circulating a $6 million book proposal of his autobiography and that McCall would assist him in writing the book. Upon learning of the intended book proposal, a *Post* story set the record straight: " 'We simply had no idea,' said Jody T. Allen, Outlook's editor… Had she known about the book proposal, Allen said, 'we would have made it clear that Nathan was working with Louis Farrakhan. Readers, she said, 'should have known that this was not some *independent observer* looking at the march from the outside.' " The *Post* also "made it clear" in a noticeably framed editor's note on the op-ed page: "An article on the Million Man March by Nathan McCall should have disclosed that McCall's agent had approached a publisher about the possibility of his co-authoring an autobiography of march leader Louis Farrakhan. Outlook was unaware of this proposal until last week." McCall was quoted as saying that "there is no book… It's an idea… The news has falsely implied I am working with Farrakhan and that's just not the case." But Ombudsman Geneva Overholser used McCall as an example of the *Post*'s ability to scrutinize itself and not just others: "From time to time we show that we *can* print stories that embarrass us. Just last week media writer Howard Kurtz noted that an Outlook piece on Louis Farrakhan by Nathan McCall, a Post reporter on leave, had failed to disclose them McCall is planning to write a book with Farrakhan."

McCall was portrayed as less than objective. Perhaps what he wrote about the racial hierarchy and Dr. Martin Luther King Junior may also have been objectionable:

> The Million Man March represents a kind of therapy for black men…
> a chance to come together and confront our shortcomings and

celebrate our strengths... and... get a little bit of this tension off of our chests. The strain inside us comes from interrelated forces operating within and outside African-American communities nationwide; it's a confluence of social, economic and political powers that seem to be working in unison to bring us down... And none of those pressures shows any signs of letting up. I follow news accounts of those constantly high unemployment, poverty and death rates...

But the depression that many black men feel is not just confined to the so-called underclass. I see plenty of hard-working, law-abiding middle-class and professional blacks - men who play meticulously by the white man's rules -frustrated and enraged because they see those rules manipulated to white advantage... I suspect that, for some white Americans, complaints about Farrakhan are a smoke screen to conceal their blanket contempt for any black man who attempts to lift us up. White America may now pledge allegiance to the memory of Martin Luther King but black America has not forgotten that King, who preached love, peace and every other noble virtue that we claim to embrace, was intensely disliked and opposed by many whites when he was alive. His plan for a march on Washington 32 years ago was also described as divisive, unnecessary, [and] potentially violent.

Page 65 - Media's "agenda" to diminish Minister Farrakhan's power

Since association with a leader of "such bigotry" did not discourage "unaccountable" numbers of Black men from marching, *the flip side of the media's hierarchical coin was to separate the marchers from Farrakhan.* Black men, portrayed as not being able to think for themselves, were perceived on the Washington Mall as asserting their independence from Farrakhan. Marchers seen as a mindless mass by certain writers were seen by others as having minds of their own - *which could be read.* The media's failure to understand the reality of Black Americans is further seen in the interpretations of what the marchers on the Mall were thinking and feeling and doing. The unconscious arrogance and paternalism of numerous writers was disclosed in their assumptions, generalizations and distortions of the reality of the marchers and Farrakhan. The

165

perceptions of these writers were, in reality, projections of their own biased agenda. That agenda: to diminish the power and influence of Minister Louis Farrakhan to unify and lead people of color at the bottom of the hierarchy to create an equitable balance of power.

Page 78 - Author Winthrop Jordan's research supports 1555 date for beginning of slavery in U.S.

[Washington Post Staff Writer Ken Ringle] himself would do well to take a refresher course on Black history. He apparently misquoted Farrakhan in stating the latter suggested it "was momentous" for the Washington Monument to be "555 feet high... because if you added '1' to it, you got 1555, 'which was the year we [black people] arrived in Jamestown as slaves.'" Ringle was also incorrect in assuming that "this will come as news to historians, since the first permanent English settlement in North America wasn't founded until 1607 and the first blacks didn't arrive until 1619." Excerpts from Farrakhan's speech, published in *The New York Times* indicated he stated that "1555 [was] the year our first fathers landed on the shores of Jamestown, Virginia as slaves." Whatever the name of those shores in 1555, historian Winthrop D. Jordan's classic book on slavery in America, titled *White Over Black: American Attitudes Toward the Negro 1550-1812*, states, "... After 1500 Portuguese ships began supplying the Spanish and Portuguese settlements in America with Negro slaves. *By 1550 European enslavement of Negroes was more than a century old and Negro slavery had become a fixture in the New World*". Ringle's attempt to prove Farrakhan historically wrong apparently led him to lose sight of the *historical wrong*.

Page 79 - The racist view of Abraham Lincoln towards Black people

In *his* book, *Lies My Teacher Told Me: Everything Your American History Textbook Got Wrong,* historian James W. Loewen writes,

> In conversation Lincoln, like most whites of his century, referred to blacks as "niggers." When responding to Stephen Douglas's race-baiting in the Lincoln-Douglas debates, Lincoln himself sometimes descended into explicit white supremacy: "I have no purpose to introduce political and social equality between the white and black races. There is a physical difference between the two, which in my

166

judgment will probably forever forbid there living together upon the footing of perfect equality, and inasmuch as it becomes a necessity that there must be a difference, I as well as Judge Douglas am in favor of the race to which I belong, having the superior position... I am not, nor ever have been in favor of bringing about the social and political equality of the white and black races [applause] - that I am not nor ever have been in favor of making voters or jurors of Negroes."

Loewen writes that historians do a disservice to students in not portraying Lincoln in the fullness of who he was:

> Textbook authors protect us from a racist Lincoln. By doing so, they diminish students' capacity to recognize racism as a force in American life. For if Lincoln could be racist, then so might the rest of us be. And if Lincoln could transcend racism, as he did on occasion, then so might the rest of us... If textbooks recognized Lincoln's racism, students would learn that racism not only affects Ku Klux Klan extremists but has been "normal" throughout our history. And as they watched Lincoln struggle with himself to apply America's democratic principles across the color line, students would see how ideas can develop and a person can grow...
>
> Lincoln... knew full well that the United States was conceived in slavery... Nevertheless he began, "Four score and seven years ago, our fathers brought forth on this continent a new nation, conceived in liberty and dedicated to the proposition that all men are created equal."
>
> Thus Lincoln wrapped the Union cause in the rhetoric of the Declaration of Independence, which emphasized freedom even while many of its signers were slaveowners. In so doing, Lincoln was at the same time using the Declaration to redefine the Union cause, suggesting that it ultimately implied equal rights for all Americans, regardless of race.
>
> In addition to noting that many signers of the Declaration of Independence were slaveowners,

Loewen also writes,

> Americans seem perpetually startled at slavery. Children are shocked to learn that George Washington and Thomas Jefferson owned slaves. Interpreters at Colonial Williamsburg say that many visitors are surprised to learn that slavery existed there - in the heart of plantation Virginia! Very few adults today realize that our society has been slave much longer than it has been free. Even if you were know that slavery was important in the North, too, until after the Revolutionary War. The first colony to legalize slavery was not Virginia but Massachusetts.

Page 82 through 86 - Documenting Million Man March Crime Free, Sea of Peace, Produced by Farrakhan

Undoubtedly, the Million Man March contributed significantly to Farrakhan's popularity - and to his legitimacy as well. Contrary to the assumptions of a vast number of writers and newspaper columnists, a survey conducted on the day following the march indicated that "Farrakhan is more popular than other prominent black political figures, including Jesse L Jackson and General Colin Powell. He was far more popular than President Clinton who was elected in 1992 with the overwhelming support of black voters." A story published in the *New York Times* story reported,

> What was clear was that the event - which, the Park Police said drew a throng of 400,000 to the nation's capital - captured the attention of much of the country. Officials of the Cable News Network said today that 2.2 million households tuned in to Mr. Farrakhan's... speech - meaning that more people watched the two-hour-long address on CNN than any other special this year, including Mr. Clinton's State of the Union Message and the Popes address to the United Nations. "We got the kind of numbers that basic cable only sees from first-run movies," said Howard Polskin, a vice-president of CNN."

Moreover, the tendency of various writers to separate the marchers from Farrakhan, as if they attended the March in spite of its "controversial originator," is not supported by a survey conducted by *The Washington Post*. The newspaper's polling sample of 1,047 marchers found that "the black men who came to Washington... were younger, wealthier and better-educated than black Americans as a whole, and... were far more willing to see Nation of Islam leader Louis Farrakhan assume a more prominent leadership role in the African American community." The survey also found that "a third of those interviewed said a major reason they came to the Mall was to 'demonstrate support for Louis Farrakhan' but only 5 percent said Farrakhan was the biggest reason they made the trip." Still, the report continued, "Farrakhan was clearly the star of yesterday's march - and perhaps an emerging force in the national politics, the survey suggests. *Nearly 9 in 10 participants said they had a favorable impression of Farrakhan and a favorable view of the Nation of Islam.*"

It was also reported that "even some of Farrakhan's critics praised his success in attracting hundreds of thousands of black men for a peaceful rally that called for renewal in the black community." His appeal to marchers to join organizations in their communities when they returned home received an enthusiastic response. Three days after the March, Earl Shinhoster, interim director of the NAACP, was reported to have said that his organization "has received hundreds of calls from people wanting to join the group - an outpouring he attributed to Farrakhan's speech." Thus, in response to Farrakhan and Reverend Benjamin Chavis' call for the reconvening the following month of the National African American Leadership Summit, Shinhoster was quoted as responding, "The NAACP welcomes the call by Minister Louis Farrakhan for a meeting within the African American leadership to implement a call outlined in his eight-point address during the Million Man March." The NAACP had refused to endorse the March and to attend previous meetings of the National African-American Leadership Conference. In fact, it was assumed that "the Chavis-brokered alliance with Farrakhan was one of the issues involved in his dismissal... as executive director of the National Association for the Advancement of Colored People."

Farrakhan's plan to register 8 million new voters "got an unusual greeting from several mainstream political organizations, which in the past have routinely denounced any effort with which Farrakhan was associated." Don Fowler, Chairman of the National Democratic Committee, was quoted as saying, "We in the Democratic Party applaud efforts to get people registered... We believe that this broadens the base to democracy, and the more democracy the better." Haley Barbour, Chairman of the Republican National Committee, stated, "Republicans believe in increasing voter registration and participation among all Americans." And "Alex Herman, an assistant to President Clinton, said, 'Any time we have more of our citizens involved in the process of voting and making their voices count, it is a good thing for the nation.'"

Farrakhan appeared to take on the aura of a reigning celebrity. It was reported that he announced the "aggressive national voter registration drive" at a news conference "as hundreds of people waited on the sidewalk just outside... to get a glimpse of Farrakhan or snap his picture. As he emerged from the building, surrounded by Nation of Islam bodyguards, Farrakhan threw a kiss and waved to the cheering crowd."

The *Washington Post* survey may have come as a shock to then Republican presidential candidate Robert Dole who was quoted as saying, "There are probably a lot of well-intentioned people coming to Washington... And I like to talk about self-reliance, about picking yourself up, cleaning up our cities and getting kids off drugs. But I don't think Farrakhan should be the leader of the march. He spreads suspicion, separation and hate *wherever he goes*.

Farrakhan, the originator of the March, who looked at all those Black men and saw "a sea of peace," did not "spread suspicion, separatism and hate" on the Washington Mall. *New York Times* writer Michael Marriott reported,

> From dawn to dusk, there was no evidence of drug deals and the drive-by shootings or crack pipes and gang colors. The throng was as good natured as a church meeting. Police made only one arrest at the rally: for disorderly conduct. What much of America witnessed on the evening news was the site of hundreds of thousands of black men, respectable and responsible, in search of solace and solutions.

Washington Post staff writers Michael A. Fletcher and Hamil R. Harris reported that "the crowd on the Mall and adjoining streets... [was] basking in a day of peaceful solidarity... It was a day a spontaneous embraces, public tears and straight-in-the-eye greetings - the opposite of the nervous, sidelong glances that some men said they customarily employ to avoid confrontation." Another *Washington Post* news story reported, "At one point, two lines of buses stretched for blocks, said a police officer, who marveled at how polite and upbeat marchers were despite waits of two hours or more to depart." The story also stated, "Most of downtown" Washington was reported "as empty as a summer Friday" partly because of the fear of Black marchers: "A few said they went to work even though friends and relatives, urge them to stay at home. 'People in D.C. were concerned about the traffic, and everybody else -my parents and my sister - were concerned about violence,'" said a 28-year-old woman who works for an investment company.

The peaceful behavior of the marchers and contrasting fear of them are reported by *New York Times* writer Karen De Witt. She wrote,

> By midafternoon, the crowd stretched from the west steps of the Capital to the Washington Monument and was, by and large, somber, disciplined, relaxed and friendly... "It's been very peaceful," said Quintin Peterson, a public information officer for the Metropolitan Police Department here. "It's been very good. No problems. No incidents. We've been handling traffic, and it's been very good, very smooth."
> Despite what appeared to be a peaceful crowd, skittishness about possible conflict prompted several downtown office buildings to issue notices that the buildings would be locked as if it were a weekend as a precautionary measure, and that occupants should use special security keys for entry. One jewelry store closed; one white businesswoman wondered whether it was safe to walk three blocks to her office.
> Wendy Bader, a lawyer with the Federal Labor Relations Authority, two blocks away from the march site, said her mother, who lives in New Jersey, had told her to stay home from work. "She was afraid of violence because she thought the crowd was going to be a lot of young black males, the kind of people would be followers of Farrakhan and anti-white," said Ms. Bader, referring to Louis Farrakhan, the Nation of Islam leader...

171

Another lawyer, hurrying to her office, said: "this is even lighter than on a Saturday. I think a lot of people just didn't come in." But the woman, who was white and spoke on condition that her name not be used, offered another reason for the lack of pedestrian and vehicular traffic. "I think a lot of people were afraid for their safety," she said. "The women in my office, they thought there was a potential for a violent outbreak - a kind of K.K.K. showing. "

Another *New York Times* story reported, "Even by the agency's [National Park Service] own accounting, the Million Man March, which won praise from police for being peaceful and orderly, ranked as one of the largest demonstrations in the capital's history." The National Park Service apparently sought to prevent the Million Man March from becoming "one of the largest demonstrations in history."

Page 89 - 90 - Minister Farrakhan as a threat to "white racial hierarchy"

Why has Farrakhan been branded a pariah by mainstream media? This writer believes it is because he represents a serious threat to America's racial hierarchy. The hierarchy cannot control or buy his accommodation or "integration" as a Black leader. He dares to point out and challenge the "white supremacy" of the "founding fathers," forcing White America to recognize and deal with the fact that many of the signers of the Declaration of Independence, which declared freedom and equality for all, were themselves slave holders, and that even "Honest Abe" had a racist "wart" or two that can no longer be covered up. Farrakhan also has the power to initiate a call that led at least twice, and possibly three or more times as many African-American men to respond as the U.S. Park Police counted - in spite of all the print aimed at discrediting the Nation of Islam leader and derailing the March.

Furthermore, Farrakhan and all other Black men - and Black women - share the reality of an oppression about which he especially has clarity, an impression that far transcends any anti-Semitism or other bias of which he may be guilty; an oppression which certain European Jewish-Americans, no matter how few, participated in as owners of enslaved Africans, and continue to participate in by virtue of *their whiteness* being there invisible means into the mainstream of America's hierarchical life.

The threat Farrakhan poses to the White-favored hierarchy of access and power is seen in the United States government's refusal in 1996 to allow Farrakhan to receive a $250,000 prize "as winner of the Muammar Ghaddafi International Human Rights Award... for orchestrating last October's Million Man March." Nor was it a surprise that the United States government prevented Farrakhan, at the same time, from accepting a donation of $1 billion from Colonel Ghaddafi of Libya. The government believes Libya to be a supporter of terrorism and thus the bars "the transfer of any money between Libya and the United States."

Farrakhan was quoted as defending the $1 billion gift: "We are not terrorists... We are not trying to do anything against the good of America. What we want to do is good for our people and ultimately good for our nation." The good that Farrakhan wanted to do, he reportedly said, was to "use the money for voter registration drives, charitable contributions and economic development for black people." The first person to receive the Human Rights Award, established in 1989, was "President Nelson Mandela of South Africa. Other winners include American Indians and the children of the Palestinian uprising against the Israeli occupation. "

One billion dollars would give Farrakhan tremendous economic and political power and make him that much more of a unifying force among Black persons and other people of color. America's White-dominated hierarchy is against any such threat to the racial status quo. The hierarchy probably fears, and for good reason, that the money would be used to change the balance of power between White and Black persons. Farrakhan himself was quoted as saying "that he was not allowed to accept the $1 billion gift from Libyan leader Muammar Ghaddafi because Washington was afraid of the power it would bring." He stated at a news conference,

> There is fear first of a black man who is gaining influence and is a man they do not control. Second, if we have accomplished what we have accomplished so far without money then they are afraid of what we can accomplish if we did have money... The American people are captive to those in power who manipulate them by falsehood. With $1 billion we could effectively affect the thinking of all of the American people.

173

Page 94-95 - Million Man March as threat to racial hierarchy but Minister Farrakhan mishandled

A primary role of mainstream media is to protect and maintain the White-favored hierarchy of access, wealth and power. The Million Man March represented a threat to the hierarchy: it was conceived by a Black leader whom the media could not intimidate, seduce or otherwise control; a Black leader critical of the "white supremacy" pervading the very hierarchy the media is committed to denying and maintaining; a Black leader who could spearhead the unifying and empowering of one million African Americans in the common cause of creating a level political and economic playing field. Contrary to the media's focus on the "controversial originator" of the March, this writer believes that Farrakhan *is feared as a unifying, more than a divisive force*. Thus *The Washington Post, New York Times* and *The Boston Globe* "rained" on Farrakhan's "parade. "

These print media portrayed Farrakhan as a pariah in an attempt to select for African Americans their rightful leaders. To march in Farrakhan's "parade" would be to associate with his "anti-white," "anti-Semitic," "sexist," "anti-gay," "separatist," "hate-mongering," message. A double standard was used to demonize Farrakhan: the media emphasized his "homophobic," "sexist," "anti-Semitic" message while ignoring the homophobic, sexism and anti-Semitism of far more powerful groups in American society. Moreover, Farrakhan was associated with White supremists and disassociated from traditional and revered Black leaders. Select Black male and female leaders were enlisted and elevated in the campaign to discredit Farrakhan and undermine the March. Those leaders opposing the March and those supporting it became a continuing feature of a "controversial" and "divisive" "parade" - the former given positive and prominent coverage and the latter subjected to criticism. When the "fiendizing" of Farrakhan did not discourage an incredible outpouring of Black men on the Washington Mall, the media proceeded to the flip-side of the coin: they separated "the message" of the marchers from "the messenger." Marchers portrayed by certain writers as a mindless mass to be "summoned" by Farrakhan were described by other writers as having minds of their own that differed from Farrakhan once they arrived on the Mall. This attempt to undermine Farrakhan's prominence and power is also seen in the coverage of his speech: his "message" to all those Black marchers was repeatedly trashed, ignored or replaced by a now-revered Black leader dead for more than two decades. In raining on the Million Man March's "parade," the White-controlled media revealed an inability or intent not to understand the reality of African Americans.

Page 97-Million Man March powerful unifying force

The Million Man March represented the powerful unifying force of African-Americans that shook the foundation of the nation's racial hierarchy. The March transcended every bias the guardian media rained down on its "parade." Interest benefiting from racial hierarchy feared not a divisive force, but a unifying one. The hierarchy thrives on divisiveness and is threatened by unity-hence the polarizing role of its guardian media's coverage of the march. The unifying power of the Million Man March will be seen in the extent to which, as Farrakhan said, African-Americans go back home and transcend differences, join organizations, register voters and work together for the common good - "committed to the ongoing struggle for a free and empowered community, a just society and a better world." In America's racial hierarchical society, a level political and economic playing field is not created by access *to* power but by the access *of* power. It is hoped this research paper contributes to that end.

Is Minister Farrakhan Being Asked to Do with No Resources What Chicago Can't (or Won't) Do with Tens of Billions of Dollars?

By Phillip Jackson
Founder and Executive Director
The Black Star Project

The Honorable Minister Louis Farrakhan was criticized Thursday in a Chicago Sun-Times newspaper column by a Black columnist, Mary Mitchell, because the Minister said that the Fruit of Islam (F.O.I.) would protect Beyoncé Knowles if the Miami Police won't do its job to protect her because it is offended by her performance at the Super Bowl that included a song that featured costumes and lyrics from The Black Panther era.

Ms. Mitchell's major criticism was that Black people are dying in Chicago and if Minister Farrakhan has resources, he should use them to stop "poor Black men and women" from dying on the streets of Chicago, and not use them to protect Beyoncé. Her exact words were "Farrakhan's threat of using the F.O.I. to protect Beyoncé is not only a joke, it is a slap in the faces of all the women who are risking their lives everyday trying to save young people." She also called the strong men of the Nation of Islam "hustlers" of the Final Call newspaper and "sellers" of bean pies, and she spoke of the F.O.I. as a "prop"!

Apparently, Ms. Mitchell really doesn't understand The Nation of Islam and is ignorant about Minister Farrakhan's history of protecting women, or she has another agenda. So, I have a few questions for Ms. Mitchell.

Chicago is getting ready to hire another Police Superintendent at an annual salary of about $300,000. Is she suggesting that Minister Farrakhan get that salary? If so, I am all for that. There are about 12,000 policemen in Chicago (mostly White), that consume about $1.5 billion of the city budget. The level of crime in Chicago suggests the police force is not effective at stopping crime. Is she asking the F.O.I. to recruit 12,000 good men and women to earn this money at about $100,000 each per year to protect our city? If so, again, I am all for that. Does she know that policing alone won't stop the violence and killing in any community no matter who is policing? Is she ready to turn over $3.5 billion to the Nation of Islam in Workforce Development and Human Service dollars to support the mission to reduce violence in Chicago? If so, I agree with her.

Poor education feeds crime and violence. The education that most Black children get in Chicago is equivalent to or less than an education received in a Third World country. Is she suggesting that the current Chicago Public School budget of about $6 billion be advanced to the University of Islam to better manage educational outcomes for Chicago students? If so, this is a great idea!

If she does not want the Nation of Islam to receive an approximate $11 billion transfer of city funds to fix problems that others are currently being paid $11 billion dollars to fix, then she is not serious and has another agenda! How can she expect Minister Farrakhan to fix these problems with not even a NICKLE from her nor a DIME from the city?

Minister Farrakhan and the Nation of Islam are currently donating hundreds of millions of dollars in services to cities and towns across America in many ways-both tangible and intangible. In services alone to reclaim felons from prisons across this nation, one could argue that the Nation of Islam should be paid billions of dollars for services previously rendered.

Ms. Mitchell doesn't really want these problems fixed. She doesn't really want to help the people on the block. Her column on Minister Farrakhan is "the slap in the face" that she talks about to serious people doing the serious work to save Black people's lives, and her viewpoint lets the people off the hook who are responsible for and being paid billions of dollars while failing to fix these issues.

Attacking Minister Farrakhan won't fix the problems of violence and killing in Chicago. Working with him will, if she is serious about these issues!

Imam Michael Saahir Wrong on Minister Farrakhan...again!

And those who believe say: Why is not a chapter revealed? But when a decisive chapter is revealed, and fighting is mentioned therein, thou seest those in whose hearts is a disease look to thee with the look of one fainting at death. So, woe to them!—Holy Qur'an Surah 47 Ayat 20

An Indianapolis Imam has written an open letter to the Honorable Minister Louis Farrakhan. His letter was penned to express an unnecessary concern that the Minister's bold and inspired message, delivered in Miami, Florida, recently, was a call for a race war. I would like to address him, his concerns and some general misconceptions about the history of the Most Honorable Elijah Muhammad and the Honorable Minister Farrakhan.

The Imam's concerns are unnecessary for several reasons.

It should first of all be established that the Imam is wrong for claiming that the Most Honorable Elijah Muhammad never made use of the theme "Justice or Else." The theme "Justice or Else" was boldly emblazoned atop the masthead of the inaugural issue of the Nation of Islam's revolutionary news organ the *Muhammad Speaks* newspaper in October 1961. And now the Minister's final call is for "Justice, Or Else" on 10.10.15.

Secondly, all of the Nation of Islam's history both before and after 1975 is indicative of the Nation of Islam's role within American society as a self-respecting, law-abiding peaceful people. Prior to the departure of the Most Honorable Elijah Muhammad in 1975 various law enforcement agencies went on record to document how much of a valued resource the Nation of Islam was in their respective cities.

"One thing I can say—wherever Muslims go, crime goes down. We policemen are always happy to have them in a community; it makes our job that much easier."—**Chicago Deputy Police Superintendent Sam Nolan (January 1974)**

"As a large group of people, the Muslims tend to be law-abiding and seem to have a rehabilitating influence in the community." —**Thomas W. Chochee, Police Chief Compton California (February 1974)**

"Addicts must be treated as persons and not statistics, and to the Harlem State Senator that means therapy, rehabilitation and employment. He said that the State chief executive could learn a lesson from what the Nation of Islam has done to remold ex-drug addicts by giving them a sense of pride in self and kind." — referring to **NY State Senator from Harlem Sidney Von Luther (March 9, 1973)**

"The Muslims have done more to rehabilitate narcotics addicts than any corrective agency in the country." —**NY State Senator from Harlem Basil Patterson, at the National Society of Afro-American Policemen's tribute to the Nation of Islam (July 5, 1969)**

Post 1975 Minister Farrakhan's message has boldly challenged the white elite power structure. All in that hierarchy of power, wealth and influence have deemed him to be a threat. Yet the record is clear. Just like his spiritual father, the Most Honorable Elijah Muhammad, Minister Farrakhan has been a rebuilder, a restorer and a peacemaker.

Most notable in this area of establishing and maintaining peace in the society, is the formation of an unarmed protection and security apparatus that was affectionately dubbed "The Dopebusters." The Dopebusters—or as they were officially known, NOI Security Agency—began in 1988 in Washington, D.C.'s Mayfair Mansion apartment complex. Because of their tremendous success in eliminating the drug trafficking and violence in the areas they patrolled, their legend spread, causing them to eventually broaden their operations to many major cities throughout America.

When Jewish pressure intervened to remove Minister Farrakhan's peace forces— despite their unmatched success in eradicating the drug crime that had plagued the country's public housing—it became necessary for congressional hearings to take place. During those hearings Housing and Urban Development (HUD) director Henry Cisneros, a Cabinet-level official, made the following commentary about the "Dopebusters."

> "since the security firms first began their work in 1988 and throughout the review we have undertaken in this instance, there have been no complaints filed against these firms regarding any

inappropriate religious activities. In fact, we have conducted **over 1,000 interviews of residents and management, and they illustrate that these security guards have been effective in transforming many drug-ridden properties into places which are now safe and peaceful."**

Cisneros' weighty testimony as the top leader of a division of the United States federal government mitigates any concerns over Minister Farrakhan and his followers being associated with acts of violence. Director Cisneros went on to push back against the notion being promoted by U.S. Representative Peter T. King of New York that the federal government doing business with Minister Farrakhan's followers was equivalent to doing business with a hate group. According to Cisneros:

> "The FBI Domestic Terrorism Unit does maintain an internal list of groups known to have committed terrorist acts, which is at times used as an indicator of hate groups or hate crimes. Organizations such as the Aryan Nation are on that list. **The Nation of Islam is not.** In addition, in the last 5 years, the United States prosecuted more than 50 criminal actions against members of so-called hate groups, alleging violations of civil rights. Although these hate crimes prosecutions have involved members of the Ku Klux Klan, the Aryan Nation, and skinheads, **none of the actions have involved members of the Nation of Islam. This is a point of law, a definable, observable point of fact."**

Moreover, even with the controversial relationship that Minister Farrakhan has with members of the Jewish community, there has never ever been so much as a bloody nose produced as a result. Jewish rabbi Bruce Khan noted that any fear of physical violence coming as a result of Minister Farrakhan's words and message is an unnecessary concern. Rabbi Khan attended the Million Man March. He wrote afterwards that **"the people who listen to him [Minister Farrakhan] do not go chasing down Jews, or gays or Whites or Koreans to beat them and murder them... They are sufferers who know how tough it is to get a fair shake as Black people. They want that to change. They hear in Minister Farrakhan's words inspiration and instructions to begin to bring** about that change. That is the message on which he focuses and on which they focus. That is not the message on which the media focuses."

I would ask Imam Saahir, who is a brother that I respect, to review in totality the Minister's message in Miami. Were he to do so, he would see the real threat is the Minister's call for an economic withdrawal from the Christmas holiday buying season. He is calling Black America to the same act of unity that Dr. Martin Luther King Jr., James Baldwin, Adam Clayton Powell and Ossie Davis called for in 1963-participation in a "Sacrificial Christmas."

I believe that a more thorough study of the Minister's history would help the Imam to have a greater appreciation for Minister Farrakhan's work, which is in harmony with that of the Most Honorable Elijah Muhammad. It is wrong for Imam Saahir to lift the history of the Most Honorable Elijah Muhammad in a way that opposes Minister Farrakhan. For years, various members of the Sunni community have condemned Minister Farrakhan for his promotion of the teachings of the Most Honorable Elijah Muhammad. They have essentially said "get rid of Elijah and get with the Qur'an." Now when the Minister invokes the Holy Qur'an to guide and pastor to the suffering victims of injustice, Imam Saahir takes a distorted view of the Hon. Elijah Muhammad to "correct" the Minister.

This is wrong and offensive!

The world knows that there has been no one more committed to the teachings of the Most Honorable Elijah Muhammad since his departure in 1975 than Minister Farrakhan. He is THE source for any who sincerely want to learn just what Elijah Muhammad and the Nation of Islam are all about. For when you look at Minister Farrakhan, you are looking at not just a theoretician but one whose theoretical understanding of his teacher's message has been refined through his courageous practice and implementation of that message. Being both theoretician and practitioner, Minister Farrakhan is guided by more than what may be written down in books or articles. For ever since he stood to rebuild the Nation of Islam in 1977, he has traveled the path blazed for him by the Most Honorable Elijah Muhammad. And this has furnished the Minister with an unmatched insight into his teacher's words, actions and programs. If you want to know Elijah Muhammad, you must inquire of Minister Louis Farrakhan. To do otherwise is to accrue a sterile, academic and incomplete portrait of a man that in over 80 years the academy has failed to understand.

Being the best student of the Most Honorable Elijah Muhammad, Minister Farrakhan is often misunderstood, just as his teacher was many years ago. Imam Saahir's concern over the Minister calling for a race-based indiscriminate retaliation against white people is unnecessary. The Minister has never advocated that violence or harm be done to innocent people: he is calling for Economic Withdrawal, a strategy of unity in keeping with the Rev. Dr. Martin Luther King, who said in his magnificent last message titled the Mountaintop Speech, "We don't have to argue with anybody. We don't have to curse and go around acting bad with our words. We don't need any bricks and bottles. We don't need any Molotov cocktails. We just need to go around to these stores, and to these massive industries in our country, and say, "God sent us by here, to say to you that you're not treating his children right.... As Jesse Jackson, has said, up to now, only the garbage men have been feeling pain; now we must kind of redistribute the pain." The Imam's misconstrual and misinterpretation of the Minister's message is similar to the misunderstanding and misapprehension by those who may have misinterpreted the Most Honorable Elijah Muhammad in some of his bold prophetic utterances during his historic Uline Arena address in 1959.

No one in his right mind would ever say that Elijah Muhammad was suicidal. Yet his words in the Uline arena address might be misinterpreted in a way that makes one think he was urging his audience toward mass suicide. His comments appear in his book *The Fall of America* and in *Message to the Blackman in America*.

On page 36 of *Message to The Blackman in America* he writes:

> "If a million of us throw ourselves in the fire for the benefit of the 20 million, the loss would be small compared to the great gain our people will make as a result of that sacrifice. Hundreds of thousands of Muslims gave their lives in Pakistan to get their nation's independence. They were successful. The black men in Africa are fighting and dying today in unity for their independence. We sit here

like pampered babies. We cannot even stand on the floor, not to mention taking a chance of crawling out of the door. We are too careful of shedding blood for ourselves. We are willing to shed all of it for the benefit of others."

This sounds like Mr. Muhammad is suggesting that a million Black people sacrifice themselves for the whole of the 20 million Blacks living in America. In his book *The Fall of America* he mentions that 10 million of us might just as well sacrifice ourselves to leave 10 million behind to enjoy the fruit of our sacrifice. In an elucidation of the aforementioned, he goes on to say on page 8-9 of *The Fall of America*: "*If you and I are deprived of justice, if the federal government will not punish our murderers and our rapers. I say to you. we must get together and find some way to punish them ourselves!*"

I strongly encourage my brother Imam to read these words of the Most Honorable Elijah Muhammad and reconsider his position about the Honorable Minister Louis Farrakhan in the light of the context and history that I am sharing with him, which expose the falsity of his poison-pen letter.

The words of the Most Honorable Elijah Muhammad as documented here perfectly harmonize with that of his best student, the Honorable Minister Louis Farrakhan, who recently in Miami said: *"The Qur'an teaches 'persecution is worse than slaughter.' Then it says, retaliation is prescribed in matters of the slain. Retaliation is a prescription from God to calm the breasts of those whose children have been slain.* **If the federal government will not intercede in our affairs, then we must rise up and kill those who kill us,** *stalk them and let them feel the pain of death that we are feeling."*

And just as Minister Farrakhan moved from the law of retaliation into an economic application of it via an economic withdrawal from Christmas, the Most Honorable Elijah Muhammad did the same. He said on page 36 of Message to the Blackman:

"We sit here like pampered babies. We cannot even stand on the floor, not to mention taking a chance of crawling out of the door. We are too careful of shedding blood for ourselves. We are willing to shed all of it for the benefit of others. I am not trying to get you to

183

fight. That is not even necessary; our unity will win the battle! Not one of us will have to raise a sword. Not one gun would we need to fire. **The great cannon that will be fired is our unity. Our unity is the best. Why are you afraid to unite?"**

I would encourage my brother Imam to bring his views into harmony with his teacher Imam Warithudeen Mohammed, who delivered a beautiful khutbah on February 25, 2000, for our annual Saviours' Day convention. In that Khutbah he said of Minister Farrakhan: **"When the brother Muslim stands upon the Qur'an, the last of the revealed books and the complete book for all times and all societies, and when he stands upon faith in Muhammad as God's last prophet and Messenger to all the worlds, mercy to all the worlds, we are to support him in that."** Surely Minister Farrakhan's words on retaliation are on the firm foundation of the Holy Qur'an.

Imam Mohammed's words point us to some of the great Islamic principles of brotherhood. Prophet Muhammad (saw/pbuh) is reported by Abu Hurairah to have said **"Do not help Shaitan against your brother."** Imam Saahir's open letter to Minister Farrakhan goes against this principle because Imam Saahir could have requested to meet with the Minister in private to discuss his points of disagreement with his words in Miami calling for justice, or else. This calls to mind the words of the great Imam Siraj Wahajj about the importance of Muslim unity and the value of Minister Farrakhan. On September 21, 2008, Imam Siraj told the *Final Call Newspaper:* **"Minister Farrakhan holds the key to the development of (Islam) in this country**—so we're going to talk about where we go from here, let us now continue the process so that we can move even further on toward the development of Islam in America **because the attack is against Islam and they don't ask you the question (are you) Sunni or Shiite, (are) you with the Nation (of Islam) or what? No. We have to recognize that the enemies of Islam are united against us,"**

Despite my respect for Imam Saahir's book titled *The Honorable Elijah Muhammad: The Man Behind the Men*, I acknowledge that he is developing a bad track record of openly criticizing the leadership of the Honorable Minister Louis Farrakhan.

On December 13, 2008, he penned a very mean-spirited open letter to Minister Farrakhan titled *Thanks, but No Thanks*. In that letter Imam Saahir wrongly attributed a motive to Minister Farrakhan of trying to interfere with Imam Mohammed's community after his passing. You reacted quite negatively to the *Muslim Journal*'s interview with the Minister. Imam Saahir took time to condemn core Nation of Islam belief's and in an arrogant self-aggrandizing stroke wrote:

> "...don't be surprised if you, Minister Farrakhan may have to sit under the feet of some of Imam Mohammed's students before you may qualify to approach us in the manner that you are trying to pursue in this interview. Imam Mohammed has taught his students well, very well."

Such words on the part of Imam Saahir are unbecoming of a man in his position. The humility of Minister Farrakhan is such that he will accept truth regardless of the person sharing it. He has said that every man or woman that he meets can teach him something that he doesn't know. But to arrogantly suggest that he is the Minister's superior is a hubristic claim that easily evaporates before the facts of history.

No. Imam Saahir was wrong on Minister Farrakhan in 2008 and he is wrong in 2015. His history and pattern of public condemnation of Minister Farrakhan undermines the work of Imam Warithudeen Mohammed in reconciling and unifying with Minister Farrakhan. Why would he want to help the Shaitan in furthering the divide among the Muslim ummah? One wonders that he should find a better use of his time in responding to issues such as the *New York Times* article condemning Islam as a "religion of rape." That is a more worthwhile cause to occupy Imam Saahir's attention. Uniting with Minister Farrakhan to combat the rising tide of Islamophobia in America would be wiser since such propaganda negatively impacts all of the diverse communities of Muslims in America.

But instead Imam Saahir has rushed to be at the forefront joining in with the enemy's propagandists in criticizing a man whom he refers to as his "Muslim brother." This wanton criticism is unnecessary, unwise and antithetical to the noble principles of brotherhood as espoused by the religion of Islam.

The Year 1974 and Why Farrakhan Is Good for Morgan State

The recent op-ed in the Baltimore Sun condemning the Honorable Minister Louis Farrakhan was a feeble attempt to dissuade students and members of the Baltimore/Morgan State community from attending the Minister's lecture on November 22, 2014. It was written by a member of the Jewish community seeking to assassinate Minister Farrakhan's character and to make his critical analysis of Jewish misdeeds in the Black community, a reason for not attending this historic event.

Minister Farrakhan has spoken to the students at Morgan State University on several momentous occasions and all with positive outcomes. As he is always such a well-spring of knowledge, wisdom, inspiration and motivation, the Morgan State students should be commended and congratulated for making such a wise choice of inviting the Honorable Minister Louis Farrakhan.

The Minister is, according to Jewish apologist Abraham Foxman, the last man standing. Foxman said of the Minister in the April 2013 issue of Haaretz Magazine

> "The only leadership that now exists in that community"—the "African American community"—"is Louis Farrakhan. Farrakhan can assemble 20,000 people several times a year,"

Why wouldn't Black college students want to listen to and be guided by the "last man standing?" It is indeed a wise choice on the part of these courageous young people. In 1974 their parents' generation came out in droves to be inspired and motivated by Minister Farrakhan. Minister Farrakhan was the keynote speaker at a Black Family Day event in 1974 at Morgan State where 30,000 students, faculty and Baltimore residents attended this electrifying event.

The Minister's message was reported on in the October 11, 1974 issue of the Muhammad Speaks (MS) newspaper. The MS coverage documented some of the highlights of the Minister's message that day as he echoed many of the powerful themes and ideas resident within the teachings of the Most Honorable Elijah Muhammad. The Minister taught the students

"You are not a man, until you learn how to love, respect and protect, your Black woman."

The Minister continued this theme of respect and protection for the woman by teaching the students that

"The Honorable Elijah Muhammad says to us that the only way we can gain the respect of the civilized world is to take that Black woman honor her, respect her, protect her..."

Minister Farrakhan was so well received by the students at Morgan State that they invited him to come back and teach them more from the wisdom of the Most Honorable Elijah Muhammad. The November 29, 1974 issue of the Muhammad Speaks newspaper reported that nearly 1000 students filled Murphy auditorium to hear Minister Farrakhan. Muhammad Speaks reporter Lonnie Kashif documents some of the powerful guidance the Minister shared with the students. The Minister said,

"...don't doubt the power of Allah to make something out of you; don't doubt the power of Allah to bring you from under the foot of white people and make them bow to you who once groveled in the dust at their feet."

The Jewish propagandist, Jay Bernstein who wrote the Baltimore Sun article condemning Minister Farrakhan's visit at Morgan State obviously has a problem with this kind of messaging being given to Black students. This kind of message motivates and inspires Black students toward an enlightened self-interest. It restores in the students a concern for their communities and gives the students an awakening that will prevent these brilliant young people from further exploitation.

Perhaps he would rather these gifted young Black students not know what Minister Farrakhan knows. He called Minister Farrakhan anti-Semitic. And since he opened that door, let's look inside it to see some of the things that Minister Farrakhan has made known about the hidden misdeeds of the Jews against Blacks. In the Secret Relationship Between Blacks and Jews series, Minister Farrakhan has made known previously hidden admissions from Jewish scholars, historians and rabbis. Some jaw-dropping revelations include:

188

"The cotton plantations in many parts of the South were wholly in the hands of the Jews, and as a consequence slavery found its advocates among them." The Jewish Encyclopedia

"It would seem to be realistic to conclude that any Jew who could afford to own slaves and had need for their services would do so.... Jews participated in every aspect and process of the exploitation of the defenseless blacks."
-Rabbi Bertram Korn, From "Jews and Negro Slavery in the Old South, 1789-1865," Dr. Korn is a rabbi, historian with degrees from Hebrew Union College-Jewish Institute of Religion, Cincinnati.

"The female slave was a sex tool beneath the level of moral considerations. She was an economic good, useful, in addition to her menial labor, for breeding more slaves. To attain that purpose, the master mated her promiscuously according to his breeding plans. The master himself and his sons and other members of his household took turns with her for the increase of the family wealth, as well as for satisfaction of their extra-marital sex desires. Guests and neighbors too were invited to that luxury."
- Dr. Louis Epstein, author of Sex Laws and Customs in Judaism

Bernstein is angry that Minister Farrakhan has exposed this history to the Black community. It is a history that needs to be told. Because unless Black people know the history of what happened to us, we will look upon one another in our miserable condition and draw the wrong conclusions.

It is ironic that in 1974 when Minister Farrakhan was at Morgan State awakening the Black students to their duty and responsibility to God, family and community, Jewish leaders were doing something entirely different.

In 1974 the Anti-Defamation League of B'Nai B'rith (ADL) and the American Jewish Congress joined forces to legally fight against Affirmative Action. In other words, while Minister Farrakhan was giving Black college students purpose and guidance for their education, Jewish groups were working to reduce the number of Black students able to enter into college. The case entitled DeFunis

v. Odegaard had been dubbed in some Jewish publications "the greatest legal battle in the history of America." The ADL had pressured a young Sephardic Jewish student Marco DeFunis Jr. to sue for entry into Washington University Law School after he had been initially denied. His argument was that the school's admission policy favored Blacks to the exclusion of qualified whites.

DeFunis v. Odegaard was at the time widely viewed as a betrayal of Black progress by supposed Jewish allies. Civil rights leaders were disappointed. Maryland Congressman Parren J. Mitchell said

> "If the court rules in favor of DeFunis, we've lost our one weapon to get Blacks into colleges and professional schools-affirmative action. No school will let us in out of the goodness of its heart, without the pressure of the law and courts backing us up."

The value of Minister Farrakhan's visit to the students at Morgan State is even more important in light of another critical event that took place in 1974. It was then that Dr. Richard Hammerschlag, a neuro-chemist working for the City of Hope National Medical Center in Duarte, California revealed ominous truths at the American Chemical Society's national meeting in Los Angeles. Dr. Hammerschlag revealed that the U.S. military was involved in genetic research to develop a weapon capable of wiping out Black people while excluding other ethnic groups.

Dr. Hammerschlag cited a November 1970 article written by Carl Larson in the magazine Military Review on the work being done to create "ethnic weapons." Dr. Hammerschlag pointed out in his presentation that new information indicates that there are "many blood proteins (known as polymorphisms) that exist in several different genetically controlled forms in human populations." And that based on this, substances can be created to adversely affect a specific ethnic population who has a particular type of polymorphism without affecting other ethnic populations. He added that as a result of "the newly developed, binary nerve gases, the possibility of genetically selective weapons becomes entirely feasible and quite probable.

What Dr. Hammerschlag pointed out in 1974 appears to have come to fruition in 2014. Minister Farrakhan said is on record warning the Black community of the creation of "race-based weapons."

The Minister said in his very popular lecture entitled Justifiable Homicide: Black Youth in Peril that

> "Another method [of depopulation] is disease infection through bio-weapons such as Ebola and AIDS, which are race targeting weapons. There is a weapon that can be put in a room where there are Black and White people, and it will kill only the Black and spare the White, because it is a genotype weapon that is designed for your genes, for your race, for your kind."

The Morgan State students, I am sure, are just as stunned as others are in the Black community that the only 2 people in America who have died from the Ebola virus are Black males. And the only countries around the world that are suffering from Ebola are Black African countries.

All of these critical issues of the day are well within the grasp of the Honorable Minister Louis Farrakhan to dissect, analyze, guide and instruct us on. We don't need Jewish propagandists interfering with who we listen to in the Black community. It's clear that if we let them guide us, we won't be in college classrooms; we will be back on plantations.

Pharaoh's Fears Alive in Jamaica:
Black Islamic Caribbean Leaders Prevented from Meeting with Farrakhan

While reading the news reports that revolutionary Islamic leaders Gerald Perreira and Imam Abu Bakr were blocked from entry into Jamaica to meet with the Honorable Minister Louis Farrakhan several thoughts came to mind.

First of all, I reflected on how Minister Farrakhan has a long history of working to produce the unity of all Blacks in the diaspora as the ultimate solution to the lingering effects of colonialism and imperialism. The Minister has also has made it a major part of his ministry the encouraging of all people of faith to unite against the encroachment and infiltration of immorality and vice upon the family unit. Caribbean critics of the Minister charged that he is divisive, yet his history paints a picture of him working to unify people of good faith and good will. Careful observation of the alleged divisiveness of Minister Farrakhan will reveal that it is only those who seek to maintain the status quo of Caribbean weakness and subjugation to the governments of Europe and America that make this charge.

The Bible says in Hebrews 4:12 that the word of God is divisive.

> "For the word of God is alive and active. Sharper than any double-edged sword, it penetrates even to dividing soul and spirit, joints and marrow; it judges the thoughts and attitudes of the heart."

And since Minister Farrakhan's message is based upon and saturated with the word of God found in both the Bible and the Holy Qur'an, it is no wonder that he is deemed divisive.

I then thought about who could give the orders to prevent Minister Farrakhan from meeting with these strong Black Islamic Caribbean leaders. It was then I remembered an account provided by Minister Farrakhan about some of his early global travels particularly to Africa. He went to Nigeria in 1986 in the aftermath of Nigeria joining the OIC. The Minister had prepared to encourage unity and tolerance between the dueling Islamic and Christian majorities of Nigeria. But the Minister was not permitted to speak. His aides were met at the place where his speech was to be held by armed military personnel who threatened to shoot them if they proceeded to enter the facility. It was later disclosed to the Minister that the U.S. State Department had circulated false propaganda against the Minister that falsely claimed he was a communist who was in league with Russian and global communist leaders and that he had come to stir up trouble in Africa.

During this same global tour, U.S. Attorney Edwin Meese said that Minister Farrakhan "should be prosecuted" if he traveled to meet with another strong Black Islamic leader-the patron saint of Africa- Muammar Ghaddafi in Libya. The Minister had condemned then President Ronald Reagan's travel ban to Libya. The Minister's plans to meet with the Libyan leader were not borne out of any outlaw tendencies within his character. Instead it was the Minister's commitment to the higher principles of his faith in the religion of Islam, specifically the principle of *ummah* or the universal community and brotherhood of all Muslims. The Holy Qur'an makes this principle clear in the following words of Surah/Chapter 49 ayat/verse number 10.

> "The believers are brethren so make peace between your brethren, and keep your duty to Allah that mercy may be had on you."

It is often the case in the religion of Islam that support for and elucidation of a concept or passage of the Holy Qur'an can be found in the sayings or traditions of Prophet Muhammad, known as his hadiths. And such is the case with the principle of ummah/brotherhood that Minister Farrakhan has always been committed to. The Prophet is reported to have said that:

> "Do not have malice against a Muslim; do not be envious of other Muslims; do not go against a Muslim and forsake him. O the slave of Allah! Be like brothers with each other. It is not allowed for a Muslim to desert his brother for over three days."

In another hadith Prophet Muhammad is reported to have said

> "The Believers, in their mutual love, mercy and compassion, are like one body: if one organ complained, the rest of the body develops a fever."

The Minister's profound commitment to the idea and principle of unity and reconciliation has been noted by the brilliant and renowned Muslim scholar Dr. Aminah McCloud, who wrote of the Minister,

> "When Farrakhan visits leaders in Iran or Libya, an uniformed observer might see only that the Minister is willfully consorting with America's enemies, rather than recognizing the visit as an expression of his commitment to ummah...
>
> In the same way that the five-times-daily prayers erase one set of class and gender issues, the notion of ummah obscures nation-state borders. This detail is critical in beginning to place some of Farrakhan's thoughts and actions within a larger Islamic context. For instance, by his continual condemnation of neocolonialism on the African continent and in the Caribbean, Louis Farrakhan demonstrates an understanding of the notion of ummah, however unorthodox his methods of expressing this understanding."

But America and the western powers in general have always feared the power of Islam among Africans and the Blacks of the diaspora. 20th century eugenicist and Harvard scholar Lothrop Stoddard makes a striking assessment within his book The Rising Tide of Color against White World Supremacy. Stoddard wrote this tome to warn the Caucasian world powers of the erosion of their global influence due to an awakening among Black Africa, Brown Arabia and India and Yellow China and Japan. Stoddard, therefore in the early 1900s is the "white man's watchman on the wall." He laments on page 97

> "Certainly, all white men, whether professing Christians or not, should welcome the success of [Christian] missionary efforts in Africa. ...all Negroes will someday be either Christians or Moslems. In so far as he is Christianized, the Negro's savage instincts will be restrained and he will be disposed to acquiesce in white tutelage. In so far as he is Islamized, the Negro's warlike propensities will be inflamed, and he will be used as the tool of Arab Pan-Islamism seeking to drive the white man from Africa and make the continent its very own."

On page 94 Stoddard quotes Sir Charles Elliott who confessed that Islam in Africa

> "...can still give the natives a motive for animosity against Europeans and a unity of which they are otherwise incapable!"

Stoddard's boldness in sounding the alarm to alert the global Caucasian and European minority of the awakening of the global Black, Brown and Yellow majority generated another thought as I reflected over the moves to thwart Minister Farrakhan's meeting with strong Black Islamic Caribbean leaders.

This thought was of the Holy Qur'an and what it describes as Pharaoh's fear that Moses and Aaron would change the religion of the enslaved Children of Israel who were under his oppressive rule. In Surah 40 ayat 26, the Holy Qur'an reads:

> "And Pharaoh said: Leave me to slay Moses and let him call upon his Lord. Surely I fear that he will change your religion or that he will make mischief to appear in the land."

Pharaoh feared Moses would change the religion of the Children of Israel and based on this fear, he desired to kill Moses. The fact that murder was in Pharaoh's mind for Moses leads us to believe that what Pharaoh feared was not what we commonly consider as religion being the rather innocuous rituals, rites, ceremonies, and dogmas of a particular faith.

If the modern Pharaoh's, which include the American government and the European colonizers of Africa, are studied, it is clear that their fear and response to Islam-with its strong Black nationalist leaders- is the equivalent of Pharaoh's fears found written of in the Holy Qur'an.

The skillful prohibition of the meeting with the Honorable Minister Louis Farrakhan, Imam Abu Bakr of Trinidad and Brother Gerald Perreira of Guyana by Jamaican authorities was a reaction to the fear that Black Nationalism and Islam might become popular throughout the Caribbean islands. For it was the Caribbean Islands, that gave birth to many Black revolutionaries in history. And as the Minister pointed out in his speech, the Caribbean is located in a strategically critical area of the globe, being a neighboring region to Cuba,

Central and South America and the United States. It is not hard to imagine America and Europe would want to prevent the birth and popularity of Black Islamic Nationalism in such an area, where the Caribbean islands might draw strength and mentorship from revolutionary pioneer Fidel Castro and the island nation of Cuba.

But again, the fear is not of the tenets of Islam or its classical "5 Pillars." It is a fear of the effect that Islam has historically had on improving the condition of Blacks who were under oppression and giving them power to develop and control their own economies-economies based on harnessing the wealth and treasure of the natural resources buried within the land.

African peoples have also historically drawn strength and courage from such core Islamic philosophies such as "persecution is worse than slaughter," "fear nothing and no one besides Allah (God)," "retaliation is prescribed in the matter of the slain," and "you are not a believer until you love for your brother what you love for yourself."

As a final thought, consider Islam's tendency to produce and support African's and Blacks of the diaspora's yearning for independence. And even though it is something of a Christian idiom, the phrase "God blesses the child who has his own" is an expression of what has been the history of Black people under the banner of Islam. And there is perhaps no one has said it better than the great son of the Caribbean Edward Wilmot Blyden while writing in his book Christianity, Islam and the Negro Race. Blyden enlightens us:

> "Mohammedanism (Islam) in Africa counts in its ranks the most energetic and enterprising tribes. It claims as adherents the only people who have any form of civil polity or bond of social organization... It produces and controls the most valuable commerce between Africa and foreign countries....there are numerous Negro Mohammedan(Islamic) communities and states in Africa which are self-reliant, productive, independent, and dominant, supporting, without the countenance or patronage of the parent country, Arabia, whence they derived them, their political, literary, and ecclesiastical institutions. In Sierra Leone, the Mohammedans (Muslims), without any aid from government-imperial or local- or any

contributions from Mecca or Constantinople, erect their mosques, keep up their religious services, conduct their schools, and contribute to the support of missionaries from Arabia, Morocco, or Futah when they visit them. The same compliment cannot be paid to the Negro Christians of that settlement. The most enlightened native Christians there look forward with serious apprehension-and, perhaps not without good grounds-to the time when, if ever, the instructions and influence from London will be withheld.

Therefore it is clear that a Caribbean region with strong Muslim beachhead would do today what it did in Africa during Blyden's time and that is produce an economic shift in power. And the Minister's Jamaica message highlighted the need and value of economic strength and independence. According to Minister Farrakhan:

The unity of the Caribbean region could produce enough wealth to develop industries out of the resources that are here. And instead of sending what you naturally produce, like bauxite, somewhere else to be turned into aluminum and then sold back to you at exorbitant prices, you could turn your own resource into its final product and be the seller of it throughout the world.

Hip-Hop, Jay Electronica and Minister Farrakhan's Call for a Cultural Revolution

"Let me tell you something. Culture - listen carefully now - culture, Muhammad teaches us, is the OUTGROWTH OF KNOWLEDGE AT A PARTICULAR PERIOD IN HISTORY. What a man's culture WAS, as he EVOLVES and he gets a new Knowledge, he develops a new tradition. New culture. New ideas. New way of life. That WAS our culture. But today we're in a new day and we're getting a new Wisdom. And WE MUST bring forth a totally new culture.

This is what we're saying: If the Black Man must create, create a new music, brother. No more blues - Black Man don't SING BLUES NO MORE!! Listen to what we're saying: NO! Black Man don't play jazz no more. Not jazz - not that stuff that comes out of our slave

day. If you are a free man, then speak to the free idiom. Make your poetry that speaks to the new. Make your art and your drama that of the new. Then you are creating a new thing that the world must come up to. Then you're the original man again. And the original man does

not copy: THE ORIGINAL MAN ORIGINATES' FOR OTHERS TO COPY.

Remember this."

-Hon. Min. Louis Farrakhan, Message at The East, January 1971, Brooklyn, NY

"Mao Tse Tung, one of the greatest revolutionaries of our time had a billion people to convert to his idea. What did he do? He saw the value of the cultural community. They took his ideas and put them in songs, put them in dance, put them in plays, put them in books and before you knew it, China became a great nation. We will never become a great nation without our artists. Our artists are the key not only to the liberation of Black people, but the liberation of humanity itself"

-Hon. Min. Louis Farrakhan, BET Interview conducted by Jeff Johnson

Hip-Hop was born in New York City.

It was born at a time when New York was being regularly saturated with the message of the Nation of Islam. In the early 1970s, New York was the scene for the early years of the ministry of the Honorable Minister Louis Farrakhan.

Minister Farrakhan was both the lead minister presiding over the Nation of Islam's work in New York City and he was also the National Representative of the Honorable Elijah Muhammad. His ministry and the message of the Nation of Islam is at the heart of what real hip-hop has always been about. As it was his ministry field that served as the womb for this "new music." A music that was not blues and not jazz but something more; this is what hip-hop or rap music is from its beginning.

New York City was a womb for the birth of the "new music" and "new culture" of Hip-Hop. And as Minister Farrakhan explained in his historic *Message at The East*, this new culture grew out of a particular knowledge during the period of its birth or inception. In New York, Minister Farrakhan worked tirelessly to fertilize the minds of New Yorkers with the message of the Nation of Islam and as a result of the introduction of this new knowledge, New York eventually gave birth to the most dominant art-form and musical expression in the past 50 years. During this period of time the Minister was on the radio airwaves preaching 6 times per week. He grew 18 temples throughout the 5 boroughs and chartered 4 Muhammad Universities of Islam. And according to Sepia Magazine, he recruited 5,000 active members for the Nation of Islam in New York. In fact, the Minister is one of the first to have a nationally "syndicated" radio broadcast. His broadcasts that were spreading the Nation's message throughout New York were sent to dozens of cities around the country through the Nation of Islam's network of radio programs in all of the cities where mosques and temples existed.

So, to say Hip-Hop has Islam in its blood is not an overstatement. Grandmaster Flash, Afrika Bambatta, Kook Herc and the Last Poets are all a part of Hip-Hop's pantheon of founding fathers, and they all have a connection to the religion of Islam as it has been practiced in America in the Black community for more than 80 years now.

As a Muslim and a hip-hop lover, I was overjoyed to see the demonstration made this year at the Brooklyn Hip-Hop Festival. The stage beheld Hip-Hop Phenom and "number 1 draft pick" Jay Electronica and one of the most accomplished and celebrated MCs in Hip-Hop today, Jay-Z. The brilliant duo was surrounded by an impressive cadre of nearly a hundred of the young members of the Nation of Islam's men's class, known as the Fruit of Islam. Social media's coverage of this event revealed diverse groups of Muslims, rappers and Hip-Hop pioneers. NOI fraternities like, the Allah Team, Lions out Of the Cage and Lost Sheep were photographed in fellowship and embrace with hip-legends like Sadat X and Lord Jamar of the group Brand Nubians.

Revolutionary academician and NOI scholar in residence Dr. Wesley Muhammad also appeared on stage with the duo in a grand display of solidarity, brotherhood and encouragement for what such a demonstration portends for Hip-Hop's future.

For some time now Hip-Hop has been at a crossroads. Some have opined that Hip-Hop is dead. Simultaneously in New York, while Jay-Z and Jay Electronica were in Brooklyn, Chuck D, of the Hall of Fame group Public Enemy was cross town in Harlem's Muhammad Mosque No.7. Chuck's appearance at Mosque No.7 rounded out a weekend of events that suggests that Hip-Hop's founding ideology of Black Nationalist Islam is poised to take a prominent role once again in the world's dominant youth culture.

And this is a very encouraging development. In the Black community, our art forms and musical expression have never been divorced from our struggle against racism, oppression, poverty and injustice. The Blues, Spirituals, Gospel and Jazz were connected to the real-life condition of being Black in America and what that necessitates of a constant struggle against forces diametrically opposed to our very existence. And Hip-Hop from its beginning was no different than its predecessor art forms in being connected to our struggle. In fact, it's not an exaggeration to describe all Black music as being cause oriented. We have sung, rapped and danced because we had a cause to sing, rap and dance about.

But today Hip-Hop really needs a re-birth; it needs to be redeemed and resurrected. Hip-Hop is no longer an art form that is identifiable with the struggle of the oppressed Black masses. You can no longer listen to the music of this generation of artists and know the important issues of the day. Hip Hop no longer reinforces in the minds of the youth, the ideas and ideals of our struggle.

Instead this beloved music of my youth has been horribly corrupted. The content of most hip-hop songs promotes gross materialism, conspicuous consumption, sexism, violence and nearly every vice imaginable. And on top of that is the open ridicule and mockery of the legacy of our struggle.

Just last year it was Lil'Wayne, one of the most talented and popular rappers today, who used the name of Emmitt Till in a sexual reference in a song. The phrase "beat it up like Emmitt Till," quickly drew the condemnation of many in the Black community. And after public outcry, Lil'Wayne apologized. His protégé Nikki Minaj used the iconic image of Malcolm X to promote a song on her album entitled "Lookin Ass Nigga." And again, the public had to complain in order for Nikki to realize the offense she had made and make an apology.

It was also quite disappointing also for Hip-Hop pioneer and mogul Russell Simmons to produce a YouTube short film entitled "The Harriett Tubman Sex Tape." The horrible parody of a fictitious sexual tryst between Harriett Tubman and her slave master again produced strong criticism of Russell's despicable attempt at humor and forced him to apologize.

This pattern of Black celebrities and artists attempting to satisfy the need for humor and entertainment with the mockery and disrespect of our ancestors is outrageous. Emmitt Till was a 14-year-old lynching victim who was so badly disfigured by racist devils in Money Mississippi that his remains were hardly recognizable as being the remains of a human being! It was his beloved Mother, a heroin of the Black struggle in America, that decided to have an open casket funeral for her son so that the world could see the extent of the terror that Black people in America were forced to live under. Historians credit Mamie Till Mobley's decision for an open casket funeral as the significant event that helped to galvanize and propel the Civil Rights movement and also inspired the Black Nationalist movement as well.

It is indeed a sad day for the Black community when our entertainers have become so disconnected from the struggle that they actually see nothing wrong with disrespecting our martyrs and saints like Emmett Till, Malcolm X, Rosa Parks, and Dr. Martin Luther King Jr.

We need a cultural revolution in the Black community.

We cannot accept that the music of today's youth instills in them contempt for the struggle of our people. We should no longer accept a cultural expression that robs the next generation of the spirit and will to fight against injustice, oppression and inequality. Just consider some of the major issues of our day, that include the rise of the prison industrial complex; the scourge of HIV on Black women; double digit unemployment for Black men; felon disenfranchisement and the abuse and sexual exploitation of women and girls. When is the last time a popular Hip-Hop artist brought attention to any of these issues in their music? When have they used their powerful platform to educate, minister, inspire and enlighten their millions of impressionable youths and young adults?

This is why the demonstration of Jay Electronica, Jay Z and the Nation of Islam at Brooklyn's Hip Hop Festival is so important. It gives to us a glimmer of hope that Hip-Hop just might be saved by being returned to its roots. It gives me hope that renewed and redeemed Hip-Hop music and culture may be preserved for my own children who were excited to see their beloved Nation of Islam in the mix with some of their favorite artists.

The excitement of my own children over this event created for me, as a father, "a teachable moment." It was for me an occasion to have a wonderful conversation with my sons about music, history, Islam and the struggle of Black people. I could look in their eyes and know that they were engaged and were listening to me as perhaps they hadn't in a long while. That experience with my own sons gave me a very personal indicator of the value of what Jay Electronica's bold demonstration represents. As I reflected over this moment in my own life I was reminded of what the Bible describes as the work of Elijah. In the book of Malachi, it says that God would send to the people Elijah and he *will turn the hearts of the parents to their children, and the hearts of the children to their parents.*

In his voluminous study of Minister Farrakhan and the Nation of Islam during the 1980s and 1990s, Swedish professor, Mattias Gardell observed that

> "Black Islamic nationalism has become widely popular among Black urban youth, and Farrakhan exerts an influence with these youths that far exceeds the actual membership of his organization. This is truly significant, given the fact that the African American urban population is a young population, with a median age of 24.9 years old for blacks compared to 34.6 years for the other city dwellers. The vitality of Black Islam as an integral part of contemporary black youth

culture is visible in the new Black independent movies, in the hip-hop movement, in artifacts and clothing, in literature and comics, in college life, in graffiti and other arts, and in gang symbolism. **Farrakhan has a unique capability ...able to reach deeply into the souls of black youths...is able to talk to them in a way that really makes them listen...this rapport enables Farrakhan to criticize and redirect destructive behavioral patterns".**

The work of the Honorable Minister Louis Farrakhan among the youth in the Hip-Hop culture is the work of Elijah being done in this modern day and time. Jay Electronica is the most recent artist to stand as a reflection of Minister Farrakhan's influence on Hip-Hop. And I join the Honorable Minister Louis Farrakhan in encouraging Jay Electronica's career as an artist and extend well wishes for his development and growth as a human being.

He should now unite with other cause oriented artists and progressive Hip-Hop thinkers and meet to confer over Minister Farrakhan's call for a Cultural Revolution. Artists like Jasiri X, Janelle Monae, Lauryn Hill, David Banner, Nas, Jay-Z, Chuck D, Professor Griff, Lupe Fiasco, Big Krit, Dead Prez, Brother Ali, Killer Mike, Problem 13, Gat Turner, KAM, H2, Immortal Technique and others should meet with Minister Farrakhan in Chicago. They should convene a Conference for Cultural Revolution. And just like the Honorable Elijah Muhammad taught of the holy wise scientists of Islam who write scripture, these artists and thinkers should write the history of arts and culture in advance. They should agree that from this point forward, the will use their respective talents and abilities to shape and mold the thinking of their people community toward noble ideals and principles.

In his brilliant analysis of the problems plaguing America, Minister Farrakhan called for a cultural revolution. The Minister's ideas on Cultural Revolution and the convening of the artistic community can be found in his book A Torchlight for America. In Chapter 6 of Torchlight for America, the Minster writes:

"The artistic community has historically been in the vanguard of social change. **What is now needed is for the artistic community to lead a cultural revolution.** On the physical level, man is what he eats.

Spiritually, "... as he thinketh in his heart, so is he... " (Proverbs 23:7) If the American people are constantly fed filth and garbage through newspapers, magazines, television, movies, plays and music; if the public, like the proverbial swine, has become a lover of filth; and if thoughts guide behavior, what do the thoughts of the American people produce? Do the thoughts of the American people produce rape, incest, murder, theft, greed, and the destruction of family and the institutions of society? I would argue that the answer is yes.

Therefore, along with summoning the spiritual leadership to convene with leadership in government, the artistic community needs to be shown its responsibilities to the overall mental and spiritual health and well-being of society and the world. Our gifts, as artists, are a blessing from God. We have the responsibility of the proper use of our gifts. Additionally, movie producers, record producers and publishers all have a responsibility to the spiritual, moral and mental well-being of the American people."

By His Stripes We Are Healed:
The Suffering of Minister Louis Farrakhan and What It Means for Black America

After a recent speech in Indianapolis, Indiana, the Honorable Minister Louis Farrakhan returned to his tenacious work schedule that, this year alone, has compelled him to travel throughout America and the Caribbean, offering his diverse audiences guidance, vision, counsel and inspiration. These events have been special moments: we have been blessed to treasure and absorb unequaled wisdom and insights, provided by a man who is now an 80-year-old veteran of the struggle for freedom, justice and equality. And not only has Minister Farrakhan been involved in extensive travel and teaching but in January of this year he began a 52-week lecture series titled "The Time and What Must Be Done." These 1-hour-long Internet webcasts have been some of the most profound messages available from any spiritual teacher, religious leader or classroom educator. And the Minister has put in the kind of preparation that speakers of his caliber normally only reserve for major addresses. Each week he devotes himself to the study of the problems of the suffering masses and allows God to inspire him with messages that he buttresses with empirical data, historical facts and complementary sources of information.

In listening to the Minister's brilliant Indianapolis speech, I reflected on his announcement of having suffered a heart attack and it causing him to take an 8-week health sabbatical. While the Minister was openly giving us a window into his personal health condition, I reflected on all that he has meant to the Black man and woman of America. I thought about all that he has meant to me and my family.

And in my mind, arose the Biblical words "and by his stripes we are healed." The Prophet Isaiah in chapter 53, verse 5, says:

> "But He was wounded for our transgressions, He was bruised for our iniquities; The chastisement for our peace was upon Him, And by His stripes we are healed."

Minister Farrakhan and the Jesus Model

From the perspective of Christian theology, this verse is a reference to the ministry of Jesus. And there is really no other scriptural personage or character that Minister Farrakhan is in more similitude to than Jesus. Black leadership has always inspired comparisons to religious figures. Marcus Mosiah Garvey, Harriett Tubman and Dr. Martin Luther King Jr. all at various times were affectionately referred to as "Black Moses." Both Jesus and Moses are important figures in Christian tradition. Jesus in the New Testament is the quintessential portrait of immense suffering that is the product of immense love. Jesus's commitment to love is widely viewed as the evolution or fulfillment of Moses's commitment to law. Similarly, the leadership record of Minister Farrakhan is marked by a commitment to profound love. He therefore follows in the footsteps and is a continuation and evolution of Marcus Garvey, Dr. King, Booker T. Washington and all the great "Black Moseses" of the past.

Where the Jesus model fits Minister Farrakhan the closest, in my opinion, is in his suffering for the salvation of his people. After all, this is what is most remarkable about Jesus: He loved people who did not necessarily reciprocate that love. Just look at some of what Minister Farrakhan has suffered in his quest to champion our causes and challenge our enemies.

Minister Farrakhan's Suffering

• 1984 U.S. Senate formally censures the Honorable Minister Louis Farrakhan.

• 1984 Friend, Colleague and Presidential Candidate Rev. Jesse Louis Jackson Jr. repudiates Minister Farrakhan's statements and distances his candidacy from the Minister

• 1985 Jewish pressure forces Black businessman George Johnson to renege on a promise to produce the POWER personal-care product line for Minister Farrakhan

• 1985 Jewish pressure forces the Black-owned Independence Bank of Chicago to reject a $5 million deposit of loan proceeds that the Minister had secured for the production of POWER personal care products

- 1993 Jewish pressure causes Black organizers of the 30th anniversary of the March on Washington to disinvite the Minister from participating

- 1994 FBI entrap the distraught daughter of Malcolm X in a murder-for-hire plot to assassinate the Honorable Minister Louis Farrakhan

- 2008 Senator Hilary R. Clinton forces Senator Barack H. Obama to renounce and repudiate the Honorable Minister Louis Farrakhan's well-wishes and moral support for his candidacy

- 2013 Friend, Colleague and longtime U.S. Representative John Conyers is forced by Jewish pressure to repudiate statements made by Minister Farrakhan during a speech at a Black Church in Detroit

In addition, the incessant lies and slander against the Minister has caused him to use these troubling words, printed in The Final Call in 2009:

> "I wish that my Black brothers and sisters would help Brother Farrakhan to get out of prison. I am not in a prison of 'steel bars'—I am in a prison of public opinion manipulated by the media and their hatred of the truth that is in my mouth that would set our people free. Help me to get out of prison. Stop looking at the Nation of Islam as though we are some enemy to Black people."

This is just a snapshot of the totality of Minister Farrakhan's suffering. Space does not permit us to be exhaustive in reciting the events that constitute a pattern in the life of Minister Farrakhan, who is indeed a suffering servant.

Consistent with the Jesus model, Minister Farrakhan has endured his suffering and rebuke and has not become bitter as a result. He "often takes blows without returning them," yet he does not diminish his work in the struggle for liberation. In fact, he increases his activity; he increases his love. And there are none who come to him seeking his love, forgiveness and respect who leave disappointed. When Minister Farrakhan is repudiated by his own people, he forgives them. He encouraged Black people to vote for the Rev. Jesse L. Jackson even after he had repudiated the Minister. He forgave Representative John Conyers, who, when pressured by out outside forces, had repudiated the Minister. When Qubilah Shabazz was arrested for seeking to assassinate the Minister, he defended her and helped raise money for her defense. Often times in any relationship, there are rough spots and individuals take turns being the bigger person, yet from my observation it is Minister Farrakhan who is always willing to be the bigger brother. He is always willing, to borrow the phrase, "take one for the team." And unfortunately, his brotherly love is not always reciprocated.

Pattern of Defending a Defenseless People

Consider how Jewish apologist Daniel Pipes has written and observed the phenomenon of Black people who get into trouble seeking out Minister Farrakhan and the Nation of Islam. According to Pipes, there is "a well-established pattern of African-Americans who, finding their reputation in tatters, turn to the Nation of Islam, which then provides them with solace and help. This phenomenon is most apparent in jails, where blacks since the late 1940s have been converting in large numbers." The groups and persons who fit this pattern are too numerous to list.

Minister Farrakhan's influence, as was on display at the historic Million Man March, is well into the millions. And those whom he influences are themselves sources of influence for millions more. In fact, the Rev. Dr. Jeremiah A. Wright once likened Minister Farrakhan to E.F. Hutton, because when he speaks, people listen. So, when he speaks up to defend those who may be entertainers, politicians, athletes, professionals or even lesser-known persons and groups, he positively affects the quality of their reputations among the masses of the people. In defending such high-profile persons, the Minister redirects the public's attention to the hidden hand behind their apparent ruin. This has the effect of healing their reputations and putting such persons on the path to rehabilitating their souls as well as their careers. And there is perhaps no greater example of this than in the case of former Washington D.C. mayor Marion Barry. Mayor Barry's high-profile case of public corruption would have been the death knell for the average politician. But Mayor Barry was helped and aided by Minister Farrakhan, who re-directed attention away from Mayor Barry's sins to the corrupt forces and strategies at work to deprive the nation's capital of progressive Black leadership.

Of Minister Farrakhan, Yale Divinity School Professor Andre C. Willis has written: "There is simply no Black person in the world that has — over so many years — been as consistent, as unrestricted, and as forthright in defending the humanity of Black people throughout the world against its attackers."

Why Won't They Defend Farrakhan?
Yet when Minister Farrakhan, our modern "Black Jesus," is being crucified in the press and censured in the Senate, none of those whom he has stood up for and spoken in defense of ever lift their voices to defend Minister Farrakhan.

This is quite disturbing. Especially when you factor in all that Minister Farrakhan has accomplished, all while facing at times very serious health challenges. Early in his ministry he overcame a bout with Tuberculosis. In 1993 he announced to the world that he was suffering from prostate cancer. Years later Minister Farrakhan announced to the world that he was suffering from receiving one of the highest doses on record of radiation seed implant therapy. The excessive amount of radiated seeds inserted into the Minister to destroy his cancer also caused severe damage to the minister internally. And this was the cause of a 14-hour surgery that he underwent in 2007 is called a pelvic exenteration.

The fact that no major Black figures ever come to the defense of Minister Farrakhan against his critics might be the most damning evidence of the absence of real freedom for Black people in America. Especially if the words of journalist William Raspberry are true, when he wrote that "Farrakhan says what so many black people believe but have learned not to say in public..." If this is true, who taught Black people not to say in public what they believe in their hearts? That sounds like textbook slavery to me. For all other ethnic groups in America seek no outside approval of who they choose to speak for them and who will be their leaders. Perhaps if we are too afraid to say what we believe, we could at least officially endorse Minister Farrakhan as speaking for us, and come to his aid and defense when he is under assault.

It's clear that at the glorious age of 80 years old, Minister Farrakhan is not stopping. He is working harder today than ever before. I personally fear what will happen to us as a people if we don't stand up for the Honorable Minister Louis Farrakhan after he has always stood for us. So, I will stand up for Minister Farrakhan like I wish others could have stood up for Jesus and all the great heroes of the past. What about you?

Sean Hannity's Lies Hide Minister Farrakhan's Call for Holiday Boycott

Fox News character Sean Hannity is pushing an idea that the Honorable Minister Louis Farrakhan should be arrested for inciting a riot. In this way Mr. Hannity continues to "out" himself as one of the chief media enemies of the Black community.

While listening to this emblem of yellow journalism, I thought to myself, if Mr. Hannity cared anything about the enforcement of law and justice why didn't he ask for the arrest of some the world's major war criminals like Benjamin Netanyahu. Mr. Netanyahu's vicious war against the Palestinians has literally torn up Gaza. In the most recent Palestinian-Israeli conflict, Israel killed 2139 Palestinians (490 children) compared to only 71 Israelis. And while Mr. Netanyahu was giving the order to bomb hospitals and schools, Mr. Hannity and FOX News sought to present every kind of justification for Israel's crimes against humanity.

If Mr. Hannity was so interested in preventing rioting and violence, he wouldn't be encouraging the arrest of the of the Honorable Minister Louis Farrakhan. Minister Farrakhan is a man widely viewed as a peacemaker. In 1996, Philadelphia Mayor Edwin Rendell petitioned Minister Farrakhan to come to Philadelphia to prevent a potential race war within that city. And throughout the years Minister Farrakhan has helped rival gangs resolve their disputes as well as settled various "beefs" in the hip-hop world. The Minister's record is clear and shows forth how he has made peace making and conflict resolution a fundamental component of his mission to awaken, resurrect and restore the Black community.

No! If Mr. Hannity was so concerned about what is taking place in the streets of many of America's major cities, he would address the root causes of the riots. There is no fireman who has to put out a fire that doesn't want to know what caused the fire. And if it happens that his training and skill detect the possibility for fire; he does all that is within his power to prevent the fire from taking place.

In other words, he changes the conditions in the environment that make the threat of fire possible.

This is how the great Dr. Martin Luther King Jr. responded to rioting in the 1960s. He boldly declared in his penetrating 1967 work *The Crisis in American Cities*:

> "Let us say it boldly if the total slum violations of law by the white man over the years were calculated and were compared with the law breaking of a few days of riots, the hardened criminal would be the white man."

Dr. King was honestly and forthrightly exposing the root cause of what he described as the Black man's "derivative crimes" which are **"born of the greater crimes of the white society."**

If Mr. Hannity was a good conscientious solution oriented American, he would be demanding that the murderers of Michael Brown, Eric Garner and Tamir Rice be arrested and indicted for their crimes. It is clear that it is their unrepentant actions that have awakened the sleeping giant of Black youth and those from other races and ethnicities who join them as brothers and sisters in the struggle for justice as they boldly proclaim that **Black Lives Matter!**

Mr. Hannity is so outrageous, that responding to him is almost pointless. But as a Black man, I take any all calls for Minister Farrakhan's arrest and detainment very serious. Minister Farrakhan has been called "the only leader" in the Black community by the powerful Jewish Anti-Defamation League (ADL). ADL leader Abraham Foxman's conclusion results from many years of working to foil the Minister to no avail. As "the only leader" who has not been compromised, Minister Farrakhan is in the crosshairs of all who want the destruction of the Black community. So, it is in the best interest of all Black people to rally to his defense and aid whenever he is besmirched, harangued, lied on, evil spoken of or misrepresented. For in America there is a documented history of the assassination of our heroes and heroines. And what facilitates physical assassination of great Black men and women-the champions of our liberation, is the manipulation of public opinion brought about by a media campaign of character assassination.

Mr. Hannity's buffoonery which masquerades as serious news commentary has been routinely condemned for its copious amounts of lies and falsehoods. The non-profit group Media Matters.Org includes a page on its website devoted to exposing 10 *Examples of Sean Hannity Saying Things That Aren't True*. To read about Mr. Hannity's scandalous reputation of lying on everyone including other journalists, the Supreme Court, President Obama, and even foreign governments go online to the website link at http://mediamatters.org/research/2013/02/28/10-examples-of-sean-hannity-saying-things-that/192828.

Mr. Hannity's current attempt at manipulating public opinion centers around the words of the Honorable Minister Louis Farrakhan in a message delivered at the historic Morgan State University in Baltimore Maryland. At the close of a brilliant multi-themed message to Morgan State's students-a cadre of future leaders of Black America, the Minister turned his attention to the controversy brewing in Ferguson, Missouri. Ferguson has been the flashpoint for the most recent and highly publicized episode of police brutality and murder of Black youth.

Minister Farrakhan, drawing from his spiritual base, began to examine how the Judeo-Christian and Islamic idea of retaliatory justice might be applied in the case of the murder of unarmed teenager Michael Brown by Ferguson police officer Darren Wilson.

These are the Minister's words beginning at approximately 2 hours and 50 minutes into the program.

> "In this book (Holy Qur'an), there is a law of retaliation, a law of retaliation... like for like. The Bible says, an eye, a tooth, a life. See now as long as they kill us and go to Wendy's and have a burger and go to sleep they're going to keep killing us. But when we die and they die, then soon we're going to sit a table and talk about we're tired...we want some of this earth, or we'll tear this goddam country up. "

In this section of the Minister's speech we witness what makes Minister Farrakhan the tour de force speaker that he is. It is Minister Farrakhan's ability to translate the Prophets of God's "fire and brimstone" warnings to Ancient Egypt, Rome and Babylon and boldly warn their modern counterpart-the United States of America. For example, God promised to "tear up" or destroy wicked nations in the Bible.

> "But if any nation will not hear and obey, I will utterly pluck up and destroy that nation, says the Lord." (Jeremiah 12:17)

> ""Son of man, if a country sins against me by being unfaithful and I stretch out my hand against it to cut off its food supply and send famine upon it and kill its people and their animals, ... "Or if I bring a sword against that country and say, 'Let the sword pass throughout the land,' and I kill its people and their animals, ... "Or if I send a plague into that land and pour out my wrath on it through bloodshed, killing its people and their animals, ... (Ezekiel 14:13-20)

Mr. Hannity may not realize it but he is handling Minister Farrakhan like the scribes handled Jesus in the Bible. Dr. Reza Aslan and other scholars have acknowledged that Jesus was known as a zealot. And after Jesus spoke of 'tearing up" the Jewish temple he was arrested and ultimately crucified. According to the book of Matthew:

> "The chief priests and the whole Sanhedrin were looking for false evidence against Jesus so that they could put him to death. But they did not find any, though many false witnesses came forward. Finally, two came forward and declared, "This fellow said, 'I am able to destroy the temple of God and rebuild it in three days.'" (Matthew 26: 59-61)

In other words, Minister Farrakhan spoke for God. He spoke for the Prophets. He warned the modern Babylon-the modern Egypt-the modern Rome that continued injustice is being interpreted by God as intentional provocation for the visitation of His wrath. This is what seminary students might understand as preaching with prophetic authority. In a 2011 interview with *Ministry Magazine*, preaching expert Dr. Hyveth Williams defined prophetic preaching as:

Prophetic preaching is a biblically based form of proclamation in which the preacher exercises the divine authority to be a spokesperson for God invested in them. When I speak of authority, I mean that which Jesus had. It caused "the crowds to be amazed at His teaching for He was teaching them as one having authority, and not as their scribes" (see Matt. 7:28, 29). While power is a natural derivative of authority, exercising it out of self-will is always dangerous and oppressive. But when power comes from the divine gift of authority, it becomes liberating and redemptive.

Mr. Hannity's connection to the modern Sanhedrin is documented in the Center for American Progress' study entitled *Fear, Inc.: The Roots of the Islamophobia Network in America.* This report describes "*a small, tightly networked group of misinformation experts.*" The report details this nefarious nexus of modern scribes to include Rush Limbaugh, Michael Savage, and Sean Hannity. This group with the unenviable ability to "*drench the public with misinformation*" is largely funded by contributions from Donors Capital Fund. The Donors Capital Fund is actually chaired by Jewish conservative Adam Meyerson. Meyerson is a significant member of ALEC (American Legislative Exchange Council), organization. And they have been the main force behind the establishment of the Stand Your Ground laws that were used to exonerate and justify George Zimmerman's murder of Trayvon Martin.

As the program ended, Minister Farrakhan took time to clarify his statement "we'll tear this goddam country up" to reveal an essential economic meaning. He said the following:

"You know over the next 4 or 5 days, the people down in Ferguson are not going to buy anything. Especially on Black Friday we black folk that don't have a lot of money anyway. You shouldn't give your money away to your oppressor... Now last, when I say tear up the country; you know there are so many ways to tear something; by coming out of it, not supporting it. But put it in your heart to fight with those who fight with you. All you have is your life. That is the gift of God. And you don't let anybody take it without giving your all to defend that gift... "

Mr. Hannity has chosen to emphasize before his 14 million viewers such a small part of the Minister's 2-hour message. It may very well be to hide the parts of the Minister's speech that supported and endorsed the Black Friday holiday shopping boycott. Minister Farrakhan's encouragement of the economic boycott of Black Friday led to what is being reported at this time of a historic 11% decrease in sales nationwide. If this continues on into the Christmas holiday, the protesters mantra of *No Justice, No Profits* will have become a reality. And Mr. Hannity's propaganda will have failed...miserably!

The Mis-Education of Yvette Carnell et.al.

Popular social media commentator Yvette Carnell recently took to the World Wide Web to utilize the YouTube platform to make an attempt to stall the growing momentum of the Justice or Else Movement and the increasing appeal and acceptance of the message of the Honorable Minister Louis Farrakhan. Brother Demetric Muhammad who serves on the Honorable Minister Louis Farrakhan's Research Team and is an Assistant Student Minister of Muhammad Mosque No. 55 provides the following points and documentation to refute her subsequent claims made in her 40-minute conversation with Dr. Boyce Watkins. In responding to Ms. Carnell, we take the opportunity to respond to those who may share her views, views that we reject as unjustified by the facts of Minister Farrakhan's magnificent history of service to the Black community and oppressed people throughout the Earth. We thank Dr. Boyce Watkins for giving us an opportunity to put forth critical facts to better educate Ms. Carnell and the general public.

1. Carnell claims that Minister Farrakhan has called for a race war.

This claim evaporates when one actually reviews the entirety of the Minister's Miami message. The quote in question reads as follows:

> "Death is sweeter than to continue to live and bury our children while White folks give the killers hamburgers. Death is sweeter than watching us slaughter each other to the joy of a 400-year-old enemy. Death is sweeter. The Qur'an teaches persecution is worse than slaughter then it says, retaliation is prescribed in matters of the slain. Retaliation is a prescription from God to calm the breasts of those whose children have been slain. **If the federal government will not intercede in our affairs,** then we must rise up and kill those who kill us, stalk them and let them feel the pain of death that we are feeling,"

This statement is a conditional statement and points to an obvious conclusion since self-preservation is widely considered a primal and first of the laws of nature. If federal protection for the Black man dissolves or is absent, then Black people are left without any guarantee of safety in a society that daily reminds us of our status as an unwanted former slave.

Historians know of the horrific effects of the infamous Compromise of 1877. This compromise was arrived at to settle the Presidential election of 1876, a race that was tied between Rutherford B. Hayes and Samuel Tilden. Its effect on Black people came as a result of federal troops being pulled out of the South as a stipulation of the compromise that allowed for candidate Rutherford B. Hayes to become the 19th President of the United States. The removal of federal troops from the South ended Reconstruction and paved the way for the birth of the Ku Klux Klan and other Anti-Black terrorist groups who seized upon vulnerable Black communities without any protection from their government. Popular stories of the destruction of Rosewood, Florida and Greenwood, Oklahoma (aka Black Wall St.) are just the tip of the iceberg. There are many hidden histories of the Black man's time as a self-respecting, entrepreneurial, civic minded, industrious builder of Black Towns and cities. It was the Black man and woman's early adoption of what we see today as the "immigrant model." Yet the survival of these municipalities was like any nation or state, dependent upon having a defense force and protective apparatus to secure its people and property.

Carnell's worries that the Minister will inspire the murder of all the "good white folk" are actually unnecessary. Particularly when you consider that the Minister's beautiful hours long message in Miami included the following truths: *"How can we charge others with the crime of killing us without due process and lying about it when we are killing each other? And we won't march on ourselves, nor will we even rise up to condemn ourselves for what we are doing to ourselves. And in the gangs when we kill we don't talk, so nobody is arrested and charged with murder and brought to what is called justice."*

In this unmentioned passage of his message, The Minister reacts to the Black victimizers of the Black community which if we are to "kill those who kill us" should also be targets of retaliatory justice.

No, Minister Farrakhan wasn't calling for a race war; he was giving to his pained and grief stricken Black audience an exhortation toward what is the first law of nature, self-preservation. And the fact that he has to remind us of this law is a woeful indicator of just how un-natural our oppressors have made us.

An unlikely source is available to help Ms. Carnell et.al to see that Minister Farrakhan's history of peace mitigates against any legitimate concern over a Farrakhan-led race war. In 1997 Rabbi Bruce Khan offered his observations in the aftermath of his attending of the Million Man March in 1995 in these words: *"people who listen to him do not go chasing down Jews, or gays or Whites or Koreans to beat them and murder them."*

As for as the main action directive put forth by the Minister-which was curiously absent from Ms. Carnell's critique- is his call for a Christmas holiday boycott. Similar to Dr. Martin Luther King Jr.'s insistence that Black people "re-distribute the pain" of injustice, Minister Farrakhan prescribed to his enthusiastic audience the idea of massive economic withdrawal from the merchants and bankers who make their largest profits each year during the Christmas season. We might describe it as 'Retaliatory Economic Justice.' He instructed that we buy no gifts and presents beginning with the 'Black Friday' sales holiday. He made a powerful case that this year we make Christmas once again about the love and sacrifice of Jesus Christ. His call was essentially a "mass" of Black people for the adoption of the principles of Jesus-the Christ. This is the same Jesus who is pictured in scripture as running the corrupt merchants or "money-changers" out of God's holy temple. From Minister Farrakhan's point of view, justice for the Black man and woman will remain ever elusive until the modern merchants and "money-changers" experience the pain of economic loss and injury.

2. Carnell claimed Minister Farrakhan is not a leader of Black people in America

Again, Carnell's claims evaporate before what has been the documented reaction to Minister Farrakhan's uncompromising leadership from Jewish leaders, academics and even critics. Consider the following sampling of testimonies.

> "The only leadership that now exists in that community"—the "African American community"— "is Louis Farrakhan. Farrakhan can assemble 20,000 people several times a year..." -**Abraham Foxman**

For the first time in African American history; a non-Christian leader is a significant, if not the significant leader within Black America." - **Professor Michael Eric Dyson**

"The appearance of Louis Farrakhan at Madison Square Garden on October 7 demonstrated, without doubt, that he is now America's preeminent black leader."-**Author Julius Lester**

3.   Carnell claimed that Minister Farrakhan is not a threat to white supremacy because he isn't dead yet.

This is one of the most ridiculous assertions I have ever heard. It comes from the same school of thought that tells articulate, intelligent and well-mannered Black children that they are acting white, because to be authentically Black you must be the opposite of all those worthy character traits.

According to Unitarian Universalist minister and scholar the Rev. Dr. William Alberts, PhD of Boston University, Minister Farrakhan,

> **"represents a serious threat to America's racial hierarchy**. The hierarchy cannot control or buy his accommodation or "integration" as a Black leader. He dares to point out and challenge the "white supremacy" of the "founding fathers," forcing White America to recognize and deal with the fact that many of the signers of the Declaration of Independence, which declared freedom and equality for all, were themselves slave holders, and that even "Honest Abe" had a racist "wart" or two that can no longer be covered up. Farrakhan also has the power to initiate a call that led to at least twice and possibly three or more times as many African American men to respond as the U.S. Park Police counted-in spite of all the print aimed at discrediting the Nation of Islam leader and derailing the March."

Ms. Carnell should study the thoughts of noted Professor Derrick Bell who spoke on how the white power structure is so threatened by Minister Farrakhan that they have developed what some have called the "Farrakhan Litmus Test." According to Professor Bell: *"Smart and super articulate, Minister Farrakhan is perhaps the best living example of a black man ready, willing and able to 'tell it* *like it is' regarding who is responsible for racism in this country .... **every black person important enough to be interviewed is asked to condemn Minister Farrakhan...** "*-Prof. Derrick Bell

To have a further appreciation for the fact that Minister Farrakhan's redemptive work among Black people is deemed an ever-present threat to the status quo of American white supremacy consider that in 1984 the Honorable Minister Louis Farrakhan was censured by the highest legislative body in world—the United States Senate—in a 95 to 0 vote.

Minister Farrakhan's international influence among African and Islamic leaders is an area where he is deemed a particular threat. The American government fearing the potential of Minister Farrakhan's ideas being backed by financial resources forbid the Minister from receiving the 1996 International Human Rights Award given by the people of Libya. The award worth $250,000 was going to be accompanied by a billion-dollar donation to the work of the Nation of Islam by Libyan leader Muammar Gadhafi.

I wonder what Ms. Carnell would think of Cuban revolutionary Fidel Castro who is reputed to have survived an estimated 638 assassination attempts! According to her logic Commandante Castro's longevity disqualifies him as a true revolutionary.

4. Carnell claimed that the Million Man March didn't accomplish anything for Black people in America

According to an October 10, 1996 USA Today article written by reporters Gary Fields and Maria Puente the Million Man March was directly or indirectly responsible for the following positive results

- One million new voters.
- Up to 15,000 new applicants wanting to adopt black children
- A decrease in black-on-black crime.
- Increased child support payments by black fathers.
- Increased interest among black men in serving their communities.

5. Carnell said Minister Farrakhan is responsible for the assassination of Malcolm X

This is a sensitive issue and exposes that Carnell has "drank the Kool-Aid" of the anti-Farrakhan propagandists who have worked to position a dead Malcolm X against a living Louis Farrakhan at the expense of Black youth. And there are many facts that we have prepared in two 2-hour Power Point Presentations that completely destroys the old propagandist narrative aimed at de-magnetizing the Honorable Minister Louis Farrakhan among the young within the Black community. This strategy is borne out of decades old COINTELPRO objectives that explicitly documents their goal of preventing the Nation of Islam and other Nationalist groups from gaining "youthful adherents."

Carnell should be educated in the fact that according to a January 22, 1969 memo the FBI takes credit for the assassination of Malcolm X. Jim Van derWaal and Ward Churchill discuss this memo in their book The COINTELPRO Papers. They write:

> "the accompanying January 22, 1969 memo from the SAC, Chicago, to the Director makes clear; the NOI factionalism at issue didn't "just happen." Rather, it had "been developed" by deliberate Bureau actions – through infiltration and the "sparking of acrimonious debates within the organization," rumor-mongering, and other tactics designed to foster internal disputes – which were always the standard fare of COINTELPRO. The Chicago SAC, Marlin Johnson, who would shortly oversee the assassinations of Illinois Black Panther Party leaders Fred Hampton and Mark Clark, makes it quite obvious that he views the murder of Malcolm X as something of a model for "successful" counterintelligence operations.

Furthermore, those close to Malcolm X have gone on record to make the point that Malcolm X had evolved to regret his pointing the finger at the Nation of Islam as being out to kill him. His secretary, Ms. Sarah Mitchell, wrote of her experiences with Brother Malcolm in her manuscript entitled **Shepherd of the Black Sheep**.

"His philosophy was evolving almost on a weekly basis," Mitchell said. On Feb. 20, 1965-the eve of his assassination- Malcolm X told aides that he should not have criticized Elijah Muhammad, leader of the NOI, Mitchell said. Malcolm had severed ties with the Muslim sect and had accused it publicly of the recent bombing of his house. **"He said now anyone could kill him and everyone would blame the Muslims,"** Mitchell said. **"He said, 'We've been set up, and they succeeded.'"** **Malcolm X planned to recant his criticism of Muhammad at the Harlem rally that afternoon, Mitchell said, but he was gunned down before he could do so. She disputes a widely-held belief that angry Muslims were behind the assassination."**

6. Carnell claimed that Minister Farrakhan has not done anything for Black people and has no record of leadership

Leadership among people is analogous in function to that of a head on a body. Thusly a good leader provides sight or vision; thought and guidance as well as speech and hearing. The Minister's long history of leadership is too numerous to enumerate his most significant accomplishments in such a short treatise. But the record is clear he has been an effective head.

Some commentators make a case for the Million Man March as being the most significant achievement of his leadership. Pastor Jamal Bryant recently spoke at a seminar on the subject of *The Black Church and Social Justice*. In his comments to a predominantly Christian audience he pushed back against the criticism he received for hosting Minister Farrakhan on his televised and webcast WORD Network program. He reminded his audience of the fact that no Christian leader has ever assembled a million people.

The Minister's accomplishments are numerous and the Million Man March is an easily identified victory. But when we consider all of the casualties in America's so-called War on Drugs, the Minister's work to end this scourge is another strong contender for his top accomplishment.

His male followers, as a result of his inspiration and guidance, organized themselves to form what became known as the Dopebusters. The Dopebusters, which were members of the Nation of Islam's men's class known as the Fruit of

Islam, operated in in 5 states, as different chapters of the NOI Security Agency won bids to patrol-crime and drug-infested housing projects in D.C., NYC, LA, Baltimore, Philadelphia, Pittsburgh and Chicago.

The Dopebusters were very successful as evident by the reduction of crime in the public housing apartment communities that they served. In New York at Ocean Towers, vacancy was routinely 30% as a result of the high rates of crime. After the Muslim security did their work that vacancy rate dropped to 1%. They were so effective Jewish resident Bonnie Kirshtein told the New York Times that, **"They did the best security I've seen in 20 years. If they were doing their job, what was the problem? I don't hide what I am and they treated me with the utmost respect."** Their work in Los Angeles brought about a 75% reduction in crime in the Holiday Venice Apartment Complex.

There are numerous stories that document that Minister Farrakhan's work to eradicate drugs and crime wherever the presence of his followers and his message have gone. There is a serious value in re-viewing the Dopebuster's history not just to vindicate the leadership of Minister Farrakhan, but to serve as a tried and true model that courageous Black men around the country can adopt to begin to patrol and protect their own communities.

If there was unlimited time and space I could go on and on in educating Ms. Carnell in why her views, feelings and perspective on the Honorable Minister Louis Farrakhan are wrong. What I have provided does not discuss the Minister's role in producing gang truces between rival street organizations. I haven't discussed his impact in Hip-Hop to influence the creation of socially conscious rap groups and lyrics, or the settling of "rap beefs." I haven't even discussed his single-handed rebuilding of the Nation of Islam that began in 1977 with Minister Farrakhan and only one other brother (Jabril Muhammad). His international work has also not been brought forth. Yet we have given enough for Ms. Carnell to do an about face if she is to be moved by facts and empirical data.

Whether she will or not remains to be seen, but at least she cannot say that we did not make an effort to educate her in an area where she was ignorant.

Woe Unto Charleston!
An Open Letter To The Clergy of Charleston, South Carolina

The Honorable Minister Louis Farrakhan has been recently unwelcomed in the city of Charleston, South Carolina. The Minister desired to grace the city of Charleston with his presence by including it as a part of his city to city tour in promotion of the 20th Anniversary of the Million Man March. Yet all arenas, churches and suitable spaces have rejected Minister Farrakhan and the Nation of Islam.

As a student in the ministry class of the Honorable Minister Louis Farrakhan and a member of his research group, I wanted to write to my colleagues in the ministry in the city of Charleston, South Carolina. All Black clergy whether Muslim, Hebrew, Christian or other faiths are co-workers in a unique and special vineyard filled with a burdened and pained mass of Black people that today are stunned and shocked at the new season of lynching that is manifest throughout America. As a result, we should see each other as colleagues, brothers and allies despite what may be theological or doctrinal differences. After all, the Abrahamic faiths are really more **orthopraxic** (*emphasizing the correct conduct and actions*) than **orthodoxic** (*emphasizing the correct beliefs and doctrines*). And one can easily see the grand opportunities for all men and women of faith to be united in brotherhood and sisterhood if we take to the "highways and byways" of the inner cities of America. For it is there among the pained and suffering Black community that we will find the modern Lazarus, the modern adulteress, the modern man with the withered hand, and the modern woman with the issue of blood; yes, even the modern blind man at the pool of Siloam is to be found today in the "hood."

I grew up in a wonderful Baptist church with parents who were active members of our church. My grandmother was a Sunday school teacher and church pianist. My great grandmother was the superintendent of the Sunday school, sang in the choir and coordinator of church missionaries. It was in the home of my great grandmother that I remember vividly to this day watching for the first time a movie about the life of Jesus and his crucifixion. And as a child, watching the horrible treatment being done to such a good man, I said to myself that if I had been alive during that time I would have helped Jesus; I would have been with him. Even as a child of no more than 9 or 10 years of age, it disturbed me to see the movie portrayal of the crucifixion of a man that I had been taught by my parents was the Saviour of the world. I remember dreaming about it for several days after watching that film.

I became a member of the Nation of Islam as a teenager and my membership in the Nation did not diminish my love for Jesus. In fact, it broadened my understanding of Jesus in a profound way. It helped me to understand how the suffering of Jesus in the Bible paralleled with the suffering of my own Black people inside America. It helped me understand how the suffering of Jesus served as a model for what Black leadership experienced as a result of the horrible confluence of forces seen in their being misunderstood by their own people, coupled with being opposed by the government and maligned and condemned by Jewish groups. My membership in the Nation of Islam above everything else made me to want to go beyond a posture and disposition of just being satisfied with praising Jesus. It made me to know that what God really requires is that I strive to discipline my life according to the teachings and example of Jesus.

I share this of myself so that you will understand that my letter to you is not from a place of hatred for you or a place of condemnation of any of you personally. I don't write to you as one who is not familiar with the Black Christian experience. Neither do I write to you as one who does not love, admire and see as a model for my life Jesus the Christ. I am not even writing you as a stereotypical Muslim who seeks to minimize the importance of Jesus as being just a mere 'Prophet.' Not that there is anything ordinary about a Prophet or Messenger of God, but I challenge my own Muslim brothers with what I have learned as a student of the Honorable Minister Louis Farrakhan. For it is Minister Farrakhan, who has always emphasized the Quranic teachings, that refers to Jesus in 11 different passages, as the "Messiah." In fact, Islamic eschatology focuses on the return of Jesus as one of the major events of the end of this world and the judgment of God.

I write to you as a brother.

And as your brother, I have to condemn in strong terms your rejection of the best brother that Black people have in the world today- the Honorable Minister Louis Farrakhan.

Dylan Roof killed 9 precious Black men and women who had assembled for prayer and worship at Mother Emmanuel AME church in Charleston. Yet in the immediate aftermath of this horrible act of terrorism, news reports circulated that the family members of the slain were offering Dylan Roof forgiveness. This sent a message throughout America and the world that the Black community of Charleston had literally forgiven the unforgivable. It said to the world that the Black community of Charleston was willing to accept the cold-blooded murder of some of the best members of that historic community without any demand for justice and prosecution of the guilty. It portrayed that trauma stricken community as weak, helpless and leaderless. It showed that the Black community in Charleston, South Carolina is truly a "prey in the hand of the mighty."

And I witnessed no pastors or preachers intervening to offer the perspective of God. God's reaction to the murder of the righteous, as recorded in the Bible, is strong and fierce! Recall dear pastor the Bible's book of Isaiah and its 49th chapter. In Isaiah chapter 49 verses 25-26 we read

> "For I will fight those who fight you, and I will save your children. I will feed your enemies with their own flesh. They will be drunk with rivers of their own blood. All the world will know that I, the Lord, am your Savior and your Redeemer, the Mighty One of Israel."

Yet there were no reports of Charleston clergy openly disagreeing with the family member's misguided reaction to the murder of their loved ones. And this silence and inability to apply the "meat" of the word of God is equal to **mal-practice** in the ministry.

The Bible is clear that even God hates and Jesus spoke of hate in what scholars describe as a class of his teachings known as the **"hard sayings of Jesus."** If as pastors and spiritual leaders of Charleston, South Carolina we did not draw the public's attention to the Bible where we read in the book of Ecclesiastes such passages as found in chapter 3, *"There is a time for everything, And a season for every activity under the heavens **a time to love and a time to hate**...a time for war and a time for peace.",* we are guilty of **mal-practice**.

If we didn't remind the believers of what the Bible contains about how God hates, and his Prophets hates the wicked, we are guilty of **mal-practice in ministry**. The Bible is clear that *"the Lord thy God is a man of war."* And his vengeance, wrath, anger and hatred are preserved for the wicked who act as wolves devouring the righteous sheep-like believers in God. Be reminded brothers and sisters in the ministry of the "meat" of the word of God. The meat of his word if often deemed indigestible by weak hearted men and women. Some examples of the "meat" of the word include the following verses:

> "For I, the LORD, love justice; **I hate robbery and wrongdoing.** In my faithfulness, I will reward my people and make an everlasting covenant with them. (Isaiah 61:8)

> Again, and again I sent my servants the prophets, who said, **'Do not do this detestable thing that I hate!'**(Jeremiah 44:4)

> do not plot evil against each other, and do not love to swear falsely. **I hate all this,"** declares the LORD. (Zechariah 8:17)

Even Jesus instructed the new believers who were just beginning their journey through life as his disciples while their family and friends opposed their following of Jesus by uttering this "hard saying," *"If anyone comes to me and does not **hate father and mother, wife and children, brothers and sisters-- yes, even their own life--such a person cannot be my disciple."** (Luke 14:26)*

If we as men and women of God cannot teach these passages of scripture with courage and conviction when the wicked rise up to kill the righteous, we are guilty of **mal-practice in ministry** and should strongly consider another line of work!

I fear that some of you who have been so psychologically imprisoned by destructive doctrinal dogmas will dismiss Old Testament scripture as arcane, irrelevant and antithetical to the grace and salvation represented by Jesus the Christ. But I caution you in that attitude. Because you may distance yourself from the Old Testament and its emphasis on justice and the law of God, but Jesus certainly did not. He said *"Don't misunderstand why I have come. **I did not*** *come to abolish the law of Moses or the writings of the prophets. No, I came to accomplish their purpose.* (Matthew 5:17)

Your rejection of Minister Farrakhan is a grave offense! One needs only to consider your rejection of the Minister in the light of Biblical scripture. In the synoptic gospels of Mathew, Mark, and Luke, we find the following cautionary verses on the subject of the rejection of the disciples of Jesus.

In Mark 6:11-12 we read

> "And if any place will not welcome you or listen to you, leave that place and shake the dust off your feet as **a testimony against them.**"

In Matthew 10:14-15 we read

> "If anyone will not welcome you or listen to your words, leave that home or town and shake the dust off your feet. Truly I tell you, **it will be more bearable for Sodom and Gomorrah on the day of judgment than for that town.**"

In Luke 10: 10-12 we read

> "But if a town refuses to welcome you, go out into its streets and say, 'We wipe even the dust of your town from our feet to show that we have abandoned you to your fate. And know this—the Kingdom of God is near!' **I assure you, even wicked Sodom will be better off than such a town on judgment day.**"

Here in these passages we find that a severe punishment is to be visited upon towns and cities that reject disciples of Jesus. Sodom and Gomorrah was violently razed by God and exists today only in history as a warning and cautionary tale. Yet Jesus says that when his disciples are rejected by cities, those cities have been ear-marked by God for a worse fate than Sodom!

Dear pastors and clergy of Charleston, cannot you see that the Honorable Minister Louis Farrakhan is the best disciple of Jesus present among you today? If you can't, allow me to help remove the scales from your eyes.

Forget doctrine and orthodoxy for a moment. Because Jesus was **unorthodox**; and he never used orthodoxy as a standard of judgment. In fact, Jesus was so unorthodox that the Jews of his day strongly condemned him. Even to this day, the Jewish community holds Jesus in disgust and condemnation. While Islam on the other hand, venerates and honors Jesus and his mother Mary.

Mark 9:38-40 proves Jesus attached more value to one having the correct actions than in one merely espousing the correct doctrines. That passage documents a conversation between Jesus and the disciple John. In some Bible translations, it is found under the subject heading **Intolerance Rebuked** and reads as follows:

> "Teacher, we saw someone using your name to cast out demons, but **we told him to stop because he wasn't in our group.** 'Don't stop him!' Jesus said. 'No one who performs a miracle in my name will soon be able to speak evil of me. **Anyone who is not against us is for us.**"

Consider such an enlightened perspective provided by Jesus as you reflect upon Minister Farrakhan, whom many pastors say preaches Jesus as well as or better than most Christian preachers. And he has been to the Black church a helper, a cheerleader, a friend and a companion. And some of you have personally benefitted from the Minister's love for you. Yet some of you think like John thought, that he should be stopped because he is not a part of your denomination. How foolish!

I challenge you to examine the effect of his preaching. You will find that his students and followers reflect the discipline, moral striving and a willingness to obey God just like Jesus taught and demonstrated. And while many of you struggle to bring your own congregations into what the New Testament calls a holiness lifestyle, Minister Farrakhan has modeled the way for you. The Minister is widely known for the moral reform of those who follow him. Many of us in our *pre-Farrakhan* days were drug abusers, thieves, murderers and practitioners of self-destructive lifestyles. This is the man that you have rejected.

The man you rejected made a call in 1995 for a million Black men to meet him in Washington, D.C. for the historic Million Man March. Nearly 2 million men answered that call and traveled to Washington, D.C. at their own expense. And of the nearly 2 million men, most or nearly 75% self-identified as Christian. This begs the question why did a million Christian men respond enthusiastically to the call of Muslim Minister Louis Farrakhan? As a pastor, you know that Bible scripture teaches that Jesus' sheep "know his voice" and will not follow a stranger. The Million Man March proved that **the voice for Jesus in the world today is the Honorable Minister Louis Farrakhan**!

The man you rejected has defended the most notable of Black men, women and groups whenever the white power structure moved against them to ruin their reputation and destroy their careers. In fact, the conflict with the Jewish community and Minister Farrakhan is the result of the Minister's defense of Rev. Jesse L. Jackson Sr. in his ambitious run for President of the United States. And all while the Minister has defended Black leadership he has himself been the subject of the most vicious and wicked propaganda campaign in American history. As a result of defending Rev. Jackson, he was branded an anti-Semite by the leaders of the Jewish community. As a result of defending Rev. Jackson, he was ultimately censured by the United States Senate. Yet none of this deterred him in his resolve to defend his own Black brothers and sisters.

The man you rejected has used his good name and reputation with the masses of our people to speak well of and defend and support notable Black clergy. The Minister's resume documents his support and defense of **Rev. Jesse L. Jackson Sr.; Rev. Charles Coen; Rev. Eddie Carthan; Archbishop George A. Stallings; Rev. James L. Bevel; Rev. Benjamin F. Chavis; and Rev. T.L. Barrett,** just to name a few. Whether you know it or not, when the Minister suffers being beaten up by the media, the Jews and the U.S. government but at the same time defends, supports, guides and finds ways to help you, you are witnessing him reflect the principle in the phrase *"by his stripes we are healed."* Again, this proves that Minister Farrakhan is living the principles and character of Jesus while most are just satisfied to "praise his holy name." Maturity should teach us that praise alone is not enough. If praise is not followed by carrying the teachings and example of Jesus into practice, it is nothing more than an empty exercise in vanity.

The man that you rejected spoke at the Million Man March and refused to use the occasion as a recruitment tool for the Nation of Islam. Instead he gave the following humble instructions to the million men. "

> "Every one of you must go back home and **join some church, synagogue or temple or mosque that is teaching spiritual and moral uplift.** I want you, brothers; there are no men in the church, in the mosque. The men are in the streets and we got to get back to the houses of God." Which one of you as pastors would have enjoyed such an audience and steered your listeners to fill the pews of another congregation or religion?"

The man that you rejected went into the treasury of the Nation of Islam to extend a grant of funding to the Rev. Dr. Charles Steele for the upkeep and maintenance of the Southern **Christian** Leadership Conference. To which, the Rev. Dr. Steele exclaimed

> "I can honestly say, if it was not for Minister Louis Farrakhan, the SCLC would be out of business."

This is just some of the sterling record of the man that you rejected –the Honorable Minister Louis Farrakhan. You know that he has been a great blessing to you. Your rejection of him is shameful, disgraceful and a manifestation of cowardice.

Brother and Sister Pastors, your rejection of Minister Farrakhan is an offense that demands repentance.

You would do well now to beg God's forgiveness for your rejection of Minister Farrakhan. Repent and become the bold and courageous man or woman of God that a time like this demands. Repent and join Minister Farrakhan along with your congregations for the Justice or Else rally in Washington, D.C. on October 10, 2015. Repent and join the Minister in having what Dr. Martin Luther King Jr. called for in 1963 which is a "sacrificial Christmas." This is a call for you and your congregations to unite with the Justice or Else Movement and show the world just "what would Jesus do" in a time like this. We are keeping our money in our pockets this year and expect you and your congregations to participate with us in an economic withdrawal of the Christmas spending season. Lastly, you should make haste in hosting the Honorable Minister Louis Farrakhan in your city at his earliest convenience. Extend to him an invitation to speak in the city of Charleston as soon as possible! This is critical, otherwise, you place your city into that horrible category that Jesus warned of--a city whose fate is so horrible, it will make God's destruction of Sodom and Gomorrah seem mild by comparison.

As-Salaam Alaikum (Peace Be Unto You),

Defiance! The Spirit of Farrakhan Affects Athletes and Entertainers

Rapper and pop culture 'Phenom' Kanye West is emerging as yet another prominent Black person to have been positively affected by what is present in the atmosphere of a spirit of revolutionary defiance emanating in and through the Honorable Minister Louis Farrakhan. Kanye recently spoke strong words of defiance at a Chicago concert to thousands of his fans. Kanye even revealed to the thousands in his audience that he had taken counsel with Minister Farrakhan and as a result, he would not be apologizing to Abraham Foxman for saying that *"Black people don't have the same level of connections as Jewish people."* Foxman claimed that Kanye's words were classic anti-Semitism. And in truth, nothing could be more absurd. Kanye's words were merely a statement of the obvious. And without apologizing, Kanye has since clarified his remarks and by saying that they may have constituted an *"ignorant compliment."*

What Kanye is exhibiting deserves analysis and encouragement. His close association with Minister Farrakhan during this controversy is sure to be condemned. For years Blacks in all professions have been cautioned to stay away from Minister Farrakhan. The phrase *Farrakhan Litmus Test* has been used to describe how one's favorable view of Minister Farrakhan could be used against them. Failing the Farrakhan Litmus Test might mean the loss of a contract, being overlooked for a job promotion or failing to be confirmed as a justice on the Supreme Court. The brilliant professor Derrick Bell once observed this phenomenon as such:

> "Smart and super articulate, Minister Farrakhan is perhaps the best living example of a black man ready, willing and able to 'tell it like it is' regarding who is responsible for racism in this country .... **Every black person important enough to be interviewed is asked to condemn Minister Farrakhan."**

Athletes and entertainers are the most influential of all professions in the world today. And there is an expectation that Black athletes and entertainers remain politically neutral. In his great book 40 Million Dollar Slaves, author William C. Rhoden discusses how this came about by examining the politically neutral career of the most high profile athlete of all time, Michael Jordan. Rhoden condemns Jordan's misuse of his powerful fame and popularity by noting that,

"...Black athletes like Jordan have abdicated their responsibility to the community with an apathy that borders on treason." Michael Jordan has become a model for the athlete or entertainer today who seeks riches, fame and success along the path of least resistance. Following this path ensures Black athletes and entertainers a certain level of success in their careers in exchange for not using their success as a platform to champion causes that benefit the Black community.

Film producer Bill Spiegel has recently debuted the latest documentary on the life of famed boxing champion Muhammad Ali. The film entitled The Trials of Muhammad Ali emphasizes the struggles of the world's most popular athlete in the areas of faith, family, profession and principles. This film is so profound, that it can be easily considered the best movie about Muhammad Ail ever made. This film exposes us to the eternal value of Muhammad Ali that lies in his example of defiance and resistance to racism and injustice. This film reminds us of that there was once another model for success in sports and entertainment long before the Jordan model had become the standard.

But Ali's principled stance against the war in Vietnam was not an organic epiphany. Spiegel's film helps us to see that at his core, Muhammad Ali was a young talented fighter who had become profoundly affected and impacted by the Honorable Elijah Muhammad and the Nation of Islam. Being inspired by the Nation of Islam and Mr. Muhammad's teaching, Ali carved a path to riches, fame and success while standing for his beliefs and championing causes that would benefit the Black community.

Jewish organizations have always been keenly interested in the accumulation of wealth among Black people, while at every turn seeking to control it. They have a long history of being accountants, managers and agents of Black talent. As a result they have a fear of the message and presence of the Honorable Elijah Muhammad and the Nation of Islam. Because the Nation's message emphasizes that as Blacks, we pool our money among ourselves and grow our own economic strength, and that we fight all who interfere with this process. Jewish professor Marc Dollinger wrote once that

"Despite the NOI's political marginalization, American Jewish Committee officials still feared Muhammad. His charismatic personality, willingness to confront racism in the most dramatic rhetorical terms and ability to inspire even non-believing African American listeners concerned Jewish leaders. The NOI leader, they feared, could earn the respect of his Black audiences, even if they chose not to join his movement."

Nowadays, the Honorable Minister Louis Farrakhan is the source of this fear among Jewish interests. Abraham Foxman in April said in Haarertz Magazine that "*The only leadership that now exists in that community*"—the *"African American community"*— *"is Louis Farrakhan. Farrakhan can assemble 20,000 people several times a year..."* So, like his teacher before him, Minister Farrakhan is feared for his ability to, to *"inspire even non-believing African American listeners."* Minister Farrakhan has a long-standing relationship with all sectors of the arts and culture community, beginning with his own career as a trained classical violinist and pioneering Calypso singer and performer. In Spiegel's film on Muhammad Ali we learn that some of Ali's earliest exposure to the Nation of Islam message was as a result hearing a musical record performed by Minister Farrakhan entitled *"A White Man's Heaven Is A Black Man's Hell."* In the Minister's ministry, he has always made outreach to Blacks in arts and culture a priority. Minister Farrakhan has delivered keynote messages to Hip-Hop summits where he passionately explained to the artists their leadership role and responsibility to use their talent in a socially conscious way. The Minister has patiently worked with artists and athletes to enlighten them on the importance of ownership and economic independence noting the sad legacy of former entertainers who end their lives broken and penniless.

Kanye's words in defiance to Abe Foxman calls to mind Minister Farrakhan's words to the rappers during these summits to be more than just entertainers. In fact, there are numerous examples throughout the sports and entertainment world that suggest that many have been affected directly or indirectly by the spirit of defiance and courage displayed by Minister Farrakhan. Minister Farrakhan has personally advised and counseled many athletes and entertainers. Others are simply inspired to make a change in their personal life or to make a business move based on what they have heard in the Minister's speeches.

Minister Farrakhan inspires us all. The word *inspire* means to "breathe in." When one is inspired by Minister Farrakhan, they are literally *breathing in* the revolutionary ides of Black unity, independence, self-respect, resistance to injustice and inequality, and speaking truth to power, among others. And the Minister's 59 years of teaching, organizing and activism has saturated the atmosphere of ideas so much so that we find traces of his ideas in the seemingly non-related activities of various athletes and entertainers.

When we hear of Jay-Z and Beyoncé traveling to Cuba for business against the advice of the government, we think of Minister Farrakhan's travels to Cuba and embracing of Fidel Castro against the official policy of the American government. Kanye's stance against Abraham Foxman reminds us of Minister Farrakhan's stance against the ADL beginning in the 1980's with Jesse Jackson's presidential campaign. The move of Lebron James, DeWayne Wade and Chris Bosh to engineer their own trade to the Miami Heat against the wishes ownership reveals an outside the box kind of thinking that is reminiscent of much of Minister Farrakhan's preaching.

We also see Minister Farrakhan's spirit in the message rap lyrics of Common, Kanye West, Jasiri X, Immortal Technique, Public Enemy and countless others over the years. When Essence magazine interviewed the very talented Ms. Janelle Monae on her signature modest wardrobe attire she said that *"Showing my skin is not what makes me sexy...I like skirts and dresses just like everyone else, but I had a message I needed to put out there. It was up to me to show people and young girls there was another way."* Janelle's thoughtful words echo Minister Farrakhan's spirit and insistence that Black women represent themselves before the world as modest, dignified and beautiful.

For sure, there are not enough artists who are willing to defy industry standards and the false expectation that Black athletes and entertainers remain politically neutral. One can only hope that Kanye becomes stronger and more refined in his approach. One can only hope that other artists see the value in becoming socially conscious and cause-oriented. Each is blessed with a powerful platform whereby they could reach millions of people with cause-oriented messaging if they did not fear loss. And this is why the Muhammad Ali model is an important study. Ali did temporarily lose millions of dollars in income, but in the end, he triumphed both professionally and personally. If Black artists and athletes will adopt the Ali model instead of the Jordan model, Black America could experience a much-needed cultural revolution. The time is now.

Minister Farrakhan Delivers Powerful Message to West Point Cadets

Written by Muhammad Speaks New York Correspondent Leroy 23X, November 24, 1972

When Minister Louis Farrakhan represented the Honorable Elijah Muhammad at West Point recently, it signaled the end of a yearlong campaign by the Black cadets to get their invitation to the Muslim Minister approved by the institution's administration.

The Nation of Islam had received the invitation a year ago from the Behavioral Science Club, a cadet group consisting of both Blacks and whites, but with the Black cadets in the majority. The invitation, however, was not passed by the administration until this mid – October; and Muhammad Speaks was informed that the invitation, like that of an earlier one to Congressman Ron Dellums, was probably reviewed by authorities higher than those at West Point before the Minister was allowed to speak.

And unlike speakers invited by the academy's administration, Minister Farrakhan's engagement did not have a large budget for publicity on the sprawling grounds of the institution. Yet, the resulting turnout of 470 cadets, administration personnel and non- military guests was called "fantastic" by a Black West Point officer, who also added that it was the largest audience for a speaker who was not pushed by the administration. In his opinion the increasing interest to learn more about the most powerful Black man in America is what brought the 330 Blacks in the audience to hear his representative.

Alluding to the determined campaign to get the Messenger's teachings on to the academy's grounds, Minister Farrakhan said that his speaking there was a historic one.

"I'm sure that something must be happening for a Black Muslim to be at West Point," he declared. "I understand that it took quite a while to get us here, but whoever is responsible for us being here among our Brothers, we thank you for permitting us to talk to our Brothers since it is they who Muhammad wants to reach with His message."

"To you my dear Brother cadet, don't be lulled to sleep by the fact that you're at West Point, there's no place in the west where you are respected. And if you don't

239

wake up and get knowledge of yourself in the east points, you won't get back among your own kind with respect."

The Muslim spokesmen then told the attentive audience that as military men who are taught "duty, honor and country" and who understand moral codes, they could appreciate Muhammad's drive to acquaint the Black man of America with the laws of civilization, "so that he may come up from the mud and stand up again as a man."

Speaking in a much milder tone than is customary for him, Minister Farrakhan's words yet had the same piercing effect as his other lectures. In fact, he had to caution the Black cadets on two occasions, after he detected uneasiness in some of their faces over what he was telling them in the presence of whites.

He said that no atmosphere is peaceful when one withholds his true feelings. He said that his frank "wake up" talk was not meant to be disrespectful to the whites; "We're not to be smart", he continued," "we're trying to level off on the Black man here so that he can stand up and be counted as someone among the respected peoples of the earth."

Minister Farrakhan proceeded to tell the Black cadets that there was nothing at West Point that would make them a complete Black man. West Point, he said, could give them a straight back, teach them how to soldier, to take orders, but that it had nothing that could straighten out the Black man's mind.

"How come in the year 1972," he asked, "you answer to the name Robinson, Brown, and Smith when the cadet role is called? Those are not you're names. The knowledge of a man's name comes to him from his father. Robinson, Smith and Brown were not your fathers. They were Englishmen; how did they become your fathers? Maybe you're in the wrong army.

"With every white cadet whose parents are from Europe and whose parents speak the language of their European ancestors, you will find that white cadet being able to speak that language to some degree. Well how come the Black man in America has no knowledge, whatsoever, of any word in his own mother tongue? Now cadet, if you don't know your name, your language, and possess no knowledge of your cultural roots, then you are a victim of amnesia.

You have lost your mind and any decision that you make in that state is not valid. Because if he were in his right mind he would see that he belonged to himself and should be free from his oppressor and unite with people like himself.

He emphasized his point of the Blackman being raised(reared) by the white man, and of the effects this had on the Black man's morals and love of self. He said that in the absence of the true father and mother, "the natural guides" Black people could not expect their oppressor to give them anything resembling the truth. A man who won't treat you right, he declared can't be expected to teach you right.

The National Representative of the Honorable Elijah Muhammad then addressed himself to the whites in the audience. He stated that the present generation of whites can never expect to understand Black people until they know what their forefathers did to Blacks.

"You can't say, 'Well I wasn't back there then,' that's true. But the mere fact that the Black man is in this condition in America today is a witness against your fathers. And, if you, the children of the father, will not do justice by the children of the slave, then their condition remains a witness against you."

Then he returned his attention to the Black cadets. He told them that the discipline they were learning was good for them because the Black man was militant by nature.

He stated that white people knew that Black people were born warriors and it was for this reason that whites did not like for Islam to be taught to Blacks. He quoted a white writer as saying that Islam brought out the "warlike propensities" in the Black man. Whites, he continued know that Black men are tough warriors, and added that the discipline was good preparation for the Black cadets until they received the Messengers teachings. These teachings, he said would enable them to fulfill their obligation to their people.

You have a commitment to make to your people, and that is to advance yourself in such a way, that you can, in "turn, advance your people." The wrong philosophy, he explained is "to think in terms of individualism. Muhammad teaches us that when we gain knowledge, we become the servant of our Brother who doesn't have that knowledge. It is our duty to share our knowledge with our Brothers, this allows us to walk in equality."

Minister Farrakhan said that Islam teaches the Muslims to respect authority and that this training included accepting the authority of Blacks. In referring to the Fruit of Islam's brotherhood, he said that it was the first time in America that Black men had other blacks to look up to and respect, and who were not placed over them by whites. He said that the submission shown to the Muslims required a completely different mind, than that produced through America's slave process. He told the cadets that they might as well gear themselves to taking orders from Blacks, … because your days of taking orders from others is coming to a fast close."

He said that while West Point is teaching an honor code in a corner of America, Messenger Muhammad was teaching an honor code, to men, women and children in every city where Blacks are found. He said that the Muslims do not have a West Point, but that their teaching institution was called Muhammad's Temple. He concluded his hour – long lecture with a warning to the Black cadets. "I don't think you have a good future in the army", he stated. "As prophecy doesn't show much good coming from the army. I must tell the truth. You know the books says Pharaoh's army got drowned, and that book is not just talking back there, its talking up here in the present day and times."

Then he answered several questions from the Blacks and whites present after which he received a standing ovation. Among the Black officials attending the lecture were Lt. Colonel Lloyd McAfee, and Hugh Robinson, former military assistant to President Lyndon Johnson; and Majors Dave Jackson and Carl McCarden. Among the white military personnel present were several commanding officers of cadet regiments and Brigadier General T.R. Seir who is the Commandant of Cadets and the second in command at West Point.

A Portrait in Humility: What Does Minister Farrakhan Think About Himself?

The following are excerpts from the book Closing the Gap: Inner Views with The Honorable Minister Louis Farrakhan by Jabril Muhammad page 70-72)

"I was telling Brother Jabril [two nights earlier] that no matter what people say of me and how people are saying things all over the world, I feel like a little boy inside of a mature man. Now look at that picture: a little boy inside of a mature man. As the man is getting older and wiser, the people outside are relating to this mature man who is representing Allah(God), the Honorable Elijah Muhammad, Prophet Muhammad and the Truth, but, on the inside there is this little boy who is almost oblivious to the kudos and the praise and all that is being said to the mature man on the outside. The little fellow on the inside may want to play. He may want to do somelittle silly thing. He is not even aware of the greatness that Allah (God) is making of him. He is just happy being a little boy on the inside of this mature man.

I keep thinking, as I look at myself, no matter what people say, "how great he is, yet I see myself jus like I was when we (looking at his wife) were back in Roxbury, Massachusetts and I am this little fellow respectful of my elders and always willing to do little things to help this one and that one; never taking myself seriously. That is my protection. The little boy on the inside is protected from all of the praise and the kudos, fame, popularity, adulation, and acclamation, on the mature man growing on the outside.

The little fellow, if there is a carton that could be drawn of a man growing in stature and the lines in his face and the wisdom that he speaks and the audiences cheering, and on the inside there is this little boy playing hopscotch or playing with his marbles and he is oblivious to the people outside saying great and wondeful things about him. He is hitting that marble. He isjust doing his "little boy" things.

So, no matter what people say; no matter how much they praise me; it does not affect me, because it only reaches the head of the old man, but the little fellow on the inside didn't hear it. He doesn't know it. You know? I don't know why I made that picture; but that's the way I feel inside.

243

Even though I know these words that you [Jabril] write are true and I know I am the representative of this Messianic dispensation; I know that I am that. I know that. I know that. But, then, I don't know it. Do you know what I mean? I know that I am becoming a very great man. But I am not aware to the point where I am carried away with myself, because the little boy on the inside does not allow it.

You know how old people can sit at a table and talk and the little boy is looking for a way to get away from table so he can do "little boy" things? Am I making sense? [We all laugh; for he is crystal clear and in a very touching and sensitive manner.] That's a heck of a picture, isn't it?

So I don't know what games people have on their minds, but little children do ot [arrogantly] judge people. Little children have a way of looking at people, they may not go to everybody, but they are innocent. And because they are innocent, they have to be protected. That's that little fellow within. Now, the old guy might be wise enough to protect the little fellow within, but I think the little fellow within the old fellow outside just looks mature and sound mature and affects the world as a mature man; but on the inside, he's just a little boy, innocent, and will never be affected by the praise of the people.

And when death overtakes him, he won't know anything of his so-called greatness. He will only know he is grateful that he was blessed to live to serve a great God, Allah, and a great cause, Islam, and a great teacher, the Honorable Elijah Muhammad.

I was telling Brother Jabril how young people get fame and fortune quickly and lose it almost as quickly as they get it. It destroys them, because it really takes time to produce greatness. Real greatness; just takes time.

And so God, in allowing me to grow, I don't care if millions of people applaud me and cheer me, the little boy inside is oblivious to that. He hardly hears it and that is not his interest. His interest isin the game of marbles; not really marbles but, you know; I just don't know how to explain it."

Historical Timeline of U.S. Government Attacks on The Nation of Islam in America

1939-Security Index of the FBI begins; it will eventually contain 673 members of the Nation of Islam and only 476 members of the Communist party

1942-The Honorable Elijah Muhammad was arrested on charges of sedition

1956-FBI leader J. Edgar Hoover request permission from Attorney General Herbert Brownwell to install surveillance equipment at the home of Elijah Muhammad

1957-Wire taps installed at residence of the Honorable Elijah Muhammad at 4847 S. Woodlawn Avenue in Chicago

1959-The FBI launches a full-scale media campaign against the Nation of Islam. This included the use of publications such as Time, U.S. News and World Report, Saturday Evening Post

1961-Wiretap and microphone were installed in the Phoenix residence of the Honorable Elijah Muhammad

1962-FBI begins new counterintelligence initiative by sending anonymous letter to NOI members depicting that the Honorable Elijah Muhammad was living an affluent life while the believers remained poor.

1964-February memo from FBI revealed their plans to foment and exacerbate tensions between Malcolm X and the Honorable Elijah Muhammad.

1965-FBI informants on scene and integral part of the assassination of Malcolm X; memos reveal FBI informants in the top levels of Nation of Islam leadership and within the inner-circle of Malcolm X's OAU and Muslim Mosque Inc. groups

1967-Elijah Muhammad named as target in the newly established COINTELPRO-Black Nationalist Hate Groups program of the FBI. This intensifies and prolongs the FBI's aggressive tactics to neutralize the Nation of

Islam. Under COINTELPRO the Nation of Islam was the victim of negative propaganda via bureau friendly journalists; suffered the infiltration of informants and provocateurs; endured its efforts to recruit youthful members being frustrated; and experienced the bureau's use of anonymous mailings to NOI members and leaders that sought to cause members to leave the organization and leaders to fight and hurt one another.

1984-U.S. Senate votes 95-0 to censure Minister Louis Farrakhan

1994-FBI informant Michael Fitzpatrick lures Qubilah Shabazz, daughter of Malcolm X into murder plot against Minister Louis Farrakhan.

2007-Department of Homeland Security admits to illegal surveillance on the Nation of Islam

Minister Farrakhan vs. America's Toughest Minds

What follows is an analysis of Minister Farrakhan's triumphant victories over the most brilliant minds that American journalism has to offer. It is offered to provide a picture of just who it is that the Minister has faced in public interviews over the years so that we might marvel at how Allah blessed Minister Farrakhan with victory and a growing appeal. None of their training, accomplishments, honors, connections or popularity and confidence could help these journalists succeed in destroying the Minister's magnetism among the people. This is an important fact base in determining how to market Allah's Divine Message that resides within Minister Farrakhan.

Without Letters but Learned:

The Bible and the Holy Qur'an agree that Jesus is the Messiah. Both books attest to the fact that Jesus was vehemently opposed. From the Biblical narrative, his enemies are categorized as being the Pharisees, Sadducees and the Scribes. According to the Online Etymology Dictionary the word *scribe* is a verb that means *"to write."* In the Hebrew language, it is the word *sopher* which means *"writer, scholar."* In Latin, its root is from *scribere*, which means "to write." In the Bible's history, the Scribes who opposed Jesus were "professional interpreters of the Jewish Law."

So, the history and etymology of the scribes highlights how this group embodied the combination and intersection of the fields of law, writing and the Jewish religion. This connection is relevant and analogous to the profession of journalism in America today. In fact, the basic training and education of lawyers and journalists is often identical. This is because undergraduate law students are advised to choose a major that emphasizes research, critical thinking, writing and close reading. In addition, the major media companies in America are headed by Jewish CEOs.

Minister Louis Farrakhan has been handled in the same way that the scribes handled Jesus. In the Bible, the Jewish leadership, called *Sanhedrin*, had a meeting that is recorded in St. John Chapter 11. The Bible quotes their fear of Jesus after he had raised Lazarus from death:

> "What are we accomplishing?" they asked. "Here is this man performing many miraculous signs. If we let him go on like this, everyone will believe in him, and then the Romans will come and take away both our place and our nation."- St. John 11:47-48(NIV)

The subtitle heading for these verses of scripture is *The Plot to Kill Jesus.* Jesus' crucifixion was therefore planned in the aftermath of his demonstrated ability to give life to the dead. Jesus' crucifixion was planned because the Sanhedrin feared the popularity of Jesus' message. Jesus pointed out their wickedness and their misuse of the people. He condemned their evil monetary practices that had desecrated the holy temples of God. And they saw in Jesus the end of their influence, control and power. So, they sought to kill him.

Minister Louis Farrakhan has closely followed Jesus. He has demonstrated the Jesus Leadership Model. And as a result of his desire to follow the Jesus that both Bible and Holy Qur'an call the Messiah, he has acquired unique and extraordinary abilities. This is undeniable. No one enlightens and positively impacts the Black community like the ministry of Minister Louis Farrakhan. In fact, it is not an exaggeration to describe Minister Farrakhan's ministry as indispensable and vitally necessary for Black survival. Minister Farrakhan is to Black America what Islam was to Europe in the Dark Ages. He possesses the guidance, the programmatic thrust and the philosophy necessary to bring the Black community out of our slavery-induced darkness. The historic 1995 Million Man March is one of the many *"miraculous signs"* performed by the Minister that demonstrates this. For in one day the Minister increased voter registration, adoption of Black children; he helped reduce Black on Black crime and sparked an increase in Black men joining community based organizations and houses of worship.

The plot to crucify Minister Farrakhan has always included the effort to destroy his strong appeal and attraction. The strongest and most powerful of journalists have played the part of the modern scribes. They have often been used to try and destroy the magnetism of Minister Farrakhan that, like Jesus, if allowed to continue *"everyone will believe in him."* These mighty journalists who were trained in research, critical thinking, writing and close reading, all were used in a critical aspect of Minister Farrakhan's crucifixion. Their job was to mock him and make him a caricature. Their job was to poke holes in his message and show his ideas to be unsound and unpopular. But in each case, they failed miserably.

None of the celebrated modern scribes were able to accomplish the goal of destroying Minister Farrakhan's magnetism among his people. And what is fascinating and seldom considered is the high levels of formal education held by these celebrity journalists contrasted against the absence of any high level educational degree held by Minister Farrakhan.

Tim Russert of NBC's Meet the Press held a B.A. in Political Science and a Jurist Doctorate also. He was bestowed a total of 48 honorary degrees and was the recipient of the Edward R. Murrow award as well an Emmy award and numerous other awards in journalism.

Mike Wallace of CBS's 60 Minutes also held a B.A. from University of Michigan where an investigative journalism fellowship bears his name. His biography says that he "earned 21 Emmy Awards, five DuPont-Columbia journalism awards, five Peabody awards and the Paul White Award, the most prestigious award given by the Radio and Television News Directors Association. He also won the Robert F. Kennedy Journalism Award grand prize and television first prize in 1996, and was inducted into the Television Academy Hall of Fame in June 1991."

Sam Donaldson graduated from the Mexico Military Institute.

Ted Koppel of ABC's Nightline holds a B.S. degree from Syracuse and an M.A. from Stanford University. A member of the Broadcasting Hall of Fame, Mr. Koppel has won every major broadcasting award including 40 Emmy Awards, eight George Foster Peabody Awards, 10 DuPont-Columbia Awards, and two George Polk Awards. His 10 Overseas Press Club Awards make him the most honored journalist in the Club's history. He has received more than 20 honorary degrees from universities in the United States.

David Broder's bio includes: "He received his bachelor's degree and an M.A. in political science from the University of Chicago. He was a fellow of the Institute of Politics of the John F. Kennedy School of Government at Harvard University and a fellow of the Institute of Policy Sciences and Public Affairs at Duke University. Broder was awarded the Pulitzer Prize in May 1973 for distinguished commentary. Broder has won numerous awards, including the White Burkett Miller Presidential Award in 1989 and the prestigious 4th Estate Award from the National Press Foundation in 1990, which also honored him with the Distinguished Contributions to Journalism Award in 1993."

Phil Donahue holds a B.A. from University of Notre Dame. He won 9 Emmy Awards and is an inductee into the Academy of Television Arts and Sciences Hall of Fame.

Barbara Walters graduated with an English degree from Sara Lawrence College and has won numerous awards.

Cokie Roberts holds a B.A. degree in political science from Wellesley College.

George F. Will- In 1986, the *Wall Street Journal* called him "perhaps the most powerful journalist in America." His biography notes: "Will was educated at Trinity College in Hartford, Connecticut, Oxford University and Princeton University, where he earned his Ph.D. He has taught political philosophy at Michigan State University, the University of Toronto and Harvard University. In 1977, he won a Pulitzer Prize for commentary for his newspaper columns."

Richard Engel holds a B.A. from Stanford University in international relations. "He speaks and reads fluent Arabic, which he learned while living in Cairo. Engel has also traveled extensively in the Middle East and can comfortably transition between several Arabic dialects spoken across the Arab world. He is also fluent in Italian and Spanish."

Minister Louis Farrakhan went to college but did not complete it. His teacher is the Honorable Elijah Muhammad, whom only completed the third grade. But what Mr. Muhammad taught Minister Farrakhan has equipped him and prepared him in such a way that the sharpest and cleverest of journalists fail in their attempts to derail is powerful message. In fact, amidst his crucifixion at the hands of the modern scribes Minister Farrakhan has routinely enjoyed approval ratings that any politician would envy. Time magazine's cover story in 1994 Ministry of Rage, featured an interview and survey of Minister Farrakhan's appeal and attraction among American Blacks. The surveys found that nearly 2/3 of all Black people agree that Minister Farrakhan speaks the truth!

All that we have written must naturally produce in the minds of Minister Farrakhan's opposers, the same question that the Jews asked about Jesus in the Bible *"How has this man become learned, having never been educated?"-John 7:15(NASB)*

Measuring Minister Farrakhan's Electronic Impact
(Top YouTube Clips as of January 31, 2013)

Every time Minister Farrakhan speaks live and in person, there are thousands of people who come out to see him. Through various YouTube channels, Minister Farrakhan has been able to reach millions of the American people. This extending of Minister Farrakhan's reach has greatly upset his and our enemies. This chart is offered to demonstrate the growing audience of the Minister even though his enemies would like us to believe that his appeal is waning; they want to portray the Nation of Islam as irrelevant. Look at the numbers and see otherwise.

TITLE	HITS	CHANNEL
Farrakhan warns, advises Obama on Libya	644,701	FCNN
Minister Farrakhan Exposes The Secrets of Freemasonry (1 of 2) (Feb 27, 2011)	546,542	Ahmad770
Minister Louis Farrakhan: State of Black America (Part 1)	444,180	FCNN
Tavis Smiley Questions Minister Farrakhan On President Barack Obama (Part 1 of 5)	414,822	Ahmad770
Snoop Dogg thanks Minister Farrakhan, Nation of Islam for supporting peace, hip hop	378,378	FCNN
Minister Farrakhan Exposes The Secrets of Freemasonry (2 of 2) (Feb 27, 2011)	358,924	Ahmad770
Minister Farrakhan on the Illuminati, The Secret Relationship Between Blacks & Jews, &U.S. History	320,289	Ahmad770
Minister Louis Farrakhan: State of Black America (Part 2)	318,654	FCNN
Farrakhan on "Coalition of Demons" attacking Libya, Africa (June 15, 2011)	280,672	FCNN
Tavis Smiley Questions Minister Louis Farrakhan On President Barack Obama (Part 2 of 5)	238,761	Ahmad770
Farrakhan Exposes Bankers and America's Hidden Agenda	230,934	Ahmad770
Minister Farrakhan's Saviours' Day 2011 Keynote Address	226,072	FCNN
Minister Farrakhan: "That's A Murderer In The White House!"	219,003	Ahmad770

BEST Preaching EVER! Farrakhan Speaks at FellowshipMissionaryBaptistChurch	215,015	Ahmad770
Tavis Smiley Questions Minister Louis Farrakhan On President Obama (Part 5 of 5)	212,491	Ahmad770
March 31, 2011 – Farrakhan Press Conference on Libya, Pres. Obama and Col. Gadhafi	209,763	FCNN
Tavis Smiley Questions Minister Louis Farrakhan on President Barack Obama (Part 4 of 5)	201,889	Ahmad770
Tavis Smiley Questions Minister Louis Farrakhan on President Barack Obama (Part 3 of 5)	201,786	Ahmad770
Farrakhan Speaks on Pres. Barack Obama, Judas & the setup of Jesus, Greed, and Zionism	187,099	Ahmad770
Farrakhan responds to Pres. Obama endorsing Gay marriage	186,063	Ahmad770
Farrakhan on LeBron James and Jewish Control (July 11, 2010)	184,954	Ahmad770
Farrakhan responds to charge of anti-Semitism (Al-Jazeera)	174,464	FCNN
Hate rhetoric against Obama & his family – Election 2012	154,450	FCNN
Minister Farrakhan: "Whose Fruit Are We"	153,830	FCNN
Jesus Saves: Exposing The International Bankers	138,892	Ahmad770
Minister Louis Farrakhan Exposes 9/11 and Questions Official Story (Part 1)	136,600	Ahmad770
Minister Farrakhan Blasts Media & Reporters During Interview Commercial!	134,735	Ahmad770
Farrakhan Warns, Advises Obama on Libya	134,231	Ahmad770
Minister Louis Farrakhan Explains The Star of David	132,699	Ahmad770
A Corrupt Government	132,067	Ahmad770
Minister Farrakhan on Ghaddafi & Libya (Feb 27, 2011) (1 of 2)	130,014	Ahmad770
The Untold Story of Hurricane Katrina	124,990	FCNN
Minister Louis Farrakhan asks, "How can you forget?"	124,671	Ahmad770
Minister Farrakhan Lights It Up at Howard University (April 2, 2011)	120,482	Ahmad770

The Fall of The Dollar (The Fall of America)	118,125	Ahmad770
Minister Farrakhan's Prophetic Warning to Wyclef Jean on Leading Haiti	115,806	Ahmad770
The Murder of Malcolm X – What Really Happened?	106,255	FCNN
What Are You Trying To Force Us To Do? PT 1	103,582	Ahmad770
Minister Farrakhan on Ghaddafi & Libya (Feb 27, 2011) (2 of 2)	102,094	Ahmad770
Impeach Bush Regime for High Crimes (Farrakhan, Al Jazeera)	96,544	FCNN
Louis Farrakhan: The Conspiracy of The International Bankers (Part 1)	96,148	Ahmad770
Louis Farrakhan and Cathy Hughes Interview on TV One (May 9, 2010) – Part 1	94,759	Ahmad770
Farrakhan: Hip Hop & The Power of Cultural Expression	92,764	FCNN
Jewish leaders demand Farrakhan denounce "Secret Relationship" book	86,832	FCNN
Wise Intelligent: Connecting Hip Hop, culture and the struggle	85,993	FCNN
Farrakhan on Obama's signing of NDAA (National Defense Authorization Act)	80,353	FCNN
Farrakhan: President Obama is a "front man: for Criminals	75,773	FCNN
Phil Donahue Interviews Minister Louis Farrakhan	74,469	FCNN
TI Speaks @ Nation of Islam's SD2009	71,508	FCNN
Min. Farrakhan in Chicago Prison (Pt. 1)	71,144	FCNN
Farrakhan Full Speech: War on Libya, Africa (Harlem, NY)	64,463	FCNN
Farrakhan's Exclusive 2013 Interview... Topics: Barack Obama, Django Unchained and more	63,351	FCNN
Farrakhan on Scientology	52,832	FCNN
Farrakhan warns, advises Obama on Libya (1)	44,813	FCNN
The Million Man March Pledge	35,646	FCNN
Farrakhan Exposes the "Black Anti-Semite" Myth	33,717	FCNN
Min. Farrakhan in Chicago Prison (Pt. 2)	32,398	FCNN
Farrakhan addresses American Clergy Leadership Conference	31,666	FCNN

Farrakhan Questioned on Libya & More: WPFW/Pacifica Radio Interview	31,281	FCNN
Minister Farrakhan on Ron Paul & Exposing the Federal Reserve and International Bankers	14,919	Ahmad770

The Best Helper of The Honorable Elijah Muhammad

On the back cover of the book Message To The Blackman in America there is a quote from Reader's Digest that reads as follows: *"This mild-looking man (Elijah*  *Muhammad) is...the most powerful Blackman in America. He offers a new way of life. Muhammad prompts even his severest critics to agree when he says he attacks "traditional reasons the Negro race is weak.""*

There are many acknowledgements of the power, influence and beneficial presence of the Most Honorable Elijah Muhammad like the one above. And all who have marveled at Mr. Muhammad's abilities include their acknowledgement that he was able to accomplish what he did through the many followers that he had throughout America. Getting work done through the efforts of others is the essence of leadership.

The Honorable Elijah Muhammad's most popular helpers and followers were his powerful ministers who allowed Mr. Muhammad to sit in Chicago and direct the activity of temples/mosques, businesses and institutions all over the country. And statistically there was no more prolific, productive and popular minister for Mr. Muhammad than Minister Louis Farrakhan of Muhammad's Temple/Mosque No. 7 in New York City.

Minister Louis Farrakhan served as the Most Honorable Elijah Muhammad's National Representative and Minister of Temple/Mosque No.7 in New York. His work in New York is legendary. In New York City, he established 18 temples /mosques of Islam throughout the area of the 5 boroughs. He set up 4 Muhammad Universities of Islam. His average Sunday meeting attendance was 1,000 and his average Wednesday meeting attendance to the mosques was 600 persons coming out to hear him deliver the life-giving teachings of the Most Honorable Elijah Muhammad.

But the most impressive metric of Minister Louis Farrakhan's work in New York is that according to Sepia Magazine, he inspired some 5,000 Black and Hispanic people in New York City to join the Nation of Islam. (Hobbs 1975)

These statistics are critical in quantifying Minister Farrakhan's impact in New York City which was the city that he was assigned to oversee for Mr. Muhammad. But what can't necessarily be quantified is how as the National Representative of the Honorable Elijah Muhammad and the Nation of Islam, he was inspiring thousands to join the Nation of Islam around the country in other cities that aired on local radio stations, Minister Farrakhan's speeches for the Nation of Islam National Radio Broadcast.

Minister Louis Farrakhan is therefore empirically proven to be the best helper that the Honorable Elijah Muhammad had prior to 1975 and post 1975. With respect to New York City, it should be noted that Mr. Muhammad viewed this city as the key city from which he could potentially influence the entire 22 million Black people in America. Consider the following quote from the Most Honorable Elijah Muhammad found in his early series of articles entitled Mr. Muhammad Speaks published inside the pages of the Pittsburgh Courier newspaper.

> "Once Harlem is united into the Brotherhood of Islam, she could command the whole 20 million American dark people. She only needs to rid herself of worthless orators who have no constructive program for this half a million-dark people. We the Nation of Islam have been given that constructive program and by all means, we intend to give it to our people in Harlem, New York. The readiness in the eyes and actions of the people of Harlem tell you and me that these people are now ready... "

Based on the above quote, it is natural for us to conclude that Mr. Muhammad would assign this key city to his most capable, strongest and productive of ministers. And history proves that this is exactly what he did. The Most Honorable Elijah Muhammad expressed his approval and praise of his Minister- Minister Louis Farrakhan- by directing the entire Nation of Islam to continue to 'hear' Minister Farrakhan.

"I want you to pay good attention to his preaching. His preaching is a bearing of witness of me and what God has given to me. This is one of the strongest preachers I have anywhere in the bounds of North America. Everywhere you hear him, listen to him. Everywhere you see him look at him. Everywhere he advises you to go, go. Everywhere he advises you to stay from, stay from. So, we are thankful to Allah for this great helper of mine, Minister Farrakhan. He's not a proud man. He's a very humble man. If he can carry you across the lake without dropping you in, he doesn't say when he gets on the other side, "See what I have done?" He tells you, "See what Allah has done." He doesn't take it upon himself. He's a mighty fine preacher. We hear him every week and I say, continue to hear our Minister Farrakhan." -Hon. Elijah Muhammad, July 30 1972, Theology of Time Lecture Series

Today there are those who would feign a love or devotion to the Honorable Elijah Muhammad while condemning his best helper the Honorable Minister Louis Farrakhan. This is a logical fallacy, for how could one love another and hate someone who is the best helper of the one that they love? This defies logic. Especially when you consider that while one could hate Minister Farrakhan; it is Minister Farrakhan who is a better helper of the Honorable Elijah Muhammad; more so than any other person who would even claim to love Mr. Muhammad.

The above quote from the Theology of Time Lecture series used the phrase "continue to hear our Minister Farrakhan." The website Dictionary.com defines the word continue as a verb that means:

> "to go on or keep on, as in some course or action; extend; to last or endure; to remain in a particular state or capacity; to remain in a place; abide; stay; to go on with or persist in; to cause to last or endure; maintain or retain, as in a position"

The connotation in the above quote is that followers of the Honorable Elijah Muhammad should continue to listen to, feed from, follow and act in obedience to Minister Louis Farrakhan. Scripturally this is key, considering that the Bible includes a verse of scripture that says "faith comes by hearing and hearing by the word of God." (Romans 10:17). Essentially the Most Honorable Elijah

Muhammad is saying that if his followers want to remain faithful, they would find that which would sustain their faith perpetually in the unmatched and unequalled ministry of the Honorable Minister Louis Farrakhan. And I personally bear witness that this is indeed true.

A Timeline of Jewish Attacks Against The Nation of Islam and Minister Farrakhan

- In **1942**: A secret ADL of B'nai B'rith file entitled "Temple of Islam Infiltration" states that a "Negro employed by us" prove "quite instrumental" in an FBI raid on the Chicago mosque resulting in 82 arrests.
- In **1959** A Time Magazine article accuses the NOI of "anti-Semitism"
- In response to the **1959** Time Magazine article, the head of the Anti-Defamation League of B'nai B'rith, Arnold Forster, admitted in a secret memo that "Time magazine notwithstanding, we have no documentable evidence of anti-Semitism on the part of the Temples of Islam movement or Elijah Muhammad." He affirmed that they are "not anti-Jewish per se." Yet Jewish organizations publicly continued to label the NOI as anti-Semitic.
- In **1959** The American Jewish Committee sent Black spies from the Urban League to Mr. Muhammad's Newark, New Jersey, appearance.
- In **1960**, the chairman of the American Jewish Congress, Nathan Edelstein, wrote that "We doubt whether the bulk of its followers are presently committed to anti-Semitism."   A Jewish scholar Marc Dollinger who studied this racist Jewish phenomenon offered a compelling explanation: "Despite the NOI's political marginalization, American Jewish Committee officials still feared Muhammad. His charismatic personality, willingness to confront racism in the most dramatic rhetorical terms and ability to inspire even non-believing African American listeners concerned Jewish leaders. The NOI leader, they feared, could earn the respect of his Black audiences, even if they chose not to join his movement."
- In **1963**: The Jewish Chronicle of Pittsburgh labeled the NOI "the anti-Semitic Negro extremist group known as the 'Black Muslims."
- In **1972** American Jewish Committee under Phillip E. Hoffman release report condemning the "Black Muslims" as using the Muhammad Speaks newspaper to project "a constant drumbeat of inflammatory anti-Zionism and anti-Israel and anti-Semitic propaganda." The report also noted "Only one movement (The Black Muslims), though looked upon by disfavor by the major black civil rights groups, remains strong,

consequential, strong, cohesive, influential and it is a movement that encompasses a significant strain of anti-Semitism.

- In **1984** Nathan Pearlmutter (ADL) referred to Minister Farrakhan as a new "*Black Hitler.*" This was in the aftermath of Minister Farrakhan's defense of Rev. Jesse Jackson. The group Jews Against Jackson and its Director Fern Rosenblatt called for the ruining of Rev. Jackson. Rev. Jackson also suffered firebombing of his campaign offices.

- In **1984**, when The Honorable Minister Louis Farrakhan was censured by the United States Senate in a 95-0 vote for alleged acts of anti-Semitism. The charge of anti-Semitism served to thwart the Nation of Islam Security companies; the POWER Products personal care line; and the National African American Leadership Conference (NAALS)

Minister Farrakhan as a Defender of Black People

Throughout the years Minister Farrakhan's love for Black People has been witnessed as he has looked beyond their faults and ministered unto their needs. Below is a listing of many of those who have been beneficiaries of Minister Farrakhan's defense. These episodes in the history show Minister Farrakhan using his good name and reputation to defend prominent Blacks who have found themselves in trouble. Jewish author Daniel Pipes commented on this phenomenon in a blog post on his website; an excerpt from his blog post is below

"The *New York Post* reports today that "Michael Jackson last night became a member of the Nation of Islam." Of course, this development takes place in the aftermath of Jackson's being arrested on Nov. 20 in connection with child-molestation charges and now being out on $3 million bail.

If this report of his conversion proves to be accurate, it would fit a well-established pattern of African-Americans who, finding their reputation in tatters, turn to the Nation of Islam, which then provides them with solace and help. This phenomenon is most apparent in jails, where blacks since the late 1940s have been converting in large numbers. Famous converts in trouble include:

- *Tawana Brawley*, who converted after her much-publicized claim of being raped by a gang of white men turned out to be a hoax;
- *Mike Tyson*, the heavyweight champion jailed for rape,
- *Benjamin Chavis*, who converted after his eviction from the National Association for the Advancement of Colored People, in large part for having paid off a mistress with NAACP funds.
- *Kenny Gamble*, the music producer whose life fell apart as he faced a payola investigation in 1975.

Other blacks in disgrace do not make the full step to conversion but become closely affiliated with the NOI, which provides them too with political and moral support. Prominent beneficiaries include:

- *Alcee Hastings*, an impeached Federal judge;
- *Marion Barry*, the mayor of Washington, D.C., convicted for drug-taking;
- *George Stallings*, a Catholic priest accused of child molestation; and
- *Gus Savage*, a U.S. congressman from Illinois charged with sexual harassment.

Finally, some blacks in difficult straits merely dip into Islam, without developing a formal relationship – such as O.J. Simpson, who read the Qur'an while incarcerated."

-Daniel Pipes; December 18, 2003, updated Jun 27, 2010
http://www.danielpipes.org/blog/2003/12/michael-jackson-and-blacks-in-stress-who

1. Mayor Marion Barry
2. Mike Tyson
3. Rev. Jesse Jackson
4. Michael Jackson
5. O.J. Simpson
6. Rep. Alcee Hastings
7. Julian Bond
8. Rep. Cynthia McKinney
9. Rep. Earl Hilliard
10. Tawana Brawley
11. David Dinkins
12. President Barak Obama
13. Rev. Charles Coen
14. Rev. Eddie Carthan
15. Qubilah Shabazz
16. Malcolm Shabazz
17. Charles Rangel
18. Congressman Mel Reynolds
19. Mayor Willie Herenton
20. Congressional Black Caucus
21. Mayor Kwame Kilpatrick
22. Benjamin Chavis
23. James Luther Bevel
24. Father Michael Pfleger
25. Rev. T.L. Barrett
26. Alderman Dorothy Tillman
27. Harold Washington Cultural Center
28. Imam Jamil Al-Amin (H.Rap Brown)
29. Bloods and Crips
30. Vice Lords and Gangster Disciples
31. From Gangs to Street Organizations
32. Hip-Hop Community
33. Stan Tookie Williams
34. Sistah Souljah
35. Bishop George A. Stallings
36. Rep. Bobby Rush
37. Steve Cokely
38. Arsenio Hall
39. Bill Cosby
40. Oprah Winfrey

41. Harold-Washington

264

Stoned for Good Works, Propaganda Keeps Hidden Minister Farrakhan's Stellar Record of Leadership

Jesus answered them, Many good works have I showed you from my Father; for which of those works do ye stone me? —John 10:32 KJV

It is ugly and egregious that Minister Louis Farrakhan's current campaign to promote peace in the streets is being attached to an alleged history of anti-Semitism. Nearly every publication that has covered the Minister's efforts has felt the need to rehash baseless lies, seeking to destroy the magnetism between the Minister and the People.

When watching the love, excitement and admiration of Black people who live in the crime-ridden streets of Chicago to the live, physical presence of Minister Farrakhan, one can't help but think of another legendary Black man who made his ministry in the "highways and byways"—Jesus of Nazareth. The New Testament records that it was the poor who "heard him (Jesus) gladly. (Mark 12:37)"

Back then it was the Jewish Sanhedrin that opposed Jesus' public ministry. Today it is the ADL and its Zionist affiliates that oppose Minister Farrakhan. The Bible's history of Jesus is very important in any analysis of the phenomenal presence of Minister Louis Farrakhan. This is because Minister Farrakhan is unique. Most religious and secular leaders within America's Judeo-Christian landscape are comfortable deifying Jesus as an object of worship. Minister Farrakhan as a Muslim enacts what can be defined as a Jesus Leadership Model. The Jesus Leadership Model is characterized by a leader's ability to demonstrate self-sacrifice, longsuffering, courage and magnetism.

Much of what Minister Farrakhan and the Nation of Islam have suffered at the hands of the Jewish/Zionist leadership is detailed in the preface of the book *The Secret Relationship Between Blacks and Jews, Volume 2 (TSRV2)*. *The Secret Relationship between Blacks and Jews* contains eye-opening revelations and records of the Anti-Defamation League of B'nai B'rith admitting in internal memos that the NOI is not anti-Semitic, while at the same time publicly leading a smear campaign against the "Black Muslims," falsely labeling the NOI "anti-Semitic."

> "*Time* magazine notwithstanding, we have no documentable evidence of anti-Semitism on the part of the Temples of Islam movement or Elijah Muhammad." —*Arnold Forster, ADL President*

> "We doubt whether the bulk of its (NOI) followers are presently committed to anti-Semitism." — Nathan Edelstein, American Jewish Congress chairman

The above quotes are Jewish admissions that their hatred of the NOI did not arise out of any legitimate cause for concern.

Jewish scholar Marc Dollinger is quoted in the book. He offers an explanation as to why these Jewish groups were "hating" on the Honorable Elijah Muhammad. Dollinger writes:

> "Despite the Nation of Islam's political marginalization, American Jewish Committee officials still feared Muhammad. His charismatic personality, willingness to confront racism in the most dramatic rhetorical terms and ability to inspire even non-believing African American listeners concerned Jewish leaders. The Nation of Islam leader, they feared, could earn the respect of his black audiences, even if they chose not to join his movement."

The more recent history of Minister Louis Farrakhan details how he has been feared and attacked in the same way as his teacher the Honorable Elijah Muhammad. Remember that in 1984 the Reverend Jesse Jackson campaigned for the presidency of the United States of America. At that time *Time* magazine reported:

> "A group called Jews Against Jackson... pledged publicly to disrupt his candidacy. Two of its members were arrested for interrupting his announcement speech on Nov. 3 in Washington, D.C. A window in Jackson's New Hampshire campaign headquarters in Manchester was smashed, and his campaign offices in Garden Grove, Calif., were fire bombed. Jackson's life has been threatened." To this Minister

Farrakhan responded to defend Reverend Jackson: "If you harm this brother, I warn you in the name of Allah this will be the last one you harm. Leave this servant of God alone."

Following his courageous defense of Reverend Jackson, Minister Farrakhan began being attacked by a multiplicity of Jewish voices. Nathan Pearlmutter of the Anti-Defamation League of B'nai B'rith (ADL) and Nat Hentoff of the *Village Voice* referred to Minister Farrakhan as a new *"Black Hitler."*

This began Minister Farrakhan's crucifixion on the cross. In Roman times, crucifixion on the cross was meant for pain and humiliation. And while the charge of anti-Semitism is meant to embarrass and injure the public profile of the person so charged, it also signifies the crossing out, thwarting, undermining and sabotaging of Minister Farrakhan's plans to help suffering Black America. In other words, the Zionists set out to murder the Minister's plans and programs.

Minister Farrakhan was pinned with a crown of thorns when in 1984, pressure from Jewish groups caused the United States Senate to vote 95-0 to censure Minister Farrakhan for alleged acts of anti-Semitism. The crown of thorns put on the head of Jesus signified that instead of being adorned with the honor, dignity and respect of a royal crown, Jesus would be mocked and ridiculed and suffer the pain of the thorns of a false crown. The modern Sanhedrin sought to falsely crown Minister Farrakhan with an official, governmental designation— "anti-Semite."

Jesus, according to the Bible, had his hands nailed down and Minister Farrakhan had his economic initiatives destroyed. Jesus was a carpenter by trade, so to nail down his hands was to hinder his ability to construct, build and repair. This would destroy a man who made his living through the work of his hands. And even though Jesus gave up his profession to devote himself to his ministry, it is easy to see that the nailing of his hands would destroy him economically. Symbolically, the Jewish leadership has thwarted the Minister's ability to build up the Black community spiritually and economically.

And every time Minister Farrakhan begins an economic program, his efforts are stymied by the ADL and those that it controls. When Minister Farrakhan received a $5 million-dollar loan from an African head of state, Libyan leader

Muammar Gadhafi, he started a personal care product line called P.O.W.E.R. (People Organized Working for Economic Rebirth). His purpose for the funds was to develop an economic base in the very lucrative Black hair and personal care product industry. This initiative was crossed out when Jewish distributors threatened Mr. George Johnson of Johnson Products that they would not distribute his products any longer if he followed through on his agreement to Minister Farrakhan to manufacture the products. In addition, because of Jewish pressure the Black-owned Independence Bank of Chicago demanded that the Minister take the $5 million dollars that he deposited with them out of their bank.

As part of his crucifixion Jesus was pierced in the side of his body. In Minister Farrakhan's case, it was the body of his organization. His followers and the communities they serve suffered when the ADL pressured the U.S. Housing and Urban Development (HUD) to end security contracts with NOI Security. Many remember when the male members of the Nation of Islam organized themselves to perform security patrols in some of the most drug-infested and crime-ridden apartment complexes in the country. The Muslim brothers of the Fruit of Islam (FOI) established security companies to provide safety and security to poor people living in public housing. But Jewish pressure on the Congress thwarted this successful economic and social services initiative by the Nation of Islam. Republican Jack Kemp and former first lady Barbara Bush were among many who praised the Nation of Islam for their work in securing vulnerable neighborhoods.

This analogy concludes by considering the interference Jewish groups have made to hinder Minister Farrakhan's movement among his people. This can be likened to nailing his feet to the cross. And when one's feet are nailed, movement is hindered. Minister Farrakhan's desire has been to go among his people to teach them and to bring them a better quality of life. His desire has been to make the Black man and woman of America the equal of the best of civilized people. There are many examples of Jewish groups protesting the leaders Black people choose to listen to and follow. A classic example of this is when in 1993 Minister Farrakhan was disinvited to speak at the 30th anniversary of the March on Washington. He was invited initially and then disinvited after Rabbi David Saperstein complained. The Black organizers of that march gave in. They disinvited the man whom divine providence blessed two years later to convene the largest March in American history—the Million Man March.

The case of Minister Louis Farrakhan's crucifixion is part of the terrible legacy of the Crucifixion of Black Leadership. It's time for our affliction to end.

The Crucifixion of Black Jesus
History's "Dark-Skinned" Revolutionaries, Their Shared Values,
Shared Enemies and Shared Fate

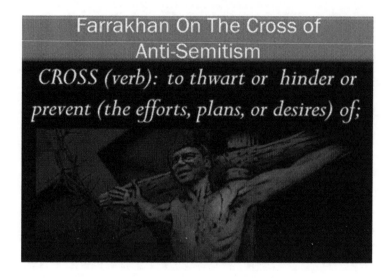

I can remember as a child growing up and at an early age becoming acquainted with the mentality of Black self-hatred that has become a cultural norm among Black people in America. The hatred of Black skin, kinky black hair and in general all physical features deemed African among the very people who possess those features is unfortunately not unusual in Black communities even in 2010. As I write this I refer to incidences when children called other children things like "Black Jesus" or "Black African." You could often hear this whenever any kind of juvenile name calling was done for amusement or meanness.

Now for young children in the 80's "checking" one another with insults like "Black Jesus" indicated a fundamental and formerly long held belief that the real Jesus was White.

Jesus is an important figure in Christianity, Judaism and Islam. In the Black community, he is of extreme importance because most Blacks in this country self-identify as being Christian. There are numerous Churches and denominations of Christianity that make up the religious landscape of America's inner-cities and suburbs. In fact, on the mantle piece of many elderly Black people's homes is a picture of John F. Kennedy, Dr. Martin L. King Jr., and

"Jesus". The myriad of pastors, ministers, reverends and bishops stand in their pulpits and, among other matters, articulate the plan of salvation that involves a belief in Jesus as the Son of God and that he was crucified for the sins of the world, and that he was raised from the dead and ascended into heaven to be with God the Father.

There is however a problem with what is taught and understood concerning Jesus. The leading religious scholars and theologians find it difficult to reconcile the history of Jesus with what is written in the New Testament of the Bible. In a book titled The 5 Gospels the leading researchers and professors in the field of study devoted to the life of Jesus write that 82% of what is attributed as being the words of Jesus in the New Testament, the historical Jesus never said! This group including Dr. Robert Funk, Karen Armstrong, John Dominic Crossan and about 150 other scholars call themselves the Jesus Seminar. They attribute that 84% of the deeds attributable to Jesus in the New Testament were never done by the actual man Jesus of 2000 years ago!

The conclusions of the Jesus Seminar are consistent with what Dr. Patricia Eddy writes in her book Who Tampered With the Bible? *"What is not generally understood, however, is that individual evangelists and sects actually altered the words and actions of Jesus to fit their own purposes."* Both of these books are witness bearers to the Honorable Elijah Muhammad and Honorable Minister Louis Farrakhan who say in the point No. 3 of *What The Muslims Believe* that "the Bible has been tampered with and must be reinterpreted so that mankind will not be snared by the falsehoods added to it.

Ethnicity of Jesus

If Jesus was white, then none of us in the Black community would be upset. After all, we have lived thinking that he was white at least since the days of Black slavery in America. However, Dr. Robert Eisler cites Jewish Historian Flavius Josephus' physical description of Jesus:

> "Both his nature and his form were human: for he was a man of simple appearance, mature age, short growth, three cubits tall [about 4 and a half feet, based on the Jewish cubit], with scanty hair, but having a line in the middle of the head after the fashion of the

271

Nazoreans, eyebrows meeting above the nose so that the spectators could take fright, with a long face, a long nose, and with an undeveloped beard, **dark skin**, and hunchbacked." (The Messiah Jesus and John the Baptist According to Flavius Josephus, Robert Eisler, Ph.D.; The Dial Press, New York; pp. 425-429)

This is a historical physical description of Jesus as a short "dark skin" man. But despite the tampering throughout the Bible, this description is consistent with the various clues in the Bible of Jesus physical description. John, on the isle of Patmos in the book of Revelations describes Jesus as having feet the color of burnish brass and hair like wool (Rev1:14-15). The Gospels describe him as being of the seed of David (Romans 1:3) according to the flesh and declared to be the son of God. If this is so, then Solomon who is David's son and therefore an ancestor of Jesus is described as being "black but comely (handsome) o you daughters of Jerusalem (Song of Solomon 1:5)." Another clue of Jesus ethnicity is that while the census was being taken and Herod had decreed to kill all boy babies Mary and Joseph were able to hide in Egypt (Matthew 2:13)

Judge A Man By The Quality Of His Enemies

There is an old saying that you don't judge a man by who his friends are but you judge a man by the quality of his enemies. In the Holy Quran Allah says in Surah 6 Verse (Ayat) *112:*

"And thus did We make for every prophet an enemy, the devils from among men and jinn, some of them inspiring others with gilded speech to deceive (them). And if thy Lord pleased, they would not do it, so leave them alone with what they forge"

Jesus in the New Testament has a public ministry of 3 and ½ years. During that short time period, he had angered several significant sectors of power and drawn out the enemies that, at least from the Qur'anic perspective, were made by Allah (God) for his own special purposes. If they were made by Allah, God, then they are not ordinary enemies. It is easy to understand that an enemy made by Allah, the supreme being, who is all-wise(al-Hakim) and is referred to in the Holy Quran as the Best Knower would be an enemy whose strength and power would be in proportion to the strength and power that Allah, the supreme being, would deposit within the prophet. Therefore, Jesus in the scripture can be deemed a tremendously powerful and influential figure because his enemies and opposers were the most powerful entities of his day. Within the ranks of the Jewish community were arrayed the Pharisees, Sadducees and Scribes. The New Testament states that Jesus was tried at the home of the High Priest Caiaphas and found guilty. And in the final drama we see the alliance between the Roman authorities and the Jewish Sanhedrin Council to crucify Jesus- the righteous teacher.

Why was Jesus so vehemently opposed? Or better yet why am I writing about it in 2010? There are literally scores of volumes of scholastic literature on this subject from a variety of prolific scholars and writers from around the globe. From my vantage point, there is however no connection made in the available literature between Jesus' crucifixion and the crucifixion of Blacks in America, particularly the "dark-skinned" revolutionary men who comprise Jesus' modern ethnic bretheren.

The Honorable Minister Louis Farrakhan is such a "dark-skin" revolutionary. We might not consider him "dark-skin" in a literal way as much as we can definitely acknowledge him as being a revolutionary voice and personage raised from among the literally "dark-skinned" people. He is opposed like Jesus by certain Jewish leaders and is opposed by certain governmental divisions as well. I should note at this time that the New Testament does not reveal any legitimate reason for the opposition to Jesus. In fact, in the 3rd Chapter of John we read that the Sanhedrin Council knew Jesus had been sent by God! "*1Now there was a man of the Pharisees named Nicodemus, a member of the Jewish ruling council. 2He came to Jesus at night and said,*

> "Rabbi, we know you are a teacher who has come from God. For no one could perform the miraculous signs you are doing if God were not with him." (NIV)

Lazarus As The Mentally Dead Black Masses

In the 11th Chapter of John we are further exposed to the illegitimate nature of the plot to kill Jesus. It was after Jesus had raised Lazarus from the dead that we read of the Sanhedrin Council's sinister plot. *47Then the chief priests and the Pharisees called a meeting of the Sanhedrin.*

"What are we accomplishing?" they asked. "Here is this man performing many miraculous signs. 48If we let him go on like this, everyone will believe in him, and then the Romans will come and take away both our place and our nation." (John 11:47-48 NIV)

It is significant that it was after the resurrection of Lazarus when the plot to kill Jesus was put into action. Lazarus was believed to be dead, but Jesus said that he wasn't dead, he was just only sleeping. Jesus then begins to raise him through the word of his mouth, which suggests that Jesus was correct in his initial assessment.

Black people in America were once called Negroes. The word Negro in Latin is the same as the word "Necro" which means 'death'. "Necro" is a common prefix for words relational in some way to death (i.e. Necrosis, necropolis, necrophilia). It might be understandable that Blacks would be dubbed Negroes (Dead) in light of the process employed to make of proud, independent Africans the chattel slaves of America. Most who have only a cursory knowledge of slavery are familiar with the slave traders and the slave masters but don't know much of the most crucial functionary in the Transatlantic Slave Trade, "the slave maker." It was his sinister work of taking the African and breaking him mentally the same way wild animals are broken. This process of breaking the African mentally was celebrated and touted as an accomplishment by Senator Henry Berry on the floor of the Virginia House of Delegates when he stated in 1832:

> "we have as far as possible closed every avenue by which light may enter the slaves mind. If we could extinguish the capacity to see the light our work would be complete. They would then be on the level of the beast of the field and we would be safe."

The mental death produced by the "closing of every avenue of light" or learning that took place during slavery is therefore comparable to the "sleeping" death that Lazarus experienced in the New Testament. Jesus then was able to awaken him from his death (sleep) with the right combination and configuration of words likewise the resurrection from mental death of Blacks in America would be by means of the right combination and configuration of words.

The Honorable Elijah Muhammad has been quoted as saying "what I have given you is a wake-up message." The master of that wake-up message and as a result

274

the principal raiser of the mentally dead Black masses is the Honorable Minister Louis Farrakhan. This is an undisputable claim especially when you consider the 1995 Million Man March which produced approximately 1.8 million men on the mall in Washington, D.C. This, the largest gathering on the mall in American history, signaled an awakening of Black men to the values atonement, reconciliation and responsibility which are the very antithesis of the values deemed necessary for them to be made slaves and members of the permanent underclass. To be a slave and a member of the permanent underclass requires self-destructive, irreverent and irresponsible attributes that are often apparent in many sectors of the Black community today.

COINTELPRO As The Modern Roman Authorities

In reality it was J. Edgar Hoover, the infamous 20th Century leader of the F.B.I. who headed up the infamous counterintelligence program (COINTELPRO) that used the language "messiah" in his memorandums that outlaid what became known as denial objectives aimed at neutralizing all major Black leaders and organizations. To achieve these ends, he utilized the tremendous financial resources of the U.S. Government to disrupt, frustrate and extinguish the efforts made by "dark-skin" revolutionaries and the various Black organizations they led. Marcus Garvey, Dr. Martin Luther King Jr., Stokely Carmichael, Malcolm X, Honorable Elijah Muhammad, Huey Newton, Maulana Karenga and others of their kind were all targets of the U.S. Government. From Hoover's vantage point the position of Black leader was the de facto position of Messiah and that meant each Black leader and organization was marked for crucifixion. As for Minister Farrakhan and the Nation of Islam, the Department of Homeland Security as recent as 2007 appeared to be operating from the deceased Hoover's playbook when it was found to be illegally targeting the NOI for domestic espionage.

The FBI under Hoover utilized what can be considered a modern, sophisticated form of crucifixion. We should remember that crucifixion, as it is detailed in the New Testament, was a public form of punishment, designed to not only inflict pain and death upon its victims but also humiliation. This kind of harsh execution, death on the cross, not only killed the victim but also killed their reputation and created for them a perpetual "dishonorable mention" in the minds of the spectating public. Crucifixion on the cross was to put fear in the hearts of the people and demonstrate what would become of any who dared to believe in and follow the revolutionary leader. It can be argued that the public humiliation, disgrace and fear it produced was the real object of the crucifixion since the fear of the revolutionary leaders was never based on any history of violence or crime. The real fear is that the popularity of the revolutionary leader grows to the point where the "whole world will believe in him" and adopt his cause as their cause, his mind as their mind and thereby rendering the applecart of oppression irreparably upset.

Consider the following excerpted from FBI internal memorandum that spelled out the COINTELPRO activities aimed at Black Nationalist organizations:

> "The purpose of this new counterintelligence endeavor is to expose, disrupt, misdirect, discredit, or otherwise neutralize the activities of Black Nationalist, hate-type organizations and groupings, their leadership, spokesmen, membership, and supporters, and to counter their propensity for violence and civil disorder.
> The pernicious background of such groups, their duplicity, and devious maneuvers must be exposed to public scrutiny where such publicity will have a neutralizing effect. Efforts of the various groups to consolidate their forces or to recruit new or youthful adherents must be frustrated. No opportunity should be missed to exploit through counterintelligence techniques the organizational and personal conflicts of the leaderships of the groups and where possible an effort should be made to capitalize upon existing conflicts between competing Black Nationalist organizations. When an opportunity is apparent to disrupt or neutralize black nationalist, hate-type organizations through the cooperation of established local news media contacts or through such contact with sources available to the Seat of Government, in every instance careful attention must be given to the proposal to insure the targeted group is disrupted, ridiculed, or discredited through the publicity and not merely publicized.
> Intensified attention under this program should be afforded to the activities of such groups as the Student Nonviolent Coordinating Committee, the Southern Christian Leadership Conference,

Revolutionary Action Movement, the Deacons for Defense and Justice, Congress of Racial Equality, and the Nation of Islam. Particular emphasis should be given to extremists who direct the activities and policies of revolutionary or militant groups such as Stokely Carmichael, H. "Rap" Brown, Elijah Muhammad, and Maxwell Stanford." (From Director to 23 Field Offices, Aug. 26, 1967)

In another memorandum courtesy of the Freedom of Information Act we see the ramping up of the COINTELPRO activities with the specifics of the desired outcomes detailed:

"The Counterintelligence Program is now being expanded to include 41 offices. ... For maximum effectiveness of the Counterintelligence Program, and to prevent wasted effort, long range goals are being set.

1. Prevent the coalition of militant Black Nationalist groups. In unity, there is strength; a truism that is no less valid for all its triteness. An effective coalition of Black Nationalist groups might be the first step toward a real "Mau Mau" in America, the beginning of a true black revolution.

2. Prevent the rise of a "messiah" who could unify, and electrify, the militant Black Nationalist movement. Malcolm X might have been such a "messiah;" he is the martyr of the movement today. Martin Luther King, Stokely Carmichael and Elijah Muhammad all aspire to this position. Elijah Muhammad is less of a threat because of his age. King could be a very real contender for this position should he abandon his supposed "obedience" to "white, liberal doctrines" (nonviolence) and embrace Black Nationalism. Carmichael has the necessary charisma to be a real threat in this way.

3. Prevent violence on the part of Black Nationalist groups. This is of primary importance, and is, of course, a goal of our investigative activity; it should also be a goal of the Counterintelligence Program. Through counterintelligence it should be possible to pinpoint potential troublemakers and neutralize them before they exercise their potential for violence.

4. Prevent militant Black Nationalist groups and leaders from gaining respectability, by discrediting them to three separate segments of the community. The goal of discrediting black nationalists must be handled tactically in three ways. You must discredit these groups and individuals to, first, the responsible Negro community. Second, they must be discredited to the white community, both the responsible community and to "liberals" who have vestiges of sympathy for militant black nationalists simply because they are Negroes. Third, these groups must be discredited in the eyes of Negro radicals, the followers of the movement. This last area requires entirely different tactics from the first two. Publicity about violent tendencies and radical statements merely enhances black nationalists to the last group; it adds "respectability" in a different way.

5. A final goal should be to prevent the long-range growth of militant Black Nationalist organizations, especially among youth. Specific tactics to prevent these groups from converting young people must be developed." (From Director to Field Offices on March 4, 1968)

This modern, sophisticated form of crucifixion created for the "dark-skin" revolutionaries of the Black liberation struggle the same fate as their ethnic big brother Jesus. For Malcolm X and Dr. Martin Luther King Jr. it was assassination and the subsequent corruption of their message and mission. For Marcus Garvey it was deportation. Paul Robeson and W.E.B. Dubois suffered character assassination and economic ruin. Strong Black Organizations like the Black Panther Party, SNCC, Us, Republic of New Africa and the Nation of Islam all suffered government funded infiltration and thwarting.

Jewish Leadership As The Modern Sanhedrin Council

In the same way that Jesus death on the cross was the fruit of the collaboration between the Roman authorities and the Sanhedrin Jewish leadership, the modern Jesuses of today were put on the path to crucifixion via the collaboration of the U.S. Government and the modern Sanhedrin Council. Most in the Black community would be surprised to learn that the Honorable Minister Louis Farrakhan is not the only leader tagged as being anti-Semitic. The Secret Relationship Between Blacks and Jews Volume 2 records the history of many of our great heroes and heroines branded with the much-feared designation of "anti-Semite." Page x of TSRV2 lists Booker T. Washington, W.E.B. Dubois, Marcus Garvey, Dr. Martin Luther King Jr., Malcolm X, Honorable Elijah Muhammad, President Nelson Mandela, Bishop Desmond Tutu, Julian Bond, Kwame Ture, Andrew Young, Kweisi Mfume, and Rev. Al. Sharpton and Rev. Jesse Jackson and Rev. Joseph Lowery. "Learned Black scholars like John Hope Franklin, J.A. Rogers, James Baldwin, Richard Wright, Julius Lester and Alice Walker have all been castigated as "black anti-Semites." Black entertainers like Michael Jackson, Spike Lee, Ice Cube, Arsenio Hall, Muhammad Ali, Public Enemy, and even Oprah Winfrey, if we are to believe some Jewish spokespeople, are all "black anti-Semites."

Why is being labeled an anti-Semite so feared a fate? It is because that is the means of the discrediting and ridiculing called for in the COINTELPRO memos. The accusation of anti-Semitism is used as a sophisticated form of 'crucifixion on the cross.' Consider the dictionary meaning of the word cross as a verb that means to *thwart: hinder or prevent (the efforts, plans, or desires) of.* It is no secret that having that designation attached to one's reputation thwarts their personal progress and can prevent the fruition of their plans and desires. The reason for this can be traced to Biblical scripture when one acknowledges its influential role in shaping the thinking of people in a Judeo-Christian society. The Bible in several passages says that if you bless the children of Israel, God will bless you; and if you curse the children of Israel, God will curse you.

> "I will bless those who bless you, and whoever curses you I will curse;
> and all peoples on earth will be blessed through you." Genesis 12:3
> (see also Genesis12:29, Numbers 24:9 and 22:6, Exodus 23:22).

The Honorable Minister Louis Farrakhan has done a series of 3 speeches that essentially grow out of What the Muslims Believe Point number 5 which states

> "...Furthermore, we believe we are the people of God's choice, as it
> has been written, that God would choose the rejected and the
> despised. We can find no other persons fitting this description in
> these last days more than the so-called Negroes in America."

The series of speeches entitled The Real Children of Israel (parts 1-3) brings history, scripture and empirical data to showcase and defend the Honorable

279

Elijah Muhammad's original thesis articulated in point number 5 that the Black people of America are the actual fulfillment of those afore mentioned Biblical prophecies.

We have shown in this series of articles that historically speaking the Jesus who was born among the children of Israel in scripture was a "dark-skin" revolutionary. Dr. Obery Hendricks, Professor of Biblical Interpretation at New York Theological Seminary and author of the new book *The Politics of Jesus: Rediscovering the True Revolutionary Nature of Jesus' Teachings and How They Have Been Corrupted* describes the revolutionary nature of Jesus teaching. Among the 7 components of Jesus revolutionary message uncovered by Dr. Hendricks in his excellent book are "treat the people's needs as holy," "give a voice to the voiceless" and "expose the workings of oppression" or to challenge the established order of things. The Black Jesuses that are the historical Jesus' modern ethnic brethren and who are mentioned in this article are further united with him in a brotherhood of shared values and revolutionary principles governing the work they have labored to do among Black people in America. These are the principles that I find particularly shared between Jesus and the Honorable Minister Louis Farrakhan.

In the final analysis, the Black community cannot afford to just be praisers of Jesus without learning the important lessons in the history of Jesus and its parallels to Black history in America. But how can our community learn these lessons if our community does not at the same time give birth to those who are willing to teach and share wisdom with their people? How many of us will determine that within our own circles of familiarity and influence that we will become a Jesus and become revolutionary to the ignorance and self-destruction that has become the status quo of Black life in America today. I pray that if you found value in this series of articles that you will share it with someone you love.

From Fard to Farrakhan: America's Punishment of Messianic Dissidents

Allah loves not the public utterance of hurtful speech, except by one who has been wronged. And Allah is ever Hearing, Knowing.

--Holy Qur'an 4: 148 (M.M. Ali Translation)

Can wicked rulers be allied with you, those who frame injustice by statute?

--Psalms 94:20(ESV)

"I confidently trust that the American people will prove themselves ... too wise not to detect the false pride or the dangerous ambitions or the selfish schemes which so often hide themselves under that deceptive cry of mock patriotism: 'Our country, right or wrong!' They will not fail to recognize that our dignity, our free institutions and the peace and welfare of this and coming generations of Americans will be secure only as we cling to the watchword of *true* patriotism: 'Our country—when right to be kept right; when wrong to be put right.'"

—Schurz, "The Policy of Imperialism," *Speeches, Correspondence and Political Papers of Carl Schurz*, vol. 6, pp. 119–20 (1913)

Congress shall make no law respecting an establishment of religion, or prohibiting the free exercise thereof; or abridging the freedom of speech, or of the press; or the right of the people peaceably to assemble, and to petition the Government for a redress of grievances.

—First Amendment, U.S. Constitution

Narrated by Abu Sa'id al-Khudri: The Prophet (pbuh) said: The best fighting (jihad) in the path of Allah is (to speak) a word of justice to an oppressive ruler.

—Hadith of Prophet Muhammad (pbuh) Abu Dawud Collection Book 32, Hadith Number 4330

The Honorable Elijah Muhammad taught that his teacher, Master Fard Muhammad began coming in and out of America in the year 1910. He was studying the American social, political, religious and economic landscape. Among the many things he did included him living with a Caucasian family for a while as well as studying at the University of Southern California. He would travel in and out of America for 20 years before the most important aspect of His work would commence in "Black Bottom" Detroit, Michigan. In Detroit, he began to teach Black people Islam with what many have described as a strange methodology. In September 1931, he met Elijah Poole, who became the Honorable Elijah Muhammad, and began to teach him night and day for 3 years and 4 months. This master-student relationship would prove to be of extreme importance as it was the beginnings of the most influential religious group anywhere in America, the Nation of Islam.

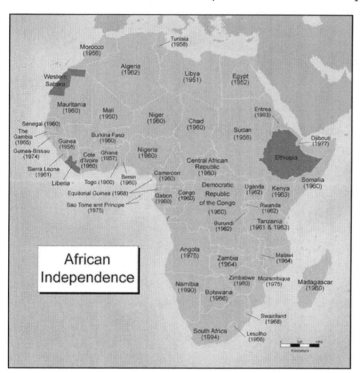

There has not been a lot of attention on the NOI's positive influence in the areas of free speech and dissent. But the Nation of Islam founder, in addition to establishing a religious tradition simultaneously produced a very significant protest movement. Within the Nation of Islam, it is believed that Master Fard

Muhammad is the source of what Lothrop Stoddard called "the rising tide of color" which moved throughout Africa and the world to stimulate and inspire the darker races to revolt against the evils of European Colonialism. Muslims believe this because of what has been taught about the world travels of Master Fard Muhammad,

> "He told me that he had traveled the world over and that he had visited North America for 20 years before making himself known to us, his people whom he came for. He had visited the Isles of the Pacific, Japan and China, Canada, Alaska, The North Pole, India, Pakistan, All of the Near East and Africa... He visited every inhabited place on the earth..." (Hon. Elijah Muhammad, Pittsburgh Courier 7, 20, 1957)

The aftermath of Fard's travels is an amazing season in the 20th Century where former European colonies, in Africa and elsewhere, fought to gain their freedom. Even the historic Bandung Conference of 1955, 400 years from the beginning of the Black American sojourn in slavery, bears the imprint of Fard's thinking. The Bandung Conference reflected a dominant theme of Nation of Islam teaching that articulates that the time has arrived in world history for the Black nation, including all the darker races of man, to rise up, unite, and throw off the yoke of European tyranny and oppression; this was a global conference where no white European countries were permitted.

There is much to be written and taught about the global impact of the mysterious man from Mecca-Master Wali Fard Muhammad. Within the Nation of Islam, the revolutionary aftermath of his world travels fits within the eschatological description of the Bible's Habakkuk chapter 3. Habakkuk 3 paints a picture of a revolutionary theophany, where the God of the enslaved Children of Israel visits them and punishes their enemies with plagues, and disaster.

Inside of America Master Fard Muhammad's mission influenced many from all races to become criers, warners and protestors of America's unjust foreign wars and corrosive domestic racism. His agitation of the poor masses angered local and federal authorities, and many who were inspired by Master Fard Muhammad's teaching were arrested and imprisoned for simply exercising the constitutionally guaranteed right to dissent or disagree with the U.S. government. Author Ernest Allen Jr. documents the history of messianic dissent among Blacks in America in his report entitled *When Japan Was Champion of The Darker Races: Satokata Takahashi and The Flowering of Black Messianic Nationalism.* An excerpt from Allen's report includes:

"In late September 1942, in a series of highly publicized raids, federal agents in Chicago arrested eighty-five African Americans. Three women and nine men were charged with sedition; the remainder were accused of draft evasion. Indicted on the former charge(sedition) were Elijah Muhammad, Linn Karriem, and Pauline Bahar of the Allah Temple of Islam [ATOI]; Mittie Maud Lena Gordon, Sean Jones, William Gordon, and David J. Logan of the Peace Movement of Ethiopia [PME]; Charles Newby (aka Father Divine Haasan) of the Colored American National Organization [CANO]; Stokely Delmar Hart, James Graves, and Annabelle Moore of the Brotherhood of Liberty for the Black People of America [BLBPA], and Frederick H. Hammurabi Robb of the Century Service Exchange."

Several days earlier, five members of the Ethiopian Pacific Movement [EPM] -- Robert O. Jordan (aka Leonard Robert Jordan), James Thornhill, Lester Holness, the Rev. Ralph Green Best, and Joseph Hartrey, an Irishman -- were indicted in New York City on the more serious charges. Less raucously, back in May, Ministers David X (aka David Jones and David Duvon) and Sultan Muhammad of the ATOI's Washington and Milwaukee temples, respectively, were detained on charges of sedition as well. In October, the head of the International Reassemble of the Church of Freedom League, Inc. [IRCFL], the Rev. Ethelbert A. Broaster, was arrested in New Orleans.) The following January, a second round of indictments occurred in East St. Louis, where Bishop David D. Erwin and General Lee Butler, two leaders of the Pacific Movement of the Eastern World [PMEW], were also charged with crimes against the State. In Newark, seven members of the House of Israel [HOI] --Brother Rueben Israel (aka Askew Thomas), Alfred Woods, Isaiah Cald, Robert Moses, Oscar Rumlin, Dawsey Johnson, and Jeremiah Ardis -- were seized as draft evaders.

This history that surrounds World War II is connected to today's events in several ways. First of all, laws such as the Espionage Act of 1917 and the Selective Training and Service Act of 1940 were used to imprison these courageous patriots that had emerged from the oppressed masses. Today we have the Patriot Act and the National Defense Authorization Act in place to legalize the same kind of wicked round up of Black Messianic Dissidents. Secondly the main ingredients of the World War II protest movement among Blacks was the message and influence of Master Fard Muhammad being carried by the Honorable Elijah Muhammad. He taught that the Japanese were the Brown brothers of the Black man of Africa and America. Today the main ingredient is the message and teaching of Master Fard Muhammad via the world-wide ministry of the Honorable Minister Louis Farrakhan. Minister Farrakhan teaches that we are the brothers of the Muslim world and must not join in with the western powers to kill our Muslim brothers.

But those are social and political connections. There is also a religious and spiritual connection. Bruce Ritter writes in his article 7 Signs of A Falling Nation that

> "In an interview with the Financial Times, U.S. Comptroller General David Walker stated that the United States government "is on a 'burning platform' of unsustainable policies and practices with fiscal deficits, chronic healthcare under funding, immigration, and overseas military commitments threatening a crisis if action is not taken soon..."

The article added,

> "Mr. Walker warned that there were 'striking similarities' between America's current situation and the factors that brought down

285

Rome, including 'declining moral values and political civility at home, an over-confident and over-extended military in foreign lands and fiscal irresponsibility by central government."

General Walker's comparison of America to Ancient Rome is in agreement with author Cullen Murphy who wrote the book *The New Rome: The Fall of an Empire and the Fate of America.* In his book Murphy describes how Rome's imprint affected the known world in colossal ways as it exported its military, culture, art, architecture, clothes, and food. Murphy adds that Roman law and Roman moral values powerfully influenced and dominated the people under its sphere. This is also true of America's global influence and power.

The comparison of America to ancient Rome is important because the Bible's Messiah, Jesus, lived under Roman authority. And while religion has sought to limit Jesus' value to a role as the *"saviour from sin,"* many modern scholars like Dr. Obery T. Hendricks are drawn to Jesus the Revolutionary and thusly see him as a natural inspiration to modern social and political dissidents. Hendricks says Jesus the Revolutionary epitomizes and embodies messianic or God conscious dissent. Hendricks identifies some of the strategies of Jesus the Revolutionary by noting that *Jesus treated the people's needs as holy; Jesus also called the demons out by name; Jesus exposed the workings of Satan, and he gave a voice to the voiceless.*

Therefore, American dissent must necessarily be of the messianic type because America's domination of the world results from her mastery of the trans-Atlantic slave trade. This commerce in Black bodies netted for America centuries of free labor and caused her to leap frog older nation-states very quickly en route to becoming the leading world superpower. Again, the messianic connection lies in America's reliance on slavery and the fact the same scenario of nations depending on slavery produced the Biblical Messiah to end it and call into judgment the slave holding nation that upheld it.

The question now is will America continue her punishment of Black Messianic Dissidents. Will she continue to frame mischief by means of law? Is Farrakhan in the cross-hairs? Are his followers to be imprisoned for supporting him in his criticism of America's unjust wars against the Muslim world? I guess for now we will have to wait and see.

10 Reasons to Support Minister Farrakhan's Presence On College Campuses

1. **Minister Farrakhan's Message of Self-Reliance is perfect for Black college students.** The *Chronicle of Higher Education* published an article, written by Ohio University professor of economics Richard Vedder, titled "Why Did 17 Million Students Go to College?" In this article Vedder documented all the Americans with high-level-education degrees that are either not working in their field or not working at all. *"Over 317,000 waiters and waitresses have college degrees (over 8,000 of them have doctoral or professional degrees), along with over 80,000 bartenders, and over 18,000 parking lot attendants. All told, some 17,000,000 Americans with college degrees are doing jobs that the BLS [Bureau of Labor Statistics] says require less than the skill levels associated with a bachelor's degree."* At least 5,057 PhDs are working as janitors. The Honorable Minister Louis Farrakhan's message is the antidote to this problem of students graduating from school and being unable to get a job commensurate with their skills, talents, abilities and education. Minister Farrakhan has long taught what a staple of NOI teachings is—that Black students should get an education that enables them to go into business, become entrepreneurs and be in a position to employ our own people. Jews do this all the time and they are successful.

2. **Minister Farrakhan teaches students to avoid the pitfalls of student loan debt. The Minister spoke recently at UC Berkeley, where students graduate with an average debt of $16,056, according to a recent NBC article written by Ayesha Minhaj.** The Honorable Minister Louis Farrakhan teaches that debt is slavery. The Nation of Islam has always taught Black people that we should be thrifty and spend and invest our money wisely. The Minister's message to the students will guide them into fields that will give them the greatest ROI or return on their investment of time, money and effort.

3. **The ban against Minister Farrakhan on college campuses is a weapon in the ongoing economic, political and social crucifixion of strong Black leadership.** *The Secret Relationship Between Blacks and Jews, Volume 2*, lists many who were victims of Jewish castigation and consequent economic retaliation only because they dared to critique Jewish behavior *and* venture into the arena of economic independence. (Malcolm X, Martin Luther King, Booker T. Washington, Oprah Winfrey, Julian Bond and Bishop Desmond Tutu et al have all been labeled at some point in their careers as "anti-Semitic.")

   The paternalistic Jewish strategy for Black self-help—known as "non-economic liberalism"—was developed by the Jewish president and founder of the NAACP, Joel Spingarn. Spingarn and his Jewish and Gentile cohorts steered Blacks far away from the world of commerce and trade and banking and finance, even though, according to the *Universal Jewish Encyclopedia*, Jews "were pioneers in the primary stages of capitalist development and therefore held a dominant position in these cultural economic functions which may be called the nervous system of capitalist economy. Banking, the stock market, export and import fall within this classification." Joel Spingarn nonetheless advised W.E.B. Dubois and the NAACP to adopt the lame-duck strategy of "non-economic liberalism." This pointed avoidance of economics has made all our efforts in the fields of politics, education and law futile, because our activities lacked a collective economic component.

4. **Zionist criticism of Minister Farrakhan is unjustified. Raising the Minister's "words" to the level of "deeds" is an illogical fallacy.** It is especially irrational when you consider that Farrakhan's words have never harmed a Jewish man, woman or child. On the contrary, Jewish views of Blacks have had harmful effects all throughout history. For instance, the so-called Curse of Ham—a Jewish Talmudic invention—alleges all Blacks and Africans have been cursed Black by the God of Abraham. This myth permitted the Trans-Atlantic Slave Trade to be carried on with religious zeal and fervor. And the Jews were sophisticated masters in this trade in Black human cargo. According to Dr. Arnold Wiznitzer, Jews *"dominated the slave trade.... The buyers*

who appeared at the auctions were almost always Jews, and because of this lack of competitors they could buy slaves at low prices." Slave trading, asserts Wiesenthal Center scholar Dr. Harold Brackman, "became a *'Jewish' mercantile specialty.*" The *Jewish Encyclopedia* adds that "Jewish commercial activity" included a "monopoly of the slave trade." In fact, a Jewish shipper had a monopoly on trade to the notorious slave dungeon at Gorée Island—the Auschwitz of the Black Holocaust. Dr. Rabbi Bertram Korn unequivocally stated: *"It would seem to be realistic to conclude that any Jew who could afford to own slaves and had need for their services would do so.... Jews participated in every aspect and process of the exploitation of the defenseless blacks."*

5. **Blacks must be encouraged to unite as Jews and other ethnic groups in America have done.** Minister Farrakhan encourages cooperation, brotherhood and operational unity in his message to the students. The idea of unity is a strong theme in the religion of Islam. Eugenicist and racist Lothrop Stoddard, quoting British naval officer Charles Elliott, wrote in *The Rising Tide of Color Against White World Supremacy* that Islam "can still give [the Black Africans] ... a unity of which they are otherwise incapable."

6. **Black youth of today are largely viewed as incorrigible. The source of influence for today's youth comes primarily from the Hip-Hop culture.** And it is Minister Farrakhan who is the godfather of the Hip-Hop culture, as his 10-year New York ministry helped birth the popular youth culture in the Bronx in 1972. Hip-Hop bears the imprint of Minister Farrakhan, for it is a hybrid art form combining spoken word, musical accompaniment and performance art. Minister Farrakhan's public life reveals a devotion to the spoken word of truth and a musical virtuosity, as demonstrated by his mastery of the violin and concert performance. His connection to the Hip-Hop community automatically grants him entry to our youth's hearts and minds.

7. **Jewish Groups attack Farrakhan but the Nation of Islam teachings are laced with concepts familiar and agreeable to Jews.** The Nation

of Islam agrees with Jews that education, economic autonomy, marriage and family, ethnic loyalty, knowledge sharing and a disciplined personal life make communities strong and constitute the path to power. The Minister's message, therefore, if internalized by the students, becomes an equalizing force propelling the Black students from ignominy and poverty to honor and abundance, thus enabling them to share company with Jews and other members of the human family that are successful— not only in business, but in all areas of life.

8. **Minister Farrakhan's spirit of revolutionary defiance is necessarily contagious.** Jesus, Muhammad, Martin Luther King Jr., Marcus Garvey and the great "change agents" of history never compromised truth and principle to avoid controversy. They all were known for "speaking truth to power." If the students internalize this spirit, they will become what the Black people of America need of a "new intelligentsia" that is passionate, principled, purified and prepared to lead our people toward a full and complete freedom.

9. **There is a need for an Anti-War Movement among Black Students.** Black, Latino and poor White youth make up the U. S. armed forces. They will be the casualties in America's projected war with Iran. America's foreign policies are influenced by the greedy multi-national corporations whose desire is to control and capitalize on the precious natural resources of other countries. These are the same corporations that enjoy close relationships with the banks that become rich through student-loan debt. It is no accident that often the only opportunity for forgiveness of student loan debt comes in the guise of a military offer to repay student loans if they join the armed forces. The voice of Minister Farrakhan, like that of his teacher the Honorable Elijah Muhammad, warns the students not to join the U.S. government's war effort in the Muslim world. Minister Farrakhan condemns America's long history of using the poor to fight the wars of the rich, and his message to the students is that they should be conscientious objectors.

10. **Minister Farrakhan awakens the students to their divine destiny.**
    Every generation must make its mark on history. Black youth are the
    descendants of the Africans brought to America to be made slaves. That
    experience of enslavement has a scriptural and religious parallel: the
    Biblical and Quranic narratives of the enslavement of the Children of
    Israel. According to both Scriptures, it was the youth of the wandering
    Children of Israel who forged the way for their entire people to inhabit
    God's Promised Land. It was the youth, led by Joshua and Caleb, who
    were unafraid of and conquered the "giants" in that land and were
    consequently dubbed the "Joshua Generation." Minister Farrakhan
    teaches that Black youth are indeed the Joshua Generation for our
    people. His message is the inspirational food that Black youth need to
    see themselves as this new generation of fearless leaders.

Is Help for Blacks, Hurt for Jews?
The Anti-Black world-view of Neil Steinberg

On September 30 Neil Steinberg released the latest propaganda attack on the Honorable Minister Louis Farrakhan and the Nation of Islam. His poisonous and uninformed article has created a teachable moment. I don't know if Steinberg is willing to learn, but I am definitely willing to teach.

His attack is strategically timed to be distributed in the immediate aftermath of Minister Farrakhan's wonderfully successful tour of New York City for the promotion of peace and an end to gun violence. Black people should, by now, begin to notice that whenever strong and uncompromising voices of Black self-help and determination begin to make progress, Zionist Jewish forces emerge to attack them. Any Black person that reads his rants against Minister Farrakhan must understand the lens through which Steinberg views the Minister and all Black people, for that matter.

Steinberg's lens is apparently the Babylonian Talmud, which is a commentary on the Torah (Old Testament) written by early Jewish Rabbis. The Talmud says that Blacks are cursed by God to be servants to Jews and that Blacks are deemed to only have value as servants of Jews. Dr. Harold Brackman of the Simon Wiesenthal Center wrote in his doctoral dissertation that Jewish Rabbis created the myth of the Curse of Ham,

> "There is no denying that the Babylonian Talmud was the first source to read a Negrophobic content into the [Noahic] episode by stressing Canaan's fraternal connection with Cush... The more important version of the myth, however, ingeniously ties in the origins of blackness — and of other, real and imagined Negroid traits — with Noah's Curse itself."

This Anti-Black worldview has been on display as recently as 2005, when the head of the Shas's Council of Torah Sages in Israel, Rabbi Ovadia Yosef, said that God sent Hurricane Katrina to destroy New Orleans because Blacks live there and were not studying enough Torah!

Moses Maimonides, who is called by the *Encyclopedia of the Jewish Religion* "the symbol of the pure and orthodox faith," wrote in his *Guide to the Perplexed*:

> "... the Negroes found in the remote South, and those who resemble them from among them that are with us in these climes. The status of those is like that of irrational animals. To my mind they do not have the rank of men, but have among the beings a rank lower than the rank of man but higher than the rank of apes. For they have the external shape and lineaments of a man and a faculty of discernment that is superior to that of the apes."

This is the lens through which Neil Steinberg views Black people. This is what Minister Farrakhan and all strong Black leaders in our history have had to fight. These Anti-Black ideas have garnered wide acceptance even within the ranks of our own people. The poetess Phyllis Wheatley wrote of her color as being a *"diabolic dye."* The slave Jupiter Hammond is an example of the great harm the Hamitic myth has had upon the minds of Black slaves. He rebuked Blacks who earnestly desired freedom with these words:

> "It may seem hard for us if we think our masters wrong in holding us slaves to obey in all things, but who of us dare dispute with God! He has commanded us to obey, and we ought to do it cheerfully and freely.... for my own part I do not wish to be free; for many of us who are grown up slaves have always had masters to take care of themselves; and it may be for our own comfort to remain as we are."

So, if Blacks are cursed with Blackness and if Black people's only purpose in life is to be a servant to the Jews, then any and all persons who seek to secure for Black people a different and more ennobled destiny must be attacked. Therefore, Steinberg and his ilk are busy demonizing the Honorable Marcus Mosiah Garvey and the Honorable Minister Louis Farrakhan. Minister Farrakhan and Marcus Garvey are exponents of what is called Black Nationalism. And it is really Black Nationalism that Steinberg wants to equate with anti-Semitism.

But what is Black Nationalism? Nationalism, according to Dr. Molefi Kete Asante, "is a relationship among people with a common heritage and with common expectations. Land acquisition is merely the ultimate stage of nationalism. The consummation and crystallization of our aspirations into an organic and systemic instrument for emancipatory politics is the first objective of systematic nationalism. This process is accomplished through historically and culturally determined actions for national expression. It contradicts attempts at national oppression through the exploitative uses of culture, science, religion, and economics. Emancipatory politics is the keystone of nationalistic struggle. It liberates the mind from the duality of marginal existence. Nationalists are therefore capable of functioning in any situation. What is necessary, absolutely necessary, is an attachment to the national idea... The correctness of systematic nationalism stems from its assault on the twin evils of race and class exploitation. This, however, is not its philosophical grounding; it is rather its activist character."

I don't know any Black person that wouldn't want this. In fact, I don't know any Jewish person that would disagree with such an ideology. Black Nationalism actually mirrors what Jews have done to secure themselves. They have land, dual citizenship with Israel, economic strength and its resulting political strength. Jews are respected and admired for their economic strength, unity, culture and values concerning education and family life. The Black Nationalist view is that Black people deserve the same, yet our Jewish friends never steered us in that direction.

Joel Spingarn and the Jewish leaders of the NAACP directed Blacks to do the very opposite of what Jews do to become successful in society. So, the NAACP and most in the Civil Rights Movement adopted the philosophy Spingarn termed "non-economic liberalism"—which encouraged and fostered a beggar's mentality in Blacks. It suggested that what Blacks desired and deserved of justice, equality and an overall better quality of life could only be achieved through picketing, marching and begging the government. This was never the model that Jews themselves employed. They developed strength through unity, self-love, entrepreneurship, and the establishment of Jewish enclaves all over America.

These are the tenets that Brother Marcus Garvey, the Honorable Elijah Muhammad and Minister Farrakhan have promoted for Black people.

Steinberg asked, "Where has Minister Farrakhan led his Nation?" I ask Mr. Steinberg, Where have Jews led Blacks? If the Jews' involvement was so beneficial to the Black struggle, why isn't the Black condition equal to the Jewish condition? Why don't we hear of the plight of the Jewish male like there is a plight of the Black male? Why is there no Jew-on-Jew crime and violence like there is a Black-on-Black crime problem? I have yet to hear of a Jewish HIV epidemic like the Black HIV epidemic statistics trumpet. And the prison industrial complex appears to have no adverse effects on the Jewish community. It is clear that Jewish paternalism concerning Black issues is for the purpose of sabotage and not salvation. It is clear that Blacks have not been given the secret to the Jewish Phenomenon of success within American society.

Instead, Steinberg and the Zionist lobby are content to fight any strong and courageous Black person who seeks to help Black people out of the miserable condition of slavery, suffering and death. *The Secret Relationship between Blacks and Jews, Volume 2,* contains a shocking list of Blacks that have at various times in their careers been labeled anti-Semites. Their only crime was advocating a position of Black self-help, an act viewed by Jews as being hurtful to Jewish interests.

Booker T. Washington	W.E.B. DuBois
Marcus Garvey	Martin L. King Jr.
Malcolm X	Hon. Elijah Muhammad
Pres. Nelson Mandela	Bishop Desmond Tutu
Julian Bond	Kwame Ture
Andrew Young	Kweisi Mfume
Rev. Al Sharpton	Rev. Jesse Jackson
Rev. Joseph Lowery	J.A. Rogers
James Baldwin	Richard Wright
Julius Lester	Alice Walker
Michael Jackson	Spike Lee
Ice Cube	Arsenio Hall

Muhammad Ali	Public Enemy
Oprah Winfrey	John Hope Franklin

What Steinberg fears is the wide acceptance of the Honorable Minister Louis Farrakhan by the masses of Black people. He had hoped that the Black masses had bought in to the notion of a "post-racial" America. He had expected that the election of a Black President of the United States of America would extinguish the light of Black people's desire for freedom, justice and equality. Steinberg's dream is that the Black community remains deprived of self-determination, unity and economic power. What Steinberg really wanted to write was how dumbfounded he is over the tenacity, durability and wide reach of the leadership of Minister Farrakhan. For it is the leadership of Minister Farrakhan that the masses of Black people now see as a torchlight, amid an ever-increasing darkness inside America.

Did Minister Louis Farrakhan Give Birth to Hip-Hop?

"Environment shapes heredity." Hon. Elijah Muhammad

The Scholars on the Origin of Rap/Hip Hop Music

Rap music has had a profound impact on the African American community in the United States. Its greatest significance, to my mind, derives from the fact that it has fostered a profound nationalism in the youth of Black America. Arguably, hip-hop has become a conduit for African American culture to a greater extent than even jazz. Where the latter could, through its polyrhythmic syncopations, embrace both the nuances and jagged edges of the collective Black experience, it could not self-consciously energize the nationalist ethos in quite the way the more lyrically focused hip-hop does.

Hip-hop, or rap music, began in the early 1970s. The first synthesis of self-conscious poetry and music can be traced, most directly, to the Black Nationalist Last Poets. Their albums The Last Poets, Chastisement, This is Madness, and others have become classics in the African American community. When one member who separated from the group, with the stage name "Lightning Rod," used a musical score provided by Kool & The Gang as a backdrop to his lyrical narrative of a day in the life of two hustlers, he had no idea he was laying the basis for an entirely new musical genre. This album, Hustler's Convention, was a mainstay in the album collection of a South Bronx DJ named Kool Herc. Almost to a person, it is agreed that hip-hop began with Kool Herc.
–Errol A. Henderson, Black Nationalism and Rap Music

As the limitations of electoral politics became glaringly and painfully apparent to the post-civil rights generation, rap artists idolized the words and works of political personalities such as Marcus Garvey, Malcolm X, and Louis Farrakhan, men whose uncompromising public personae and urban, poor/working-class roots stood as an example to those young black men whose status was undermined in the postindustrial capitalist economy. "God knows, when I heard Farrakhan, I had never heard a black man talk like that. It blew my mind, absolutely blew my mind," Hip Hop journalist/activist Kevin Powell recalled of his introduction to Farrakhan during the mid-1980s. "It was

298

intoxicating, as intoxicating as crack was for a lot of people in our community in the '80s."
-Charise Cheney, "Revolutionary Generation": (En) gendering the Golden Age of Rap Nationalism

The Nation of Islam is generally acknowledged as having a deep influence on rap music. Rappers such as Poor Righteous Teachers, King Sun, Brand Nubian, Movement Ex, and Public Enemy, frequently quote and draw inspiration from the Honorable Elijah Muhammad (founder of the Nation of Islam), Malcolm X, and Minister Louis Farrakhan. The famed boxer, Muhammad Ali, was also an early rapper.
-Catherine Tabb Powell, Rap Music: An Education with a Beat from the Street

Musician Grandmaster Flash defined hip hop as "the only genre of music that allows us to talk about almost anything. Musically, it allows us to sample and play and create poetry to the beat of the music. It's highly controversial, but that's the way the game is." Hip hop culture began in the 1970s in the Bronx, N.Y., among African-American, Latino, and Caribbean youth who created intercultural crews ("new kinds of families") of MCs/rappers, disc jockeys, break dancers, and graffiti artists whose art and style expressed resistance to postindustrial conditions and the destruction of jobs, affordable housing, and support systems in working-class black and Latino neighborhoods at the beginning of the Ronald Reagan-George H.W. Bush era.
-Professor Richard Brent Turner, The Influence of Malcolm X and Martin Luther King Jr. on Hip Hop

The real significance of hip-hop is not, however related to those rappers (amoral and obscene), but rather to the religio-politically oriented "message rap" artists, who have steadily found success since the mid-1980s.... The Hip-Hop movement's role in popularizing the message of Black militant Islam cannot be overestimated. What reggae was to Rastafarianism in the 70's... Hip Hop is to the spread of Black Islam in the 80's and 90's.... Expressing thanks and support for the Nation of Islam and Louis Farrakhan has become almost standard practice on the rap albums, and long quotations from NOI literature are often included in the lyrics.

-Professor Mattias Gardell, In The Name of Elijah Muhammad Louis Farrakhan and The Nation of Islam

Connecting The Dots on Minister Farrakhan's Presence At Hip Hop's Genesis

Hip Hop Born in New York circa 1972- All scholars and students of Hip Hop history agree that this musical art form began in the early 1970s in New York City. The Honorable Minister Louis Farrakhan was then the Minister of Temple No.7 in New York. His influence was transmitted to all of the Black citizens of New York via his 5,000 followers and his 18 satellite Temples of Islam. The Minister was also being heard on the radio 6 times per week. Such a wide and far reaching presence easily made him one of the most influential forces in all of New York City. This is important when you consider that environment shapes heredity. Minister Farrakhan's ministry was saturating the collective consciousness of Black and Hispanic New Yorkers with the revolutionary message found within the teachings of the Most Honorable Elijah Muhammad.

The Presence of Caribbean DJs help start the music- New York has long been a haven for Caribbean immigrants. Minister Farrakhan is connected to the Caribbean peoples through his parentage; his mother being from the Island of Nevis and his father being from Jamaica. The Minister has spoken often in the Islands and received warmly as a native son and head of state.

Hip Hop as hybrid of spoken word and performance art- Hip Hop is a unique and attractive art form. It is a hybrid or mixture of spoken word, performance art and musicianship. In this way, it bears the definite imprint of the Farrakhan influence. For it is Minister Farrakhan's professional career where he has demonstrated mastery in both spoken word-as the towering figure known quite simply as The Minister- and musicianship-where he has performed and still plays classical violin. Hip Hop is Minister Farrakhan's baby. Rappers to this day pay homage to him and see him as the peacemaker and strong man for Black people.

Hip Hop As Music With A Message-

As Professor Mattias Gardell points out Hip Hop begins as 'message rap.' Throughout the history of hip hop artists have written lyrics to include urban social commentary, revolutionary manifestos and homage to the giants of the Black liberation struggle. This characteristic of the Hip-Hop culture is directly reflective of the ministry of the Honorable Minister Louis Farrakhan. Public Enemy's Chuck D once wrote "Farrakhan's a prophet that I think you ought to listen to, what he can say to you, what you ought to do, is follow for now..." Hip Hop's revolutionary, truth to power quality is more evidence of the influential role of Minister Louis Farrakhan. His mighty ministry in New York City during the 1970's created a unique climate in New York where cultural, educational and artistic trends were born. To that end we consider the Honorable Minister Louis Farrakhan the Godfather of the Hip Hop cultural phenomenon.

God Gives The Minister A Vision of Things To Come
Proof of a Vision: The Honorable Minister Louis Farrakhan's MESSAGE from Elijah By Tingba Muhammad, NOI Research Group

The vision-like experience that The Honorable Minister Louis Farrakhan had in

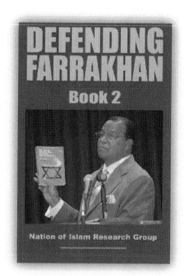

1985 is part of the instructional fabric of the Nation of Islam. Now there is conclusive supporting data discovered by the NOI Research Group that establish the factual basis for The Minister's spiritual experience. This body of data shows a flurry of secret diplomatic and military activity at the moments in time in which The Minister says his vision-like experience occurred. This evidence is drawn from, among other sources, now-declassified documents, new investigative journalism, White House records, and diary entries of the President of the United States. There is even a photograph that has been found of the very meeting in question.

Minister Farrakhan describes the event as a "more than a vision experience" and the fullness of that seminal event was catalogued in Mother Tynetta Muhammad's insightful book *The Comer by Night* and in a series of articles authored by Bro. Jabril Muhammad that appeared in the *Final Call* newspaper. Our research will address the portion of Min. Farrakhan's September 17, 1985, experience that is quoted below:

> "In this vision...Elijah Muhammad spoke to me these words: 'President Reagan has met with his joint chiefs of staff to plan a war. I want you to hold a press conference and make known their plans. And tell them that you got it from me, Elijah Muhammad, on The Wheel.'..."

The reference to *The Wheel* is highly significant in the Teachings of the Nation of Islam in that it refers to the "wheel-shaped plane known as the Mother of (all) Planes"— "a masterpiece of mechanics"—a human-built plane spanning "a half-mile by a half-mile." Launched in 1929, it was built by the man known to believers as Allah in Person, Master Fard Muhammad, the long-awaited "Messiah" of the Christians and the "Mahdi" of the Muslims. This awe-inspiring "Mother Plane" houses 1,500 smaller "baby planes," and whereas the Nation of Islam has clearly identified these aircraft, when they are seen by the general public they are referred to as UFOs. The Bible refers to these vehicles in its Book of Ezekiel (1:16) and in Exodus (13:21) as "the wheel(s)" and "a cloud by day and a pillar of fire by night."

According to the Hon. Elijah Muhammad through his Representative Minister Farrakhan, The Wheel is "a weapon that all of the technology of the Western White world can't fathom," whose purpose is to destroy the present world. So, the appearance of Elijah on that Wheel in Minister Farrakhan's vision carries a great significance—and not just for Nation of Islam members and believers. This Wheel would have intrigued Ronald Reagan himself, for in 1974 he claimed to have had an encounter with a UFO while he was still governor of California. A week later he described the event to Norman C. Miller, then Washington bureau chief for the *Wall Street Journal*:

> "I was in a plane last week when I looked out the window and saw this white light. It was zigzagging around. I went up to the pilot and said, 'Have you seen anything like that before?' He was shocked and said, 'Nope.' And I said to him: 'Let's follow it!' We followed it for several minutes. It was a bright white light. We followed it to Bakersfield, and all of a sudden to our utter amazement it went straight up into the heavens. When we got off the plane, I told Nancy all about it."

The pilot of Governor Reagan's plane, retired U.S. Air Force Colonel Bill Paynter, backed up Reagan's version of the incident with the UFO:

> "It appeared to be several hundred yards away. It was a fairly steady light until it began to accelerate, then it appeared to elongate. The light took off.... The UFO went from a normal cruise speed to a

fantastic speed instantly.... We didn't file a report on the object because for a long time they considered you a nut if you saw a UFO."

Reagan's deep fascination with this issue is demonstrated at various points in his life and so the emphatic point made by The Messenger— *"And tell them that you got it from me, Elijah Muhammad, on The Wheel"*—may have been meant specifically for Reagan to hear. And Reagan's "close encounter" was carefully concealed by the media and his handlers until after he left the White House, so Minister Farrakhan *could not have known about Reagan's experience with The Wheel* through any conventional means.

During a press conference, he held in February of 1986, it dawned on The Minister that his vision of the Reagan-planned war was in fact targeting the North African nation of Libya and its leader, Col. Muammar Gadhafi. Two months later, on April 16, 1986, Pres. Reagan did indeed attack Libya—almost seven months to the day from the Minister's September 17th experience.

What actually was happening in the Reagan White House and in the United States military during those critical months in time that correspond to The Minister's profound experience on The Wheel?

First let us consider the strategic role of Libya in world affairs that made it a target of the world's most powerful nation. It must here be remembered that Reagan was described as being "obsessed" with Libya and its leader throughout his presidency (1981–1989). Not only was Col. Gadhafi sitting on massive strategic oil reserves, but he was seeking to unite all Arab, Muslim, and African oil states, and, more troubling, he was governing a large part of Chad, which is a major producer of uranium. Gadhafi's Soviet-assisted vision for the region was diametrically opposed to the colonization schemes of the West and its Israeli representatives. And Reagan's obsession had been an American obsession from the nation's very beginning. Tripoli was the center of the first covert operation in American history—under Pres. Thomas Jefferson in 1804—and it was now the concern of the Reaganites.

The Reagan administration had been aware and approving of a 1984 assassination attempt against Gadhafi by French agents that failed. And secretly, the United States was engaged with Israel and its Arab client states in a propaganda operation that not only planted false stories in the media to link Libya with *any* "terrorist" act—bombings, kidnappings, hijackings, assassinations, etc.—but also invented the "evidence" that "implicated" Libya. Records now show that operatives of the Central Intelligence Agency (CIA) and the Israeli Mossad performed terrorist acts and blamed Libya. This, the Reaganites hoped, would turn Col. Gadhafi into a pariah, which would justify his violent removal.

In the months leading up to Minister Farrakhan's experience, evidence shows a series of political crises that foreshadowed the early September 1985 meetings of high-level military officials in the Reagan administration.

Though Reagan's published diary was clearly edited to be made compatible with official American propaganda, he demonstrates "concern" over Libya in several pre-September entries. On June 27, 1985, Reagan mentions that *"Gadhafi is talking to about a joint terrorist war against us."* On July 3: *"We are also discussing Iran & Syria a plan to take care of the Libya situation—including bombing some known terrorist training centers."* Records of the National Security Council (the body responsible for national security issues) almost mirror Reagan's diary. They similarly show that Libya was the topic of their meetings on June 25th and July 3rd. In a July 9 speech, Pres. Reagan used his most aggressive rhetoric against "a confederation of terrorist states" he identified as Nicaragua, Libya, North Korea, Cuba, and Iran. They were, he said, "the strangest collection of misfits, Looney Tunes and squalid criminals since the advent of the Third Reich"—a malicious reference designed for Israeli ears.

Then, according to journalist Bob Woodward, an emergency meeting was called in mid-July when state department officials overseas were secretly flown home to—in their words— "stop the madmen in the White House" who wanted an immediate war against Libya. For the moment, they were successful.

Between July and September of 1985 plans were developed for a joint US–Egyptian military offensive against Libya, but it was rejected only because Egypt's Pres. Mubarak did not trust the United States. The plan was dubbed "Operation

Flower," with its two components called "Operation Tulip" and "Operation Rose." Both were covert CIA operations, with "Tulip" using Libyan exiles to overthrow Gadhafi in a *coup d'état*, and "Rose" being a joint U.S.–Egyptian military campaign against the Libyan government. On September 1st, units of the Libyan military did in fact try to overthrow Gadhafi, but the rebellion was crushed and 43 senior officers were arrested.

The Meetings

Minister Farrakhan's September 17th vision referred to meeting(s) of the Joint Chiefs of Staff (JCS) earlier that month. Based on the best evidence, the secret meeting(s) probably occurred on September 3rd, two days after the failed *coup d'état* in Libya, and then again on September 9th during a secret gathering of top military leaders from nations in alliance with the United States (NATO). The latter meeting is depicted in a photograph now held at the Reagan Library (see below).

KEY FACTS
• President Reagan makes a statement

‹ Previous day | Next day ›

Monday September 9, 1985

Figure 1.September 9, 1985, meeting with NATO commanders. Could this be the meeting Minister Farrakhan was told of on The WHEEL?

On **September 3rd**, returning from vacation, Pres. Reagan met with his National Security Council, and it's Planning Group. According to Reagan's diary,

> "[Egyptian] Pres. Mubarak believes Gadhafi of Libya is a threat to all the N. African countries & mainly Egypt. We've been meeting with [him] on how we can assist him if Egypt is attacked. <u>Do we all go out & join in a war & would our people support such a move?</u> There is no

doubt Egypt & the Suez Canal are very important to our security. Still it's a complex problem. For now, we'll keep on studying contingency plans with Pres. Mubarak."

Six days later, on **September 9th**, Reagan writes: *"I welcomed the 18 Generals commanding their country's forces in NATO. They are here visiting our military bases."*

That language suggesting that the "visit" was ceremonial in nature was clearly for public consumption, but it is evident that wars were being planned and various military roles were being assigned. The "visit" of these top commanding generals is not like a convention or annual gathering. If it were ceremonial, there would be plenty of photo opportunities and chest-pounding for the non-NATO world to see—much like the Russians' annual review of their weaponry through Red Square. But the media make no mention of this extraordinary meeting (or their "visiting military bases"). Nor does Reagan say when these commanders arrived in the United States and when they departed.

If, as Reagan says, "the 18 generals" are "visit military bases"–*plural*–one must realize there are over 500 bases in America alone, and dozens of military facilities in the area surrounding Washington, DC. Their visit to the United States, some from thousands of miles away, must have been for at least several days. And it is highly unlikely that eighteen NATO commanders would come to America and not meet with the Joint Chiefs of Staff, which is made up of the top commanders of the U.S. Navy, Army, Marines, and Air Force.

This was *most likely* the meeting that The Honorable Minister Louis Farrakhan was told of on The Wheel. And it is clear that The Minister *could not have known* of it through any conventional means.

Later that day (September 9th), Reagan meets with a group of Jewish leaders for a "photo op," but with the Middle East on the brink of war the description of this meeting as *ceremonial* is suspect. At about this time the Israeli Army was placed on heightened alert on at least five separate occasions.

The March to War

Immediately following those two (or more) planning meetings, a series of events occurred that continued the march toward the April 1986 bombing of Libya.

On **September 10,** Israel released the last of hundreds of Palestinians they held, whose freedom had been the stated motive for many of the Arab "terrorist" acts against Western targets. This preemptive move is clearly made by Israel at the behest of Reagan to eliminate any righteous grievances so that the planned war against Libya can proceed as a "retaliation" rather than as an unjustified act of aggression. On **September 11th,** another suspect 20-member delegation from the American Jewish Congress goes on a "fact-finding mission" to the Middle East. On **October 18th,** Operation Ghost Rider—a full rehearsal for a strike against Libya—commenced in Newfoundland, Canada.

A bombing incident on **December 27th** at the Rome and Vienna airports kills 20 people and 5 Americans and accelerates the White House rhetoric. On **Jan 7th** Reagan blames the incident on Gadhafi, and now the die is cast and the American "retaliation" is assured.

In February 1986, it crystallizes for Minister Louis Farrakhan that the war he was told of was indeed to be launched against Libya. As he recounts:

> "From Tripoli, speaking before the representatives of approximately 80 nations, I told the vision publicly, sending back to the United States a warning to President Reagan and Secretary of State George Schultz."

On April 14, 1986, Ronald Reagan ordered a strike on five targets in Libya. And on the next day 33 attack aircraft struck Tripoli. The total number of Libyans murdered in the attack were estimated at 60, including Col. Gadhafi's recently adopted infant daughter Hana. Far more innocents may have perished, including the leader himself, *had not Minister Farrakhan relayed that divine warning—* from *The Wheel.*

Reagan boasted that "If necessary, we shall do it again." Under President Barack Hussein Obama, they did.

Farrakhan plays Mendelssohn
By Debra Hanania-Freeman and Fred Haight

In 1993, the Honorable Minister Louis Farrakhan, the leader of the Nation of Islam, astonished the world with a virtuoso performance of one of the most tender and compassionate pieces of music in the Classical repertoire, Felix Mendelssohn's Violin Concerto in E minor, Opus 64. The recently released videotape "For Love of Music-Farrakhan Plays the Violin" not only features the historic May 1993 concert, but also gives viewers an inside look at how and why that concert came to be. While there is no question that Farrakhan's startling solo performance, accompanied by the New World Orchestra conducted by Michael Morgan, is the high point of the videotape,

it is also true that, as a totality, the complete production is an artful composition. In the introductory moments, we learn that Louis Farrakhan's love of the violin and Classical music is not new or casual, but an art form he has been committed to for over fifty years. We also learn, through the words of his son Mustapha, that although circumstances had forced Farrakhan's formal training to cease some forty -four years prior to his 1993 performance, music was always very much part of his life.

Mustapha remembers a household in which he and his eight brothers and sisters were wakened to the sounds of their father's violin. Despite Farrakhan's obvious love of the instrument, the fact that he did not play publicly for some four decades was also a personal decision. At first, the young Louis Walcott was forced to abandon his formal training when he left his home in Boston to attend college in the South, where there were no Classical teachers for young blacks. In 1955, when Louis Walcott meets Elijah Muhammad for the first time, he responds to Muhammad's plea that his followers choose between entertainment and religion. It was Muhammad's view that the black people in America had enough entertainers and athletes, but were in desperate need of thinkers. Louis Walcott, soon to be Louis Farrakhan, dedicated himself to becoming a thinker and, at least for a while, put away his beloved instrument. By 1989, when the Mosque Maryam was dedicated in Chicago, Farrakhan had risen to lead the Nation of Islam, and was, depending on who was doing the talking, the most respected or most feared black leader in America. At the dedication of the mosque, Sylvia Olden Lee, a pianist and teacher of international stature (the first African-American professional musician at the New York Metropolitan Opera, where she was Vocal Coach 1954-56, and professor of vocal interpretation at the Curtis Institute of Music for more than 20 years), accompanied a fine young singer. We learn that afterwards, at a dinner at the minister's home, a string quartet played. Mrs. Lee reports that, obviously inspired by the day's events, when someone handed Farrakhan his violin, he rose to perform. Lee admits that she didn't expect much. "But," she reports, "I was absolutely startled. His performance was captivating; brilliant; prestissimos flying as he made his instrument sing along." She was so impressed, in fact, that she began to tell others. Among those she spoke to was Dr. Willis Patterson, Dean of the University of Michigan School of Music, and then head of the National Association of Negro Musicians. She asked him if he had a celebrity performer for the association's upcoming conference. When he said, he did not, she suggested he invite Louis Farrakhan. Patterson was shocked. "Can he play?" he asked her. Sylvia Lee replied, "Oh, he can play; he plays like Isaac Stern." An invitation was sent and accepted. Minister Farrakhan played the Massenet "Meditation from Thais," but the idea of performing the piece he was learning when his formal training had ended-the Mendelssohn Concerto-was born.

Minister Farrakhan wanted to play it as a gift that he would give to others for his own sixtieth birthday. Having only learned the first movement of the three-movement piece, Farrakhan dedicated the next two years of his life to studying and perfecting it. During those two: years, only those closest to him knew of his plan. He did not alter his grueling travel and speaking schedule. In fact, it was during this period that Louis Farrakhan spoke in every major city in the United States with the goal of reaching 1 million black men. Yet he found the hours he needed to practice and to study. His teacher, a Russian Jewish concert artist by the name of Elaine Skorodin Fohrman, often accompanied him. Some of Louis Farrakhan's critics claimed that he selected a piece by Mendelssohn, a Jewish composer, as a cheap trick to cover his alleged anti-Semitism., But when his son Mustapha is asked why Mendelssohn, he looks surprised. "Why Mendelssohn? It had to be Mendelssohn. He loved him."

The rest of the videotape tells a beautiful story of everything that went into the

 preparation of the concert. Minister Farrakhan's dedication to the music is only part of the story. We learn that an entire community had to mobilize to see the concert realized. A great deal of fear and slander and prejudice had to be overcome. Just before we are taken to the performance, Farrakhan tries to explain his motivation in taking on this task. He tells us, "Music, like truth, is the essence of my life. When I put down my violin to dedicate myself to my people, some of my thinking became narrow and nationalistic. But music expands my breast and I can feel not only the pain of my own people, but all of humanity. Its universality teaches of the beauty of all human beings. "He talks about how the human heart, like a fine instrument, can be crafted through the beauty of music to clear away ignorance and "lift men from where they are to where God wants them to be. People don't know Farrakhan; they don't know the soul of the man. I'd like them to. "On his choice of Mendelssohn, Farrakhan says, "The man's music was simply divine." But what of Farrakhan's music? B y this time in the video, the viewer has no doubt of the nobility of the man or the mission, despite the venomous slanders that accompany nearly every mention of his name in print. The desire to use beautiful music to heal wounds, to open doors, especially for young people who might otherwise never be exposed to an orchestral Classical performance, has to do some good. But, we also know that the Mendelssohn piece remains out of reach to even some professionals. The bowing is very complex. The piece leaps from the lowest note to the highest; there are trills; double stops; all in quick succession. Well, we think, even a tiny step in the right direction is better than nothing. Finally, we arrive at the doors of Chicago's Christ Universal Temple. It is time for the concert.

But can Farrakhan play? To quote the New York Times critic (something we almost never do in this publication), "Can Louis Farrakhan play the violin? God bless us! He certainly can." First, a word on the composition. In most Classical concertos, there is a pause between the three movements. But, in this concerto, taking a cue from the late Beethoven, Mendelssohn links all three movements together without a break, indicating that he had a strong idea of the work as an integrated whole. Farrakhan clearly comprehends Mendelssohn's intent, and succeeds admirably in developing such a concept of this work. For example, the first movement of the Concerto is indicated "Allegro" (fast) and the third movement "Allegro molto vivace" (fast and very full of life). Although the emphasis "molto vivace" does not necessarily imply faster than simple "Allegro," violinists always play it very quickly, rather than think about what the indication actually means. The result is that although the third movement of the piece is joyous, in most recorded performances, the passion of the previous movements dissipates. The movement is usually only half as long as the first and tends to become a bit fluffy and light. Farrakhan takes the movement at a slower pace, allowing it to retain its jubilancy without becoming unserious. The listener hears the echoes of the first movement in his mind's ear, just as the composer intended. (Indeed, the transition from the second to the third, an "Allegretto ma non troppo" quotes from the first movement in order to underline the link.) Maestro Michael Morgan comments earlier in the video that it is in the second movement that Louis Farrakhan's character comes out. A very interesting thing happens.

Maestro Morgan begins the movement in the slow, Adagio- like tempo in which

it is usually played. When the violin enters, Farrakhan speeds up to the Andante (walking pace) which Mendelssohn himself indicated. We see Morgan turn his head with a puzzled look before he adjusts to the soloist's tempo. This is a cantabile (singing) movement. The traditional slower tempo allows a violinist to show how well he can make his instrument sing. But the Andante tempo taken by Farrakhan, with his instrument still singing beautifully, keeps a certain edge of tension coming out of the first movement and leading into the third. The concept of the work as a whole is developed, and a respect for its seriousness maintained. Farrakhan's ability to make his instrument sing deserves attention. All good instrumental music is based on the human voice and Minister Farrakhan has the mastery of bowing technique necessary to organize phrasing as he desires. But, there is also something more.

When Minister Farrakhan addresses the audience at the conclusion of his triumphant performance, he speaks of the fact that in music, every note has a different vibration; just as every human being "vibrates" differently. He jokes that the warm-up of any orchestra sounds like pure chaos-until the oboist plays the "A" to which the orchestra tunes. But, he emphasizes, it is the composer who organizes all the tones into a beautiful harmony. What the world needs now, he says, is a divine composer "to put us together on the staff of life, so we can combine to produce beauty, harmony, and peace." In music, this quality is developed through polyphony (many voices). A single instrument, like the violin, can capture the qualities of different species of human voice, such as soprano and mezzo-soprano. This polyphony is further differentiated by the different registers that exist within each species of voice. We do not know the extent of the Minister's knowledge of vocal registration, but in the above-mentioned comments (which clearly moved the members of the orchestra); he brings in a most valuable quality from outside formal musical study per se. The

313

tendency in today's media-run culture is toward a homogenization, or flattening-out, of the differences both between unique individuals in Society, and between different voices and vocal registers in music. This habit undermines the idea that man is made in the image of God, because it flattens the quality that can only be manifested in the sovereign individual's creative mind.

A leader who works to develop creative individuals would tend to also orient toward such differentiation in music. Let's examine one example here. Mrs. Fohrman, in an early section of the video, mentions the talent Farrakhan demonstrates in playing the very difficult cadenza in the first movement. It must be noted that this cadenza is unique. Mendelssohn places it in the middle of the movement rather than the end, and it is clearly a tribute to the "Chaconne" for solo violin by J. S. Bach, a piece where Bach developed the principle of polyphony in a single instrument to undreamt-of heights. The Mendelssohn cadenza emphasizes a low voice, something most unusual. The violin most often plays in the soprano or mezzo-soprano range, but here we find the quality of a human tenor voice in its middle and lower registers! Farrakhan, though clearly capable of playing this passage with great speed, makes a point of slowing certain portions of it down, in order to make that very unique tenor voice sing, while playing the higher notes much more lightly. The videotape is highly recommended. We also think it would be a most valuable addition to the curriculum of any educational institution, from elementary school on up. And, we can only hope that Minister Farrakhan will continue to develop in this direction-something very sorely needed in music and in society today.

EIR Volume 22, Number 29, July 21, 1995

Farrakhan is Not the Problem: The Arrogance and Absurdity of America's Racial Litmus Test
By Tim Wise

Thirteen years ago, when I first started out on the lecture circuit, speaking about  the issue of racism, it seemed as though everywhere I went, someone wanted to know my opinion of Louis Farrakhan.

To some extent, this was to be expected, I suppose. It was 1995, after all, and Farrakhan had just put together the Million Man March in DC. So, when race came up, that, and sadly, the OJ Simpson trial and verdict seemed to be the two templates onto which white folks in particular would graft their racial anxieties.

Though OJ has long since faded as a matter of conversation among most, discussion of Farrakhan never seems to end. As controversy, has erupted regarding comments made by Barack Obama's former pastor, the Rev. Jeremiah Wright, Wright's occasional words of praise for Farrakhan have caused many to suggest that he, and by extension, Obama, are somehow tainted. Wright, we are to believe, is forever compromised as a legitimate commentator on issues of race and even as a man of God. And why? In large part because he has noted two basic truths that are pretty hard to dispute: first, that Farrakhan is an important voice in black America–important in the sense that millions of black folks are interested in what he has to say–and second, that he is someone whose community work with young black men has been constructive where many other efforts to reach them have failed. Although Wright has never indicated that he agrees with the more extreme comments made by the Minister over the past two-and-a-half decades (and indeed, much of Wright's own ministry and approach to issues of race, gender and sexuality suggests profound disagreements with Farrakhan on these matters), his unwillingness to condemn the Nation of Islam leader is used to write him off as an extremist and a bigot.

As someone who is Jewish, I am expected to join in this chorus, apparently. Thus, the repeated and regular queries dating back at least fifteen years from other Jewish folks or from whites generally, asking why it is that I have never, in all of my years as an antiracist activist, turned my pen (or at least my computer keyboard) on Farrakhan.

But the simple truth is, Louis Farrakhan is not the problem when it comes to racism, sexism or heterosexism in this country; nor is he any real threat to Jews as Jews, or whites as whites, contrary to popular mythology.

Much as Muhammad Ali once famously noted that no member of the Vietcong had ever referred to him by a common racial slur, as a way to explain his lack of enthusiasm for fighting in Southeast Asia, I must point out that no member of the Nation of Islam ever told me when I was growing up that I was going to hell, that my soul was an empty vessel, or that I would burn in a lake of fire for all eternity, just like all of my Jewish ancestors, because we had rejected God. The folks who did that were white Christians: teachers, preachers, other kids, and co-workers–all of them spiritual terrorists and religious bigots of the first order. And not one of them was selling a bean pie on the corner, or copies of The Final Call. Yet, we as Jews make nice with Christians just like that, who smile while they condemn us, whose sense of spiritual superiority apparently causes us no alarm, nor spurs us to denounce them for their chauvinism, while the Nation of Islam's occasional episodes of anti-Jewish sentiment send us into fits of apoplexy.

But can we get real for a moment? What ability does Farrakhan have to do me any harm, or any Jew for that matter? When was the last time those of us who are Jewish had to worry about whether or not our Farrakhan-following employer was going to discriminate against us? Or whether our Fruit of Islam loan officer was going to turn us down for a mortgage? Or whether our Black Muslim landlord was going to screw us out of a rent deposit because of some anti-Jewish feelings, conjured up by reading the Nation's screed on Jewish involvement in the slave trade? The answer, of course, is never. If anything, members of the Nation, or black folks in general, have a much greater likelihood of being the victims of discrimination at our hands–the hands of a Jewish employer, banker or landlord, and certainly a white one, Jewish or not–than we'll ever have at theirs. White and/or Jewish bias against Nation members, either as blacks or Muslims or both, is more likely to restrict their opportunities than even the most advanced black bigotry is capable of doing to us. That's because bias alone is never sufficient to do much harm. Without some kind of institutional power to back up that bias, even the most unhinged black racism or anti-Jewish bigotry is pretty impotent.

Oh, sure, a Black Muslim could attack me on the streets I suppose, either because of my whiteness or my Jewishness, so in that sense, the potential for such a person to harm me exists. But how many of us who are Jews have really been attacked by members of the Nation of Islam? Not only in absolute terms, but relative to the number who have been attacked or otherwise abused by white Christians? And why, given the likely answers to those questions, do we continue to fear the former, while spending so much time trying to ingratiate ourselves to the latter? Is their support for Israel–which is only offered because they hope ingathering Jews there will bring about the return of Jesus, at which point we'll all be sent to hell anyway–really that important? Is that all we require in order to be pimped?

Likewise, although lesbian, gay, bisexual and transgendered folks face violence regularly, and can be discriminated against legally in housing or employment, how often are members of the LGBT community singled out for these things by members of the Nation of Islam, as opposed to so-called God-fearing Christians filled with something to which these latter typically refer as "love?"

Sadly, it isn't only conservative and right-wing white folks who have chosen to make Farrakhan something of a racial Rorschach test for black leaders. To wit, the recent ventilations of self-proclaimed spiritual guru, Michael Lerner, who claimed in an April 29, 2008 e-blast from his "Network of Spiritual Progressives," that lasting damage had likely been done by Rev. Wright's praise for Farrakhan. According to Lerner, failure to clearly condemn the Nation of Islam leader is a "danger to any hopes of reconciliation between blacks and whites in this country."

But such a statement–in effect, placing the burden for racial reconciliation on black people, who must condemn Farrakhan in order for whites to be willing to dialogue–is a grotesque inversion of historic responsibility for the problem of racism in the United States.

Disturbingly, Lerner's formulation suggests it is perfectly legitimate for whites to hold blacks as a group responsible for the words of Louis Farrakhan, or the inadequate condemnation of Farrakhan by Rev. Wright. To believe that praise for Farrakhan is a deal-breaker when it comes to white-black amity, is to endorse the notion of collective blame: the same kind of thing Lerner rightly rejects when it is done to Jews. If someone were to suggest that Jewish folks' tepid condemnation of the Israeli government's repression of the Palestinians, or terrorist Jews like Meir Kahane–whose followers are welcomed participants each year in New York's "Israel Day Parade"–legitimizes anti-Semitism, or makes reconciliation between Jews and Muslims impossible, Lerner would be rightly outraged. But in his recent message, he engages in the same sloppy thinking.

Secondly, by arguing that praise for Farrakhan makes racial reconciliation impossible, Lerner essentially places the burden for solving the nation's race problem on blacks and blacks alone. Whites are not asked by Lerner to renounce popular white politicians or historical figures, even those with egregious records on issues of racial equity and justice. Only blacks must prove their sincerity by renouncing one of their own. It is as if Lerner believes Farrakhan were the reason for white folks' intransigence on issues of race; as if he honestly thinks whites had embraced the cause of racial equity until Farrakhan burst into the national consciousness sometime in the early 1980s. It's as if he thinks whites have been honest racial brokers, just waiting for blacks to come to the table of brotherhood, while blacks have been the impediment to progress because of their occasional kind words for the Minister. In other words, Lerner writes as if history never happened, or at least is of no consequence.

And speaking of history, for white Americans to condemn Farrakhan, while still admiring some of the people for whom we have affection–who have not only said but done far more evil things than he–is evidence of how compromised is the principle we now seek to impose on others. It is evidence of our duplicity on this subject, our utter venality as arbiters of moral indignation. It isn't that what

Farrakhan has said about Jews, or gay and lesbian folks is acceptable–it isn't. But the fact that his words make him a pariah, while white folks actions don't do the same for us, is astounding.

After all, Louis Farrakhan never led a nation into war on false pretense. A white American president, supported in two consecutive elections by the majority of white people did that. And still, millions of whites are riding around with those infernal W stickers on the backs of their vehicles.

Louis Farrakhan never bombed a pharmaceutical factory in Sudan–responsible for making almost all of the drugs needed to fight major illness in that impoverished nation–on the false claim that it was a lab for chemical weapons. Another white American president, supported and revered by white liberals did that. And millions of white folks have been supporting that president's wife in her quest for the same office, at least in part to return to the glory days they felt were embodied by her husband's administration.

Louis Farrakhan never overthrew any foreign governments that had been elected by their people, only to replace them with dictators who were more to his liking. One after another white American president has done that, going back decades.

Louis Farrakhan didn't bomb the home of a foreign leader, killing his daughter in the process, or arm a rebel group in Nicaragua responsible for the deaths of over 30,000 civilians, or give guns to governments in El Salvador and Guatemala that regularly tortured and executed their people. One of white America's favorite white Presidents, Ronald Reagan did that. And millions of white folks (and pretty much only white folks) cried tears of nostalgia when he passed a few years ago, after which point thousands of these went to his ranch in California to pay tribute; and they name buildings and airports for him now; and some even suggest that his face should be added to Mt. Rushmore.

Louis Farrakhan didn't say that his adversaries should be hunted down until they no longer "remained on the face of the Earth." One of America's most revered white presidents, Thomas Jefferson, said that, in regard to American Indians. And he's on the two-dollar bill that I used to buy some coffee this morning.

And even if we were to restrict our comparative analysis to extreme statements alone, the fact is, white folks who say things every bit as bigoted as anything said by Farrakhan remain in good standing with the media and millions of whites who buy their books and make them best-selling authors.

Take Pat Buchanan, for instance. Despite a litany of offensive, racist and anti-Jewish remarks over the years, Buchanan remains a respected commentator on any number of mainstream news shows and networks, his books sell hundreds of thousands of copies, and rarely if ever has he been denounced by other pundits, or grilled by journalists, the way Farrakhan has been, in both cases.

So, for instance, Buchanan has said that AIDS is nature's retribution for homosexuality; that women are "not endowed by nature" with sufficient ambition or will to succeed in a competitive society like that of the United States; and that the U.S. should annex parts of Canada so as to increase the size of the nation's "white tribe" (because we were becoming insufficiently white at present), among other things.

Most relevant to demonstrating the hypocrisy of the press when it comes to Farrakhan, however, consider what Buchanan has said about Adolf Hitler. When Farrakhan said, Hitler had been a "great" military and national leader–albeit a "wicked killer" (which is the part of the quote that normally gets ignored)–he was denounced as an apologist for genocide. Yet, when Buchanan wrote, in 1977, that Hitler had been "an individual of great courage, a soldier's soldier in the great war," a man of "extraordinary gifts," whose "genius" was due to his "intuitive sense of the mushiness, the character flaws, the weakness masquerading as morality that was in the hearts of the statesmen who stood in his path," it did nothing to harm his career, and has done nothing in the years since to prevent him from becoming a member of the pundit club in Washington. Nor would he receive the kind of criticism as Farrakhan–at least not lasting criticism–when he wrote in 1990 that survivors of the European Holocaust exaggerated their suffering due to "Holocaust survivor syndrome," and that the gas chambers alleged at Treblinka couldn't have actually killed anyone because they were too inefficient.

In other words, a white guy can praise Hitler, can cast aspersions on the veracity of Jews who were slotted to be killed, and can make blatantly racist, sexist and homophobic remarks and ultimately nothing happens to him, and no white politician is ever asked their opinion of him, or made to distance him or herself from the white man's rantings. But black folks will have to do the dance, will have to make sure to reject Farrakhan, because otherwise, apparently, we should intuit that they are closet members of the Nation, just waiting to take office so they can pop on a bow tie and put Elijah Muhammad's face on the nation's currency.

Perhaps when white folks begin to show as much concern for the bigoted statements and, more to the point, murderous actions of white political leaders as we show over the statements of Louis Farrakhan, then we'll deserve to be taken seriously in this thing we call a "national dialogue on race." Until then, however, folks of color will continue–and rightly, understandably so–to view us as trying to dodge our personal responsibility for our share of the problem. They will view us, and with good reason, as merely using Farrakhan so that we can divert attention from institutional discrimination, institutionalized white privilege and power, and the way in which white denial maintains a lid on social change, by creating the impression that everything is fine, and whatever isn't fine is the fault of crazy, militant black people, who follow crazy and hateful religious leaders.

In this way, white Americans can continue to pretend that the nation's racial problem isn't about us; that we are but passive observers of a drama concocted by others, over which only they have any control. And in this way, we guarantee the perpetuation of the very enmity we claim not to understand, the very tension we cannot comprehend, and the chasm-like divide that was created in our name and for our historic benefit, no matter how much we try and shift the blame now, heads rooted firmly in the proverbial sand.

Professor Derrick Bell's Analysis of Minister Farrakhan's "Racial Standing"

(Excerpted from Chapter 6: Rules of Racial Standing, Printed in Dr. Bell's book Faces At The Bottom Of The Well)

Fourth Rule:

When a Black person or group makes a statement, or takes an action that the white community or vocal components thereof deem "outrageous," the latter will actively recruit blacks willing to refute the statement or condemn the action. Blacks who respond to the call for condemnation will receive super standing status. Those blacks who refuse to be recruited will be interpreted as endorsing the statements and action and may suffer political or economic reprisals.

"Pretty strong stuff!" I exclaimed. "Meaning?" Geneva asked. "Well, perhaps the best contemporary example of the Fourth Rule involves the adverse reaction of many whites to the Muslim minister Louis Farrakhan. Smart and super articulate. Minister Farrakhan is perhaps the best living example of a black man ready, willing, and able to 'tell it like it is' regarding who is responsible for racism in this country. In this regard, he's easily a match for all those condescending white talk-show hosts who consider themselves very intelligent, certainly smarter than any black man.

"All these TV pros seem anxious to put this outspoken black man in his place. They have big staffs to do their research and prepare scripts filled to the brim with denigrating questions. And they have film clips carefully edited to make Farrakhan look as outrageous and irresponsible as possible.

"On camera, these self-appointed defenders of a society senseless enough to put them in their highly paid jobs, attack Farrakhan with a vengeance. Clearly, destruction and not discussion is their aim. But there's no contest. Minister Farrakhan, calm, cool, and very much on top of the questions, handles these self-appointed guardians with ease. I love it!"

"I gather," Geneva broke in, "that many black people do not concur in your assessment of the Farrakhan phenomenon."

"It doesn't matter. Whatever their views on the controversial Black Muslim minister, every black person important enough to be interviewed is asked to condemn Minister Farrakhan — or any other truly outspoken black leader. Reporters generally ask, 'Have you heard what Farrakhan said and what are you going to do about it?' Note that, with Farrakhan, it's not what do you have to say, but what are you going to do about what he said? And don't make the mistake of telling a reporter ten positive things about Farrakhan and adding one criticism. You guessed it, the story will be headlined: 'Leading Black Spokesperson Condemns Farrakhan.'" "But," Geneva objected, "Farrakhan is a Black Muslim, which most blacks are definitely not."

"It's not his faith we're asked to deal with, Geneva. It's his race and his mouth."

She laughed. "On the surface, this is strange, kind of crazy. Remember the biblical story of how little David killed the mighty Goliath. David left his sheep in the field, journeyed to the impending battle, and convinced King Saul of the Israelites to allow him to be their champion. The armor they put on him was so heavy, he took it off, and went to meet Goliath with his staff, a slingshot, and five smooth stones in his pouch. And David was not modest or shy as he told Goliath what the Philistine giant least wanted to hear: This day will the Lord deliver thee into mine hand; and I will smite thee, and take thine head from thee; and I will give the carcasses of the host of the Philistines this day unto the fowls of the air, and to the wild beasts of the earth; that all the earth may know that there is a God in Israel. "For many people," Geneva continued, "Minister Farrakhan is a black David going one on one against the Philistines who bestride the land, abusing their power and generally messing over black folk. But when Farrakhan issues his challenge, no Goliath comes forth. Rather, some of the Philistines come running, not up to Farrakhan, but to any black person of substance they can find, asking, 'Did you hear what that man said about us? What are you going to do about it?' "

"That's the question I've been asking myself, Geneva," I responded. "Why must I do something about Minister Farrakhan? Those he condemns are not without power, not without money, not without guns. A sad history serves as proof that they know how to use all three against us. Why me?

"'Oh,' I am told, 'that man is hurting your cause.' But the cause of black people has been under attack for three hundred years, not by one black man but by the dominant white society. The suggestion that our current plight would be relieved if Farrakhan would just shut up is both naive and insults our intelligence. It also reveals more about those who would silence him than they likely want uncovered." I went on with how, in 1985, when Farrakhan was scheduled to speak in New York City's Madison Square Garden, Black officials came under heavy pressure to speak out and denounce him because of earlier statements of his deemed anti-Semitic and anti-white. Some black officials spoke out. Others, while not condoning some of Farrakhan's comments, complained in interviews that they were repeatedly expected to condemn fellow blacks for offensive remarks or behavior, while whites are not called upon to react to every such indiscretion by white officials. Typical of this position, Representative Charles B. Rangel (D., N.Y.) told a reporter that Farrakhan's statements about Judaism being a "dirty' religion" were "garbage," but added, "it's easy to come down heavy on Farrakhan." Rangel expressed the hope that matters had not reached the point that, just as blacks in South Africa have to carry a passbook to go from place to place, "black Americans have to carry their last statement refuting Farrakhan. I would not, if someone said Jesus Christ is a phony, go around asking Jews to sign a statement to condemn him."

In a similar vein, the Reverend Calvin O. Butts, pastor of the Abyssinian Baptist Church in Harlem, refused to condemn Farrakhan, and pointed out that the Muslim minister criticizes many groups in strong terms, including black churches and black ministers. Butts acknowledged that many Jewish people "look askance at any slight breeze of anti-Semitism. However," he added, "if in response to Israel's refusal to impose sanctions on South Africa to protest its policies of racial separation, I jumped up and said all Jewish leaders in the United States should denounce Israel, how many Jewish people would join me in that? I don't think many."

"I agree, Geneva," I said, "with both Congressman Rangeland the Reverend Butts. Anti-Semitism is a horrible thing, but just as all criticism of blacks is not racism, so not every negative comment about Jews — even if it is wrong — is anti-

Semitism. Were I a Jew, I would be damned concerned about the latent — and often active — anti-Semitism in this country. But to leap with a vengeance on inflammatory comments by blacks is a misguided effort to vent justified fears on black targets of opportunity who are the society's least powerful influences and — I might add — the most likely to be made the scapegoats for deeply rooted anti-Semitism that they didn't create and that will not be cured by their destruction."

"Fear is not rational," Geneva observed. "Jews understandably feel that they must attack anti-Semitism whenever it appears. Farrakhan, being a frightening figure for most whites and thus vulnerable, becomes a symbol — even though, as you point out, an inappropriate one of the nation's anti-Semitism. Jews and white people generally hope that criticism by blacks will diminish his credibility, if not in the eyes of his followers, at least in the minds of those who believe that the threat he represents can be defused by our responding to their urgent pleas for black condemnation of an out-of-control black."

"It's not set out in the Fourth Rule, Geneva, but have you noticed that those blacks who utter 'beyond the pale' remarks are never forgiven. Thus, when Farrakhan attempts to explain that his statement was aimed at Israel as a state and not at Judaism as a religion, his explanation is rejected out of hand. The attitude seems to be: 'You said it, and thus you must be condemned for all time.'"

Geneva agreed. "The Reverend Jesse Jackson has experienced a similar 'lifetime renunciation' notwithstanding his frequent and fervent apologies for the regrettable 'Hymie and Hymietown' remarks he made during his 1984 presidential campaign. As I indicated earlier, I understand why a group is upset by what it deems racial or religious insults, but I doubt that I'm alone in not understanding why blacks who lack any real power in the society are not forgiven, while whites, including those at the highest levels of power, are pardoned. For example, many Jewish spokespeople complained bitterly when President Reagan went to lay a wreath at the Nazi cemetery at Bitburg in Germany, but they do not continue to harass him about the issue everywhere he goes. No one denounced Reagan as anti-Semitic for going. More significantly, neither President Bush nor the whites who support him are called on to condemn Reagan in order to prove that they are not anti- Semitic.

"We boast that, unlike communist countries, there is no censorship of the press here. But blacks like Jesse Jackson, who are subject to an unofficial but no less effective 'renunciation,' are simply not heard."

"Your renunciation isn't limited to controversial political figures," I interrupted. "The writer bell hooks complains that 'often radical writers doing transgressive work are told not that it's too political or too "left," but simply that it will not sell or readers just will not be interested in that perspective.' "

"Similarly," she continued, "one need not agree with Farrakhan that African Americans need to separate from this country to understand that, after three hundred years of trying and not yet having the acceptance here that non-English-speaking white immigrants have on their first day on this soil, we need to be thinking of (if not yet doing) something other than singing one more chorus of 'We Shall Overcome.' Whatever his rhetorical transgressions. Minister Farrakhan and his church are giving the most disadvantaged black folk reason to hope when most of the country and more than a few of us blacks have written them off. His television hosts give him credit for cleaning up a neighborhood in Washington, D.C., and yet question his motives for accomplishing what few government officials have even seriously tried."

Thinking of Geneva's earlier statement about blacks who do not agree with our position on Farrakhan, I recalled a black friend who was unmoved when I discussed Farrakhan's abilities, and said, "Even if everything you say about him is correct, he is still a bigot. Why can't I call him what I think he is?" In effect, my friend was asking, "Even given the perverse weight white society gives to black-on-black criticism, must persons of color remain silent if they strongly disagree with statements or actions by other blacks?"

"The whole racial standing phenomenon, Geneva, raises a troublesome dilemma for many black scholars. How can blacks criticize other blacks or civil rights policies with which they disagree? Must they sacrifice their academic freedom, even their First Amendment right to free speech, in order to prevent whites from endowing with super standing their assertion of anti-black beliefs they have held all along?"

"The answer," Geneva said, "is that a burden of blackness, particularly for the black scholar, is racial awareness. Black academics must weigh the value of their statements, their writings, against the fact that, like it or not, their criticism of other blacks — whether or not accurate, or fair, or relevant — will gain them enhanced or super standing. In some instances, in 1991, the Nation of Islam and its Abundant Life Clinic received a citation from the City of Washington, D.C, for expunging Washington's Mayfair Mansions of violent crack dealing. The Nation of Islam continues to patrol the area."

They may feel so strongly about an issue or an individual that there is no alternative to speaking out — despite the predictable consequences." "I don't disagree," I responded, "but those who decide that, despite all, they must speak out against blacks who are threatening to whites, must not be surprised when blacks subjected to public criticism, cry 'Foul.' And when the black critics are later criticized themselves, this is not intended to — and certainly does not — silences the black speakers, as is claimed by Professor Stephen Carter. After all, they now have enhanced or super standing. White people want to hear their views, almost ad nauseam. Rather, some of the rest of us are saying, 'Now, see what you have done. Knowing the consequences, you should have communicated your criticism in some other way.' ""Is there an inconsistency," Geneva inquired, "in your opposition to blacks who gain enhanced standing by telling white people what they want to hear about blacks, and those like Minister Farrakhan who gain, if not standing, a kind of notoriety by telling whites what they least want to hear?"

"A good point," I conceded, "but I think the statements by Louis Farrakhan and other outspoken black militants are bold, impolitic, and sometimes outrageous precisely because they are intended for those blacks whose perilous condition places them beyond the courteous, the politic, even the civilities of racial and religious tolerance. These blacks need to hear their rage articulated by those able and willing to do so. They need reassurance that others, not they, are the cause of the wretched circumstances in which they live. Professor Lucius Barker makes this point when, while noting the large differences between whites and blacks regarding attitudes toward Farrakhan, he warns: 'Sooner or later whites must understand that this type of rhetoric and behavior has been fostered by their own ongoing maltreatment of blacks in the American political social order. As long as such conditions exist, blacks understandably find themselves more receptive to many types of rhetoric and promises of deliverance than would otherwise by the case.' "

"The real paradox here," said Geneva, "is that while whites fear spokespersons like Minister Farrakhan, the risk posed by the Farrakhans in this country is as nothing compared with the risks to all arising from the conditions against which those Farrakhan rails in uncompromising terms."

"I have not talked to him, Geneva, but I rather imagine that Minister Farrakhan understands the rules of racial standing. He knows that abstract condemnation of racism and poverty and the devastation of our communities is inadequate and ineffective. He has decided that the only way to be heard over the racial-standing barrier is to place the blame for racism where it belongs. Using direct, blunt, even abrasive language, he forthrightly charges with evil those who do evil under the racial structure that protects them and persecutes us, that uplifts them regardless of merit and downgrades us regardless of worth."

Farrakhan is Innocent, FBI is Guilty
Setting the record straight in Malcolm X Assassination

"Only one movement (The Black Muslims) though looked upon by disfavor by the major black civil rights groups, remains strong, consequential, cohesive, influential..."
-Phillip E. Hoffman, American Jewish Committee, 1972

"For years the Bureau has operated a counterintelligence program against the NOI and Muhammad... despite these efforts, he continues unchallenged in the leadership of the NOI and the organization itself, in terms of membership and finances, has been unaffected."
-Chicago Special Agent in Charge FBI Memo 4/22/1968

There is no doubt; the Unites States Federal Bureau of Investigation (FBI) has been a number 1 enemy of Black America. The crowning achievement of the FBI's COINTELPRO (counter-intelligence) program, during the 60's, were the assassinations of Rev. Dr. Martin Luther King Jr. and Malcolm X.

A new film called "Betty and Coretta" that is airing on the Lifetime network is working really hard to deceive the public. This oddly timed film features the wonderful R&B singer Mary J. Blige portraying the legendary Mrs. Betty Shabazz. The writers of this film include in its script accusatory words coming from Mrs. Shabazz, portrayed by Mary J. Blige, that Minister Farrakhan was responsible for her husband-Malcolm X's death.

The desire of the writers and producers are to destroy the magnetism of Minister Farrakhan among a new generation of Black youth that are discovering the living legend for the first time for themselves on college campuses and in the streets of the hood throughout America. This film is a weak attempt to derail Minister Farrakhan's momentum.

What do they want to derail, you might ask? Minister Farrakhan at nearly 80 years of age is more prolific than ever. He has recently toured the Caribbean nations addressing the governments, professional groups and youth groups. In 2012 Minister Farrakhan visited major historically Black college campuses and even delivered a major address at the University of California-Berkeley. During the heat of the summer, Minister Farrakhan mobilized the Nation of Islam's men's class, known as the Fruit of Islam, into the streets of Chicago and America's major cities on a peace in the streets mission. And in January of this year Minister Farrakhan began a 52-week webcast lecture series entitled The Time and What Must Be Done.

These are all activities that have historically been fought by the United States Federal Bureau of Investigation (FBI). J. Edgar Hoover used untold sums of tax payer dollars to wage a war against all Black Nationalist Groups. His stated goal was to prevent the rise of a Black "messiah" who could unite Black America in a bond of brotherhood and strength. Minister Farrakhan is the modern equivalent of what Hoover feared would happen 40 plus years ago.

This movie fits rightly in the category of what Hoover described in his COINTELPRO memos as "friendly media." Consider the following quoted from the famous Church Committee Report III.:

> "Much of the Bureau's propaganda efforts involved giving information or articles to "friendly" media sources who could be relied upon not to reveal the Bureau's interests... the Division assembled a list of "friendly" news media sources -- those who wrote pro-Bureau stories. Field offices also had "confidential sources" (unpaid Bureau informants) in the media, and were able to ensure their cooperation. **The Bureau's use of the news media took two different forms: placing unfavorable articles and documentaries about targeted groups, and leaking derogatory information intended to discredit individuals.**" (Church Committee Report III)

In his very important book *Racial Matters: The FBI's Secret File on Black America 1960-1972*, Kenneth O'Reilly writes:

> "In 1968 the Miami field office of the FBI and its "friendly and reliable" media contacts began work on a far more ambitious series of **documentaries** on the Nation of Islam and other black groups."

This film "Betty and Coretta" that disrespects and mocks the great legends of Black History is straight out of the FBI playbook. It is a "friendly media" documentary that aims to ruin the Nation of Islam. But this isn't the first time that the NOI has been under attack.

It is a well-known fact that the long-term leader of the FBI, J. Edgar Hoover was a member of the Masonic Shrine. The Masonic Shriners are largely Christian white men who occupy powerful and influential positions within business, government and academic fields. They are students of the Bible, Holy Qur'an, World History and Prophecy. They are particularly known for their private veneration of Prophet Muhammad and the early history of Islam as a world conqueror.

Hoover's Shriner membership sheds light on his use of the word "messiah" in his infamous COINTELPRO memo. For in both Bible and Qur'anic prophecy, the Messiah is born from and is a blessing to the Children of Israel. The Messiah is to be a man like Moses. Moses liberated the enslaved Hebrews out of Egypt in the Biblical narrative. This led to the destruction of the Egyptian way of life and economy and produced the end of the rule of the wicked Pharaoh.

Ward Churchill and Jim Vander Wall write in their excellent expose *The COINTELPRO Papers* the following conclusion about the assassination of Malcolm X. This conclusion is informed by their meticulous research of the available documents on the nefarious government sabotage of Black movements:

> By the point of Malcolm's assassination during a speech in Harlem on the night of February 14, 1965, the FBI had compiled at least 2,300 pages of material on the victim in just one of its files on him, the NOI and the OAAU." Malcolm X was supposedly murdered by former colleagues in the NOI as a result of the faction-fighting which had led to his splitting away from that movement and their "natural wrath at his establishment of a competing entity. However, as the accompanying January 22, 1969 memo from the SAC, Chicago, to the Director makes clear; **the NOI factionalism at issue didn't "just happen." Rather, it had "been developed" by deliberate Bureau actions - through infiltration and the "sparking of acrimonious debates within the organization," rumor-mongering, and other tactics designed to foster internal disputes – which were always the**

standard fare of COINTELPRO. The Chicago SAC, Marlin Johnson, who would shortly oversee the assassinations of Illinois Black Panther Party leaders Fred Hampton and Mark Clark, makes it quite obvious that he views the murder of Malcolm X as something of a model for "successful" counterintelligence operations.

This may be a shocking conclusion, but it is the right conclusion. The FBI considered the assassination of Malcolm X a model for "successful" counterintelligence operations. And using Malcolm's assassination as a model, they proceeded to work to assassinate Fred Hampton and Mark Clark of the Black Panther Party!

They hope that they can assassinate Minister Louis Farrakhan. But Minister Farrakhan is a divinely guided man and a divinely protected man. He is completely innocent of Malcolm X's assassination. The FBI infiltrated and produced division within the Nation of Islam and worked diligently until their intended goal was achieved.

Black America must not allow itself to be deceived today, for this indeed is the day where the truth (the facts) shall make all free.

Farrakhan Vindicated!

Charges of anti-Semitism exposed as Anti-Black racism, fear mongering and money scheme

In an interview with Democracy Now's Amy Goodman, the following exchange took place with former Israeli Education Minister Shulamit Aloni.

> Amy Goodman: Yours is a voice of criticism we don't often hear in the United States. Often when there is dissent expressed in the United States against the policies of the Israeli government people here are called anti-Semitic. What is your response to that as an Israeli Jew?
>
> Shulamit Aloni: Well it's a trick, we always use it. When from Europe someone criticizes Israel, we bring up the holocaust. When in this country people are criticizing Israel, they are [called] anti-Semitic.

What Ms. Aloni is describing is the very skullduggery used against the noble work and reputation of the Honorable Minister Louis Farrakhan and the Nation of Islam. Minister Farrakhan remains the beloved champion of truth and heroic strong man of the liberation struggle for poor and oppressed peoples around the world. Yet the price he has had to pay for speaking the truth is to suffer being called an anti-Semite and all that comes with that negative designation. However, those who have falsely accused the Minister have actually revealed more about themselves and their true motives and intentions.

It is interesting that Ms. Aloni used the term "trick." According to Dictionary.com the word trick means:

> A deception. Trick, artifice, ruse, stratagem, and wile are terms for crafty or cunning devices that are intended to deceive; an underhanded act designed to cheat someone; an artifice of diabolical ingenuity.

The Most Honorable Elijah Muhammad taught that both the American slave master and the European colonizer of the Black, Brown, Red and Yellow peoples of the Earth did so using the science of "tricks and lies." Minister Aloni has confirmed the Most Honorable Elijah Muhammad's teaching in this regard by

333

revealing one such trick that has been used against Minister Farrakhan and strong Black leaders throughout history. More plainly, the trick has been on the general public who are forced to admire, respect, support and even love Minister Farrakhan in veritable secret, or otherwise suffer by being accused of allowing their admiration to provide legitimacy for an alleged "anti-Semitic hate teacher." Some are affected by the trick to the point that they have developed outright negative opinions of Minister Farrakhan on the basis of his criticism of Jewish influence.

But to raise legitimate criticism to the level of anti-Semitism is fallacy known as the straw man fallacy. When legitimate criticism is mischaracterized as anti-Semitism, it is done obfuscate or hide real issues. The so-called anti anti-Semitic watchdog groups have even been condemned by avowed Farrakhan-critic Rabbi Michael Lerner. In his book, co-authored by Dr. Cornel West titled *Jews and Blacks: Let the healing begin* he writes.

> The ADL, like the Simon Wiesenthal Center in Los Angeles, has built its financial appeal to Jews on its ability to portray the Jewish people as surrounded by enemies who are on the verge of launching threatening anti-Semitic campaigns. It has a professional stake in exaggerating the dangers, and sometimes allows existing racial or political prejudices in the Jewish world to influence how it will portray the potential dangers.

And even though Rabbi Lerner is also guilty of "straw manning" Black criticism as Black Anti-Semitism, Rabbi Lerner understands the sources of Black criticism of the Jewish community. He wrote in 1969 that

> "Black anti-Semitism is ... a tremendous disgrace to Jews; for this is not an anti-Semitism rooted in ... hatred of the Christ-killers but rather one rooted in the concrete fact of oppression by Jews of blacks in the ghetto ... an earned anti-Semitism."

In the mistreatment of Minister Farrakhan by groups like the ADL and the Simon Wiesenthal Center, Black people *en masse* have been the real victim. For all of the economic programs and unity efforts advanced by Minister Farrakhan to uplift Blacks in America from poverty and want, have been undermined by these groups whose efforts are no less racist and Anti-Black than that of the Ku Klux Klan. Maybe this is why when in 1991 Klan wizard David Duke ran for governor of Louisiana, the ADL was mute, claiming that their tax-exempt status prevented them from intervening in a political campaign.

Yet, when in 1984 Rev. Jesse Jackson ran for the office of the President of the United States of America, the ADL actively engaged in sabotaging Rev. Jackson's campaign, even working to destroy his candidacy before it got started! According to Daniel Levitas of the Center for Democratic Renewal,

> "Before Jackson announced his candidacy in 1983, but aware of his impending run, the A.D.L. quietly circulated a nineteen-page memo to reporters detailing Jackson's past statements regarding Jews."

Matters got even worse when Rev. Jackson was accused by reporter Milton Coleman for using a Jewish racial slur when referring to Jews in New York. This caused Rev. Jackson to apologize publicly to the Jewish community for using the term "*Hymietown*," to which ADL director Nathan Perlmutter responded

> "He could light candles every Friday night, and grow side curls, and it still wouldn't mater... he's a whore."

No sane person would ever accuse Rev. Jesse Jackson as being a threat to the Jewish people. Still Perlmutter attacked Rev. Jackson whose run for the presidency symbolized the collective hopes and dreams of all Black people at that time. Perlmutter cared nothing for this fact; he viewed Blacks as a perennial "underdog," for whom no one would come to their aid once condemned by Jews. His vile reference to Rev. Jackson as a *whore* is definitely a tongue- in- cheek remark. By his own admission, the ADL practiced Black-baiting for money. In its own publication, *"Not the Work of a Day": ADL of B'nai B'rith Oral Memoirs, Vol. 1*, former ADL director Nathan Perlmutter reminisces:

> A few weeks ago, I had an expose [sic] on Jesse Jackson. Quite, by coincidence, I wasn't aware of it, we had one of those mass mailings going out for fund raising. It was one of those mailings to lists that were not our usual givers. The fund-raising people tell me that in the several weeks following—these were small gifts, $20, $100, but there

335

were many of them—we never had the response to a mailing that we had in our July, 1984 mailing.

Author Micah L. Sifry in his 1993 article in *The Nation* magazine entitled *Anti-Semitism in America* seeks to hold these anti anti-Semitic groups accountable for their blatant hypocrisy in demonizing Blacks who are critical of their political and economic activities while at the same time, explaining away negative Jewish criticism made by whites.

Sifry points out that in 1990 political commentator Pat Buchanan blamed the Israel Lobby and Jewish geopolitical strategists for America's use of force against Saddam Hussein. Sifry notes that it was anti-Semitism watchdog Bill Buckley who defended Buchanan by writing that he did not believe that Buchanan was anti-Semitic but just *"attracted to mischievous generalizations."* Buchanan is interesting because he has enjoyed a popular and successful career in America as a Communications Director for Pres. Ronald Reagan and a frequent talk-show commentator. Yet he said that Adolf Hitler,

> was also an individual of great courage, a soldier's soldier in the Great War, a leader steeped in the history of Europe, who possessed oratorical powers that could awe even those who despised him. But Hitler's success was not based on his extraordinary gifts alone. His genius was an intuitive sense of the mushiness, the character flaws, the weakness masquerading as morality that was in the hearts of the statesmen who stood in his path." - St. Louis Globe – Democrat, Aug 25, 1977

Yet when Minister Farrakhan said that Hitler was "wickedly great," (literally: one who is unusual or considerable in degree, power, intensity, in the practice of evil) the ADL and Wiesenthal Center used that harangue the Minister in the media and undermine his economic initiatives.

Sifry also notes Buchanan's orchestration of President Reagan's laying a wreath at the tomb of German SS soldiers. Sifry writes,

> The Washington Post reported that Buchanan was "credited... with the President's characterization of World War II German soldiers and SS troops as 'victims' of the Nazis 'just as surely as the victims in the

concentration camps.' And that Buchanan bluntly urged Jewish leaders visiting the White House to 'be good Americans' and stop protesting Reagan's cemetery stop.'"

According to Sifry, the ADL did not even raise any objection claiming that

> "There was an allegation about an offensive note about Jews [by Buchanan] at the time that we couldn't confirm."

But Reagan-Buchanan aside, they could be considered mild in comparison to the Fred Malek-Richard Nixon anti-Semitic combination. It is amazing to consider the response of the ADL to Fred Malek and President Nixon. According to Sifry,

> *Fred Malek, a high-level adviser to then-Vice President Bush had given President Nixon a list of Jews in the Labor Department, some of whom then lost their jobs.*

To this the ADL's *Abraham Foxman called it*

> "ancient history," adding that Malek had merely been "carrying out the instructions of an individual who had [prejudiced] feelings."

We might understand Foxman's response as genuine were it not for what Sifry reveals of what the ADL wrote about the so-called individual who had [prejudiced] feelings that Malek worked for. The Watergate tapes of President Nixon reveal Nixon calling Jews kikes and lamenting their influence in the Arts and advising his staff to stay away from them. Yet according to Sifry,

> he asked the A.D.L's research director, Alan Schwartz, for a copy of all statements the league had ever made regarding Nixon and anti-Semitism. The only one he could find was issued in response to the ex-President's assertion that lobbying by Israel and American Jews was responsible for Congressional opposition to the 1981 AWACS sale to Saudi Arabia. It read, in part: "Richard Nixon is indeed a friend of Israel and his views on foreign affairs merit regard. But singling American Jews out from the broad spectrum of opposition to the AWACS sale, is at best mischievous, at worst mean-spirited."

In the light of this problematic history of the much-feared charge of anti-Semitism, the fair-minded observer is able to see clearly that what is motivating the use of this charge is not any real threat to the Jewish people and not any real anti-Semitic behavior. For when Jews in the Nixon administration lost jobs and income due to his anti-Jewish actions, he was still deemed a friend. When President Reagan and Pat Buchanan equaled the pain of German SS soldiers to those who were their victims, they are not even held accountable for such offensive behavior. So, all we have left is the traditional tried and true blue racism that Black people have never had the luxury of being forgetting about. It is the same scapegoating of Blacks that has proven to be a money-maker whenever those in power can make those they influence to give them money in the name of protecting them from a Black boogeyman. Its time-out for these games and wasting of time and resources. If Minister Farrakhan is speaking falsehood, then all you have to do is respond to his call for a public showdown with him and defeat his falsehood with your truth.

Miracle Man of The Muslims
By Sterling X Hobbs

Sepia Magazine, May 1975

He's a better orator than the late Dr. Martin Luther King Jr. He sings better than Marvin Gaye. He's a better writer than Norman Mailer. He dresses better than Walt Frazier. He's more of a diplomat than Henry Kissinger. And he's prettier than Muhammad Ali.

Who can this be? Is it Superman? No, he's Minister Louis Farrakhan, the National Representative of the Nation of Islam, the Black Muslim followers of the Honorable Elijah Muhammad, and to his loyal "flock," he is all the aforesaid superlatives wrapped up in one magnificent species of manhood. Minister Farrakhan heads the powerful New York Muslim No.7 comprised of more than 5,000 active members and in his decade of its leadership has become a legend in his time, more than surpassing in dynamism and charisma all the claims for the late Malcolm X.

Louis Farrakhan is more sought after on college campuses than both Rev. Jesse Jackson and Dick Gregory. Many times, he receives as much as $3,000 for his speeches, which he hands over to the Muslim school, the University of Islam. He addresses New York via radio six times per week and speaks regularly on the Muslim-funded national broadcast which reaches over 150 cities around the country. Regularly he receives ambassadors from foreign governments and has turned down invitations from both Idi Amin of Uganda and Fidel Castro of Cuba to visit their countries "with the full honors of a head of state." He has an open invitation to most Black-hosted television programs. He has been the subject of two TV specials. Last year Muslim Temple No. 7 published his first book, "Seven Speeches by Minister Louis Farrakhan" and later his first record – an album from his speech to over 70,000 Blacks on Randall's Island – was cut and entitled "Black Family Day 1974."

Observing Minister Farrakhan deliver a lecture is not unlike attending an exciting drama production or jamming at a rock concert. He transforms words into music and carries his listeners through thought-provoking ideology over the course which Blacks should take in economics, politics, religion and education.

He acts out and illustrates his points and the screams from women are reminiscent of the old Temptations concerts.

Many observers of the racial scene, who had written off the Nation of Islam after the death of Malcolm X and the end of Black militancy in the late 60s, now ask: "Where did this man come from?" Black Muslims will smile and say: "One morning as the sun rose in the east, New Yorkers awoke from slumber and found that suddenly the Black Muslims, like Jesus, were resurrected from the dead and were led by a minister more fiery and articulate than ever. And the Muslims became once again a power to reckon with."

My first experience with Minister Farrakhan came five years ago at the Congress of African Peoples in Atlanta. I was seated with Black poet Don L. Lee among the dashikis and African agbadas, wearing my own of course. Suddenly following an address by the late Urban League leader, Whitney Young, a host of Black Muslim brothers walked swiftly into the arena and replaced the security guards who had been provided by Imamu Amiri Baraka, coordinator of the conference.

Each of the Muslim brothers appeared to be at least 6 foot 3 and consequently Minister Farrakhan, who stands about 5 foot 9, was dwarfed in their company. My first reaction was, "Wow, you mean this little dude is Louis Farrakhan?" I had heard so much about him that I was expecting a giant, one who would be in physical harmony with the legends.

Then Minister Farrakhan began to speak. His voice thundered throughout the auditorium and each time the audience would erupt in applause, he would say, "Shut up and listen! You clap too much and think too little." And the audience loved each minute of it. In a manner, which is completely his own, he denounced the entire Baraka-inspired Pan-African movement. He called their leaders unfit and challenged them to "ask yourself the question: Am I qualified to lead Black people?" Come on up with the answer. And don't lie to yourself; you've been lying long enough!" The arena went wild, the audience loving it. Then he denounced them for their "immorality" and they begged for more. Needless to say I was awed.

I recall my first visit to his office back in 1972. I was doing an article for a community newspaper and I was as nervous as a schoolgirl in the exclusive company of Ringo Starr. But Farrakhan's manner was pleasant and comforting. He had just finished making a two-hour speech and was preparing to do yet another. Perspiration soaked his entire body as he asked, "Do you mind if I change clothes while we talk?" The minister stripped down to his shorts as I asked questions. Lester 4X, his assistant secretary came in with a fresh shirt from the Libas clothing store. The sleeves were a bit too long and Farrakhan, in mock anger, said, "Man you brought me this jive-time shirt. I ought to..." then threw his hands up as if he were about to mix it up with his secretary. "The Messenger told me to never go before the people without fresh clothes, else you'll get sick," he said. I have accompanied Farrakhan on some of his visits to college campuses and to watch him before student audiences is fascinating. He never uses notes but prefers to fire away freely. "I was born to do this work," he once said. "This is a labor of love. I love Black people and that's why I don't have to use notes. Have you ever seen a man in love refer to his notes when he's talking to the one he loves? Well, I'm in love with my Black brothers and sisters and I don't need notes because what I say is from my heart, not a notebook."

Often the Minister doesn't even select his subject matter until after he is before is audience and making his opening remarks. He is astonishingly sensitive to people's thinking and ideological leaning. At Cheney State College, for example, he was quite fiery and related much of his message in "street talk" because this is the type of campus Cheney is. Then later that same day, at Lincoln University, he was on a higher spiritual plane because Lincoln has a strong religious element on campus knowledgeable in scriptures. But the uncanny thing is that no one has to tell him this, but he feels it when he goes out and faces his audiences.

In the wake of the passing of Elijah Muhammad, there was much talk of a power struggle in the Nation of Islam and that Minister Louis Farrakhan was a prime candidate to succeed the Messenger of Allah. But he was among the first to pledge fealty to Wallace Muhammad and let all know that he has no aspirations whatsoever for Muhammad's exalted position among Muslims. In his book, "The Black Muslims in America," C. Eric Lincoln quotes him: "The Messenger has very big shoes and my feet are too small." But the distrust of him in some circles troubled Farrakhan to the point that he went to Chicago to inform

Muhammad prior to his death: "Dear Apostle, I fear turning a hypocrite to the truth." And Muhammad replied, "Brother, you don't have that to worry about – not you."

Minister Farrakhan reinforces his position with statements like: "Elijah Muhammad is my master. When he found, me I was just a dumb Negro slave, a dope user, a wine drinker and a disrespecter of the Black woman. He is the greatest, most wise man the Earth has ever produced."

He constantly reminds his audience that "without Muhammad I am nothing." He once said: "Elijah Muhammad gave Malcolm wings and after flying for so long and so high, Malcolm began to think that he was flying under his own power. I know who has given me my wings and I know who controls those wings even now. I'm sitting in the driver's seat here in New York, but Elijah Muhammad is doing the steering."

There are many Muslims who believe Farrakhan to be the modern-day equivalent of Moses' brother Aaron in the Bible and Holy Qur'an. The words and legacy of the Muhammad, they feel, will lead Black people forma 400-year bondage in America as Moses led the children of Israel from bondage in Egypt under Pharaoh. Some see a parallel between scriptural Aaron, the chief spokesman for Moses, and Minister Farrakhan.

When he was scheduled to appear on Black Journal with Elijah Muhammad on a panel featuring Imamu Amiri Baraka, Rev. Albert Cleage, Rev. Ralph Abernathy and Vernon Jordan, Minister Farrakhan shouted: "This will be Moses and Aaron conquering Pharaoh's magicians."

Beyond his oratorical skill, Minister Farrakhan has demonstrated that he is also an accomplished business administrator, personally directing the opening of nearly a score of flourishing Muslim businesses in New York. Sales figures of the New York Temple alone were well over $3 million last year.

The most visible Muslim sections in New York are around 116th St. and Lenox Avenue in Harlem where the Arabian-designed Temple No.7 is located. On the two streets, there are 15 Muslim-owned establishments. Muslim enterprises employ more than 500 people, not all of whom are Muslim. There are more than

50 businesses privately owned and operated by individual Muslims with portions of their profits donated to the Muslim cause.

Sales grosses of Muslim business units range from up to $15,000 weekly for Muslim Brand Imported Fish (the profit margin in fish is quite high, states Minister Larry 4X) to $7,000 weekly for the bean pie distribution of Shabazz Bakery in Corona. Minister Larry once said, "Without the bean pie we'd have to close down," before Farrakhan took over administration of New York Muslim businesses.

Real estate holding alone of the Muslims in New York are about $1,730,000.

To administer the New York temple and its business ventures, Farrakhan arrives at his office within the Islamic Complex at 7:30 a.m. He usually is driven in his Mercedes 600 or on days when he feels daring, he drives himself to work in either his Eldorado or Mercedes sports car. He's normally greeted by five or six brothers who act as a security force which he does not necessarily desire. Out of respect a brother will usually open Farrakhan's door or attempt to carry his briefcase and Farrakhan will plead, "Please, brother, I'm not an invalid…allow me to carry my own bag."

Minister Farrakhan was born Louis Gene Walcott in the Bronx in New York City of Jamaican parents who later moved to Boston's Roxbury section. His mother sought to give him a musical background and he became regarded as a boy-genius at playing the violin. In school, he was particularly interested in English and he searched for a more complete knowledge of the Black man's history. He was a star athlete at English High, winning track honors in the 100-yard dash.

When he was a child, his mother taught him about the lynching of Blacks in the South and she would give him books on slavery. So, moved was young Louis over Black suffering of slaves that tears would stream down his cheeks. Later Louis attended Winston-Salem Teachers College in North Carolina, and experienced the Dixie discrimination that he had read about.

Of his childhood, Minister Farrakhan remembers: "Once my showed me a picture on his wall of a man whom he said was the greatest leader our people had ever had. I stood on a chair and looked into this man's face for many long minutes. Then I asked my uncle, 'Where is this man, that I might meet him and help him?' My uncle answered, 'That man is dead.' I was so hurt that after hoping, all my young years, to meet the right man for our people, that when I found him, he was already dead. Tears rolled down my cheeks and I cried and cried because Marcus Garvey was dead."

Louis Walcott became a professional singer and actor, struggling to make it big with calypso and country songs. He still plays whenever the mood hits him or when he requires a break from the constant pressure he's under. Diners at the Salaam No. 7 Restaurant were shocked one Saturday evening to find the live entertainment supplied by Minister Farrakhan himself who, with a quartet of Muslim brothers, played the violin and sang a number of songs.

While working in a Boston night club when he was 20, a Muslim brother came up to him and announced, "Brother, God has chosen a Messenger to lead the Black man to freedom, justice and equality." Quite emotional, Louis Walcott left the night club, walked slowly down Massachusetts Avenue, crying and talking to God: "Oh God, You know I have always loved my people. Why did not you choose me?" Later he had the thought: "When God chose His Messenger I was not even born. And if God had chosen a Messenger, that choice is all right with me. Let me find the Messenger then and serve him as I would serve God."

While in Chicago in 1955 at a Muslim Saviours' Day Convention, he heard Elijah Muhammad speak for the first time and thought to himself that he didn't particularly like the Messenger's style of speech. Then something very eerie took place. Out of the thousands of people in attendance, Mr. Muhammad looked up into the row of seats where Louis was sitting and said, "Brother, don't pay attention to how I speak, pay attention to what I'm saying Brother. I didn't get the chance to go to the white man's fine schools because when I tried to go, the doors were closed. But if you take what I say and place it into the beautiful way of speaking you know, you can help me save our people."

Louis was stunned. "Man, that scared me to death," Farrakhan relates. "I thought the Messenger had read my mind." But what Louis didn't know was that Muslim captain had told Mr. Muhammad where Louis would be seated and informed the Messenger that Louis "was a college man who could help us if we get him." But how the Messenger knew what Louis was thinking remains a mystery.

Following this experience, Gene Walcott registered with the Nation of Islam's New York Temple. Louis X soon rose to become a lieutenant in the Fruit of Islam, the name given to the military training of men who belong to Islam. Every male Muslim is considered an F.O.I. after he undergoes his processing period.

Though the martial arts are taught, the greater portion of the F.O.I. classes are spent discussing proper marital relationships, proper grooming, techniques in salesmanship, and spiritual meanings of the Bible and Holy Qur'an.

The only cases where the F.O.I. is used for physical punishment is in rare cases of the abuse of a fellow Muslim, especially a Muslim sister. In this case the offender, if found guilty, is penalized according to his offenses. Once a Muslim sister's pocket book was snatched and the thief was apprehended. The beating he received left few unbroken bones in his body. I am told that an offense such as rape of a sister could possibly result in the death of the offender.

But the F.O.I. classes stress a peaceful relationship with the community at large. However, the Muslim realize that a degree of respect must be maintained and they fear if they allow transgressors to go unpunished then "Laz" – the nickname from the Biblical Lazarus used to describe non-Muslims – would declare open seasons on Muslims. But Farrakhan reminds some overzealous members of his congregation that "Allah gives you no credit for beating up your mentally-dead Black brother."

When he was known as Louis X, Farrakhan rapidly grew in stature, received a promotion and was transferred to the Boston Temple to become F.O.I. Captain. When something happened to the temple minister, "I received word that I was to minister to the people," Minister Farrakhan recalls. Ministering, at first, did not come easily to a young and inexperienced Louis X. "I was not able to relate to many of the educated persons who joined the Boston Temple as they were much more intelligent than I. And because I couldn't understand their ideas, I thought they were enemies of Islam and I drove them all out of the temple," he relates.

Realizing his mistake, Louis X wrote to the Messenger in Chicago and asked to be relieved of his position and charged with "any sins they commit wile expelled from the Temple." This display of compassion pleased the Messenger and instead of dismissing Minister Louis, he permitted the suspended brothers to return to the Temple and Louis X remained the minister. Coupled with his administrative problems, Louis X had financial difficulties to add to his woes, "I was so poor in Boston that once, when I spoke in Philadelphia, and the holes in my shoes were so large that the brothers had to drive me right up to the door of the Temple to keep the rain from soaking."

Finally, around 1960, Minister Louis, having more experience and maturity, saw his problems begin to ease. During that period Louis X recorded a song, "A White Man's Heaven Is A Black Man's Hell." He also authored two plays: "Orgena" (A Negro spelled backwards) and "The Trial." Among Muslims these were quite popular and Louis X was beginning to make a name for himself traveling throughout the country performing his two plays for community audiences.

But one evening the Honorable Elijah Muhammad asked him, "Brother do you want to be a song and dance man or a do you want to be my minister?" There was no question in his mind about his reply: "I want to be your minister, Dear Holy Apostle."

Minister Louis was moved to New York after the defection of Malcolm X, a somewhat ironic move because prior to this they had been close friends. Malcolm admitted Louis was closer to him than his own blood brothers. But Malcolm's crusade the last year of his life to undermine the work of the Nation destroyed this closeness and Minister Louis openly attacked Malcolm in Muhammad's Speaks as a hypocrite and "deadly enemy of the Black man."

Soon after this move to New York, Elijah Muhammad gave him the name "Farrakhan." The Messenger never revealed the exact meaning of Minister Farrakhan's name and to this day he is unaware of what his name means.

Minister Farrakhan is a personable man who generally likes people and enjoys sharing ideas with most anyone. This has enabled him to establish warm relationships with most community leaders in New York. Though he chooses to

346

shy away from the word "diplomat," Farrakhan is just that. But his style of diplomacy is rarely based upon shrewd deception, but rather upon honest appreciation for opinions of others. And while he may disagree with their ideologies, his love for them as brothers is felt in his voice and seen in his eyes during meetings with them. He says, "We can disagree without being disagreeable."

Minister Farrakhan's power internally is growing daily. Thousands of young Blacks have joined the Black Muslims after hearing one of Farrakhan's fiery lectures delivered in person or over radio or television. And while he was only 22 when he became a Minister, he is now revered as a "big brother" to many of the younger Black Muslims."

Is Farrakhan the New Garvey?

The new Lifetime Network film entitled Betty and Coretta is extremely offensive to Black America. How in the world could a film be rolled out during Black History Month that offers such ugly caricatures of our powerful Black heroes and there not be national outrage? How could the Sanitsky company be allowed to premier this wickedly motivated film during this very special Black History Month? Black History Month is very significant because it comes in the aftermath of the inauguration of America's first Black President's second term. And while Blacks bask in the tremendous accomplishment of President Obama, a blow to the legends of our history comes out of nowhere to sucker-punch the Black electorate when they least expected it.

As a student of the Honorable Minister Louis Farrakhan, I am intrigued by the fact that this film has all the hallmarks of the documentaries and films that were produced in the 50's and 60's at the height of the infamous COINTELPRO program of the FBI. These films were designed to destroy the magnetism and popularity of the strong Black American dissidents who were seeking to hold America accountable for centuries of mistreatment, injustice and inequality. And while this film mocks a broad group of our leaders, Minister Louis Farrakhan is depicted in the worst light. This movie places the blame for the murder of Malcolm X onto Minister Louis Farrakhan.

This horrible lie against the Minister should concern all in the Black community. Because despite there being a Black man in the White House as President of the

United States, he is burdened with trying to be everything to everybody. Therefore, his benefit to the Black community is diluted and virtually ineffectual. Minister Farrakhan on the other hand, has no such burden and is free to be a gallant strong man and hero for Black causes. Minister Farrakhan has demonstrated a great deal of love, humility and an impressive ability to forgive other Black leaders who repudiate and speak ill of him to appease white and Jewish concerns. He has always been generous in lending his credibility with the masses to defend Blacks in trouble. He openly defended Marion Barry, Rep. Alcee Hastings, David Dinkins, Rev. Jesse Jackson, Michael Jackson and numerous others. This is a function and outgrowth of his profound love for his people and what God has given him of a special wisdom that allows him to see the hidden hand of Satanic forces at work in the undoing of the Black community.

The Minister is at the root of the most powerful event in modern history. The Million Man March in 1995 brought out between 1.6 and 1.8 million Black Men of all faiths, ages and walks of life for the noble purpose of atonement, reconciliation and responsibility. That event, more than any other event, clearly communicated Minister Farrakhan's value and importance to more than just the Nation of Islam. We learned at the Million Man March that Minister Farrakhan had become the most influential man in all of America.

Minister Farrakhan's ability to attract and impact the lives of millions of people with the message of self-love, Black nationhood, and divine destiny is reminiscent of one of the great patriarchs of Black people's struggle for liberation, the Honorable Marcus Mosiah Garvey.

Marcus Garvey's United Negro Improvement Association attracted between 6 and 8 million followers. Both Marcus Garvey and Minister Farrakhan's wide appeal made them targets for the FBI's anti-messiah objectives. COINTELPRO memos outlined the specific denial objective *"to prevent the rise of a "messiah" who could unify, and electrify, the militant Black Nationalist movement."* That Hoover feared Black nationalists being "unified" and "electrified," reveals what Hoover understood of Biblical prophecy. The Bible in Ezekiel 37:10 speaks of a people referred to as "dry bones". These despondent and life-less people are the subject of the Prophet Ezekiel's ministry. Ezekiel, who is considered a type of the Messiah, causes these "dry bones" to come alive and to become "unified" into what the Bible calls and "exceedingly great army." Hoover therefore understood Black people's place within Biblical prophecy.

The behavior of the FBI towards both Garvey and Minister Farrakhan indicate that both have been viewed as the political and prophetic messiah. Minister Farrakhan might be considered the New Garvey or New Messiah as both he and Garvey bear striking similarities to one another as revealed in a 1919 Department of Justice memo written by J. Edgar Hoover.

In Race First by Professor Tony Martin a memo is included that is dated October 11, 1919 from the Department of Justice that describes just why the Honorable Marcus Mosiah Garvey was considered dangerous. In the memo Hoover is disappointed that *"Unfortunately, he (Garvey) has not as yet violated any federal law whereby he could be proceeded against on the grounds of being an undesirable alien, from the point of view of deportation. It occurs to me, however, from the attached clipping that there might be some proceeding against him for fraud in connection with his Black Star Line propaganda..."*

The Memo continues with Hoover's description of Garvey and his work:

MEMORANDUM FOR MR. RIDGELY.

I am transmitting herewith a communication which has come to my attention from the Panama Canal, Washington office, relative to the activities of MARCUS GARVEY. Garvey is a West-Indian negro and in addition to his activities in endeavoring to establish the Black Star Line Steamship Corporation he has also been particularly active among the radical elements in New York City in agitating the negro movement. Unfortunately, however, he has not as yet violated any federal law whereby he could be proceeded against on the grounds of being an undesirable alien, from the point of view of deportation. It occurs to me, however, from the attached clipping that there might be some proceeding against him for fraud in connection with his Black Star Line propaganda and for this reason I am transmitting the communication to you for your appropriate attention.

The following is a brief statement of Marcus Garvey and his activities:

Subject a native of the West Indies and one of the most prominent negro agitators in New York;

He is a founder of the Universal Negro Improvement Association and African Communities League;

He is the promulgator of the Black Star Line and is the managing editor of the Negro World;

He is an exceptionally fine orator, creating much excitement among the negroes through his steamship proposition;

In his paper the "Negro World" the Soviet Russian Rule is upheld and there is open advocation of Bolshevism.

Respectfully,

J. E. Hoover

1. *Garvey is a native of the West Indies and one of the most prominent Negro agitators in New York.* (Minister Farrakhan's parents are both from the West Indies. Minister Farrakhan as the Honorable Elijah Muhammad's minister in New York City from 1965-1975 was considered the most powerful Black leader in New York during that time. It bears noting that Hoover's use of

"agitator" is in a negative or pejorative sense. But the agitator has a very positive connotation when it describes the large cylindrical moving part inside a clothes washing machine. It is the dirt and grime on the clothes that is agitated and removed from the clothing in an effort to make the clothes clean and wearable. Black leadership therefore should take pride in being called an agitator to cleanse America of its disease of racism, injustice and inequality that keeps a stain on any global mention of the United States.)

2. *He (Garvey) is a founder of the Universal Negro Improvement Association and African Communities League.* (Minister Farrakhan in his leadership role within the Nation of Islam has articulated and espoused similar if not identical political and social positions as that of Marcus Garvey's UNIA. The Minister also served as deputy commander of the World Islamic People's Command. His leadership also produced the National African American Leadership Summit-NAALS and the Millions More Movement)

3. *He (Garvey) is promulgator of the Black Star Line and is the managing editor of the Negro World.* (Minister Farrakhan is the promoter of several cooperative economic initiatives in the same vein of Garvey's Black Star Line, for example the Power Personal Care Products Line, NOI Security, and the 3 Year Economic Savings Program. Garvey was the managing editor of the Negro World newspaper; Minister Farrakhan is the publisher of the Final Call Newspaper. Both leaders understand the power of the printed word and the distribution of positive messages in the transformation of their communities.)

4. *He (Garvey) is an exceptionally fine orator, creating much excitement among the Negroes through his steamship proposition.* (Minister Farrakhan is without a doubt, the most exceptional orator ever produced for the articulation and advocacy of Black causes. The Minister's speeches, programs and initiatives routinely produce excitement among all who listen. In 1994 Time magazine documented that Minister Farrakhan had a 67% approval rating in the Black community. It was the Minister's mighty voice that produced the great Million Man March. Statistics revealed that 80% of the men who attended were of the Christian faith. So, the power of the Minister's delivery of the divine revolutionary message is evidenced in this statistic which shows how what he speaks is not contained within the narrow confines of any one particular religion

or ideology. His voice is the universal sound that the oppressed hear and respond to as though it is the voice of God.)

Minister Farrakhan like Marcus Garvey has broken no laws. This is upsetting to his enemies who want a reason to arrest him and destroy his movement. Like Garvey he has the attention and support of millions. The Black community at-large should rally around the Minister and demand that the governments classified files on the Nation of Islam and all Black groups be released and un-redacted. Black people have suffered too much to continue on believing that our movements and our leaders are failures, turn-coats and murderers of one another. We deserved the once hidden hand of government to be revealed so that justice and healing can come as the product of our full access to truth.

Bibliography

"troubleman31", T.I. aka. 2016. *www.twitter.com.* May 11. Accessed May 12, 2016. http://www.twitter.com.

Ajanaku, Karanja. 2009. "Minister Louis Farrakhan: 'I Am Exactly What I Am'." *The New Tri State Defender.* October 22. Accessed August 13, 2013. http://www.tsdmemphis.com/index.php/news/4779-.

Alberts, William E. 1996. *Mainstream Media as Guardian of Racial Hierarchy: A Study of the Threat Posed by Minister Louis Farrakhan and the Million Man March.* Boston,MA: William Monroe Trotter Institute.

Alexander, Amy. 1998. *The Farrakhan Factor.* New York: Grove Press.

Allen, Frederick. 1985. "Farrakhan's Real Message Has Validity." *Executive Intelligence Review,* December 13: 71.

Associated Press. 1998. "Bruce Willis Calls Farrakhan a Hero." *AP News Archive Beta.* June 15. Accessed August 9, 2013. http://www.apnewsarchive.com/1998/Bruce-Willis-Calls-Farrakhan-a-Hero/id-5fbcba2e9223183a05a881b157305f11.

Badu, Erykah. 2013. "@fatbellybella." *Twitter.com.* April 17. Accessed August 10, 2013. https://twitter.com/fatbellybella.

Beiser, Vince. 1997. "Farrakhan Talks To The Jews." *Jewish World,* June 26: 26.

Bell, Derrick. 1993. *Faces At The Bottom Of The Well: The Permanence of Racism.* New York: Basic Books.

Birdman. 2016. *YouTube.Com.* April 24. Accessed May 15, 2016. https://www.youtube.com/watch?v=Zz2ToSMTWH0.

2003. *Journesy in Black: Minister Louis Farrakhan.* Directed by John Bellamy. Performed by Black Entertainment Television.

Blige, Mary J. 2013. "@MaryJBlige." *Twitter.com.* February 12. Accessed August 10, 2013. https://twitter.com/maryjblige.

Brown, Stacey. 2013. *New York Post.* June 9. Accessed May 15, 2016. http://nypost.com/2013/06/09/bill-cosby-a-plague-called-apathy/.

Cheney, Charise L. 2005. *Brothers Gonna Work it Out: Sexual Politics in the Golden Age of Rap Nationalism.* New York: NYU Press.

Comer, Matt. 2012. "Councilwoman LaWana Mayfield addresses Farrakhan controversy ." *The Clog.* November 14. Accessed August 10, 2013. http://clclt.com/theclog/archives/2012/11/14/councilwoman-lawana-mayfield-addresses-farrakhan-controversy.

Cube, Ice, interview by Michael Williams. 1993. *Ice Cube Comments on Meeting Minister Farrakhan & The Struggle Facing Black Youth (1993, Rap City)*

Curry, George. 2015. "Why Black People Answer When Farrakhan Calls." *www.afro.com.* October 12. Accessed October 24, 2016. http://www.afro.com/why-black-people-answer-when-farrakhan-calls/.

Dash, Damon. 2015. *Meeting with Farrakhan.* New Buffalo, May 18.

Executive Intelligence Review. 1985. "Young Mostly Agrees With Farrakhan." *Executive Intelligence Review,* September 13: 63.

Farrakhan, Hon Minister Louis, interview by Sway. 2015. *Sway In The Morning Radio Show* (June 7).

1997. *Gray's Ferry Unity Peace Rally.* Directed by The Final Call Inc. Performed by Hon. Min. Louis Farrakhan.

2016. *Holy Day of Atonement*. Directed by The Final Call Inc. Performed by Honorable Minister Louis Farrakhan.

1997. *International Islamic Conference.* Directed by Final Call Publishing. Performed by Honorable Minister Louis Farrakhan.

Farrakhan, Minister Louis. 1993. *A Torchlight For America.* Chicago: Final Call Publishing.

FCNN. 2011. "Minister Farrakhan, Wyclef Jean on Haiti TV & Radio ." *YouTube.* December 16. Accessed August 10, 2013. http://www.youtube.com/watch?v=v0Au2J83800&list=PL2A7710178C E5A09F.

Fields, Gary, and Maria Puente. 1996. "The Million Man March: A Movement Or Just A Moment." *USA Today,* October 10.

Franklin, Robert Michael. 2001. "Religious Belief and Political Activism in Black America: An Essay." *Journal of Religious Thought* 63-72.

Freeman, Debra Hanania. 1993. "Farrakhan Dispels Media Image." *Executive Intelligence Review,* May 21: 63.

Gardell, Mattias. 1996. *In The Name of Elijah Muhammad: Louis Farrakhan and The Nation of Islam.* Durham, NC: Duke University Press.

Gates, Hernry L. 1995. "Grading Farrakhan." *The New Yorker Magazine,* October 30: 8.

Giovanni, Nikki. 1996. "A Million Reasons To Hope." *Black Collegian* 3: 26-28.

G-Unit Radio 19. 2013. "50 Cent - Louis Farrakhan Skit ." *YouTube.com.* March 29. Accessed August 10, 2013. http://www.youtube.com/watch?v=_6Ob8v67dE8.

Henry III, William, Sylvester Monrie, Sharon Epperson, Julie Johnson, and Ann Blackman. 1994. "Ministry of Rage." *Time Magazine*, February 28: 21-27.

Hilburn, Robert. 1988. "POP MUSIC : Public Enemy's Chuck D: Puttin' on the Rap." *Los Angeles Times.* February 7. Accessed August 9, 2013. http://articles.latimes.com/1988-02-07/entertainment/ca-41167_1_public-enemy.

Hobbs, Sterling X. 1975. "Miracle Man of The Muslims." *Sepia Magazine*, May: 24-31.

Holcomb, Corey. 2016. *www.youtube.com.* March 4. Accessed May 10, 2016. https://www.youtube.com/watch?v=yfGVrtLzOMU.

—. 2015. *www.youtube.com.* October 28. Accessed May 10, 2016. https://www.youtube.com/watch?v=cD7lS47JmXo.

Hollywood, Hip. 2015. *AOL.ON.* june 29. Accessed May 10, 2016. http://on.aol.com/video/exclusive--2-chainz-and-farrakhan-set-out-to-help-the-community-518913058.

Hume, Ellen. 1984. "Storm Center: Racial Rhetoric Puts Farrakhan in Spotlight In Jesse Jackson Camp --- Black Muslim's Controversy Seems To Help Campaing, Origins of the Friendship; Influence of The Golden Rule." *Wall Street Journal,* April 26: 1.

Islam, Muhammad's Holy Temple of. 2016. *Nation of Islam.* March 15. Accessed March 15, 2016. www.noi.org.

Jestice, Phyllis G. 2004. *Holy People of The World: A Cross Cultural Encyclopedia.* Santa Barbara, CA: ABC-CLIO,Inc.

Jones, Frank Paul. 1996. "Is Farrakhan The Solution To Our Problem ." *New Amsterdam News,* October 18.

Jones, William. 1993. "Black Caucus, NOI Agree To Closer Collaboration." *Executive Intelligence Review*, October 1: 68.

Jordan, Robert A. 1983. "Jackson speech was not best at Washington Rally." *Boston Globe*, September 1: 1.

Jr., Rev. Dr.Charles Steele, interview by Eric Ahad Muhammad. 2013. *The SCLC and The Nation of Islam* (December 30).

Kane, Gregory. 1996. "What I'm about to say will no doubt get me in trouble with the Jewish community. Protesters w." *The Baltimore Sun.com.* September 22. Accessed August 10, 2013. http://articles.baltimoresun.com/1996-09-22/news/1996266058_1_louis-farrakhan-kemp-nation-of-islam.

Karenga, Maulana, and Haki R. Madhubuti. 1996. *Million Man March/Day of Absence: A Commemorative Anthology.* Chicago: Third World Press.

Larry King/CNN. 2013. "Mike Tyson Expresses His Love Of Farrakhan." *YouTube.* June 20. Accessed August 10, 2013. http://www.youtube.com/watch?v=i4ge5mOH0wo.

Lester, Julius. 1985. "The Time Has Come." *New Republic*, October 28: 11-12.

Lion, Snoop. 2013. "Snoop Dogg AKA Snoop Lion speaks of what The Hon. Louis Farrakhan has meant to his life ." *YouTube.* June 27. Accessed August 10, 2013. http://www.youtube.com/watch?v=h3S5FPAglO8.

MacNeil Lehr News Hour. 2012. "Bell: Farrakhan 'Great Hero For The People'." *Breitbart.com.* March 9. Accessed August 10, 2013. http://www.breitbart.com/Breitbart-TV/2012/03/09/Bell%20Louis%20Farrakhan%20is%20A%20Great%20Hero%20For%20The%20People.

Marsh, Clifton E. 2000. *The Lost Found Nation of Islam in America.* Eugene,OR: Wipf and Stock.

McCall, Nathan. 1995. "Makes Me Wanna March; Why I'm Coming and What All of Us Have To Gain." *The Washington Post,* October 15: C01.

Media Matters for America. 2008. "Ignoring Obama's statement on Trumpet award, Hannity suggested that Obama "associated" himself with Farrakhan ." *Media Matters for America.* January 18. Accessed August 9, 2013. http://mediamatters.org/research/2008/01/18/ignoring-obamas-statement-on-trumpet-award-hann/142222.

2000. *Saviours Day Jumuah .* Directed by Final Call Publishing. Performed by Imam Warithudeen Mohammed.

2002. *Saviours' Day Jumuah Los Angeles .* Directed by Final Call Publishing. Performed by Imam Warithudeen Mohammed.

Montgomery, Maxine Lavon. 2004. *Conversations with Gloria Naylor.* University of Mississippi: University Press.

Morris, Rev. Elisha B. 2015. *Twitter.com.* August 3. Accessed May 15, 2016. www.twitter.com.

Muhammad, Ashahed. 2011. "Farrakhan delivers a warning and offers a healing for spiritual leaders and humanity." *Final Call.com.* May 31. Accessed August 9, 2013. http://www.finalcall.com/artman/publish/National_News_2/article_78 72.shtml.

—. 2013. "Farrakhan tells students: You are chosen to build a world!" *Final Call.com.* March 26. Accessed August 10, 2013. http://www.finalcall.com/artman/publish/National_News_2/article_97 05.shtml.

—. 2009. "Farrakhan to spiritual leaders: 'God has never done His greatest work in politics'." *Final Call.com.* January 3. Accessed August 9, 2013. http://www.finalcall.com/artman/publish/article_5521.shtml.

—. 2015. *FinalCall.com.* August 14. Accessed May 15, 2016. http://www.finalcall.com/artman/publish/National_News_2/article_10 2534.shtml.

—. 2008. "Hip Hop Lives: FCN Interview with Nas." *Final Call.com.* August 4. Accessed August 9, 2013. http://www.finalcall.com/artman/publish/Entertainment_News_5/Hip _Hop_Lives_FCN_Interview_with_Nas_5051.shtml.

—. 2008. "Life and ministry of Imam W. Deen Mohammed remembered." *Final Call.com.* September 21. Accessed August 11, 2013. http://www.finalcall.com/artman/publish/National_News_2/Life_and_ ministry_of_Imam_W_Deen_Mohammed_remember_5222.shtml.

Muhammad, Ashahed. 2015. *Rapper The Game says: 'A lot of people are going to be ready to ride' with Farrakhan - #JusticeOrElse.* Los Angeles, June 2015 30.

Muhammad, Cedric. 2013. "Socialism and Muhammad's Economic Blueprint." *Final Call.com.* August 9. Accessed August 10, 2013. http://www.finalcall.com/artman/publish/Business_amp_Money_12/ar ticle_100637.shtml.

Muhammad, Jehron Muhammad and Nisa Islam. 2015. *FinalCall.com.* June 30. Accessed Month 15, 2016. http://www.finalcall.com/artman/publish/National_News_2/article_10 2447.shtml.

Muhammad, Nisa Islam. 2000. "Zionism, not Farrakhan is the problem, rabbis say." *Final Call.com.* March 15. Accessed August 9, 2013. http://www.finalcall.com/national/rabbis2-28-2000.htm.

Muhammad, Starla. 2013. "A man of integrity, consistency and sincerity." *Final Call.com.* May 15. Accessed August 10, 2013. http://www.finalcall.com/artman/publish/National_News_2/article_98 51.shtml.

Muwakkil, Salim. 2003. "Farrakhan and the Beefs of Rap." *www.inthesetimes.com.* December 15. Accessed October 24, 2016. http://inthesetimes.com/article/491/farrakhan_and_the_beefs_of_rap.

National Review. 1985. "The Farrakhan Formula." *The National Review*, November 1: 19-20.

Now, News One. 2015. *News One.* October 11. Accessed May 12, 2016. http://newsone.com/3206584/harry-lennix-on-louis-farrakhans-justice-or-else-address/.

O'Reilly, Bill. 2008. "Sticking Up for Rev. Jeremiah Wright and Louis Farrakhan." *Fox News.com.* April 4. Accessed August 10, 2013. http://www.foxnews.com/story/2008/04/04/sticking-up-for-rev-jeremiah-wright-and-louis-farrakhan/.

Osgood, Carl. 1995. "Congressman Disagree on Million Man March." *Executive Intelligence Review*, November 3: 76-77.

Parks, Phaedra. 2015. *Essence.com.* October. Accessed May 12, 2016. http://www.essence.com/video/phaedra-parks-considers-minister-louis-farrakhan-great-mentor.

Pear, Robert. 1991. "Despite Praising Farrakhan in 1983, Thomas Denies Anti-Semitism." *New York Times*, July 13: 1.7.

Pulver, Matthew. 2015. "Louis Farrakhan, rising: With rap's superstars at his side, the Nation of Islam leader steps forward in the new fight for civil rights." *Salon.com.* April 27. Accessed October 24, 2016. http://www.salon.com/2015/04/27/louis_farrakhan_rising_with_raps_superstars_at_his_side_the_nation_of_islam_leader_steps_forward_in_the_new_fight_for_civil_rights/#.

Raspberry, William. 1990. "A Visit By Louis Farrakhan." *Washington Post,* May 2: A23.

Rezendes, Michael. 1996. "Muslims' self help praised by Kemp." *Boston Globe,* September 8: A.1.

Ross, Rick. 2013. *Before Its News.* November 30. Accessed May 15, 2016. http://beforeitsnews.com/african-american-news/2013/11/a-meeting-between-the-honorable-minister-louis-farrakhan-and-rapper-rick-ross-wise-words-from-a-great-mind-2449300.html.

—. 2013. *Brother Jesse Blog.* 11 30. Accessed may 10, 2016. http://jessemuhammad.blogs.finalcall.com/2013/11/a-meeting-between-honorable-minister.html.

Sanders, Senator Hank. 2013. "State Senator Supporting Farrakhan's Visit Writes To BJF ." *The Birmingham Jewish Federation.* June 13. Accessed August 10, 2013. http://www.bjf.org/daily-updates/722-state-senator-supporting-farrakhans-visit-writes-to-bjf.html.

Scarface. 2015. *Twitter.com.* June 8. Accessed May 15, 2016. www.twitter.com.

Schelzig, Erik. 2009. "Farrakhan: Don't Be "Pacified" By Obama Election." *Huffington Post .* October 19. Accessed August 9, 2013. http://www.huffingtonpost.com/2009/10/19/farrakhan-dont-be-pacifie_n_325616.html.

Shalev, Chemi. 2013. *Haaretz.com.* April 28. Accessed May 16, 2016. http://www.haaretz.com/jewish/features/even-after-boston-there-is-more-anti-jewish-than-anti-muslim-sentiment-in-u-s-says-adl-s-foxman.premium-1.517960.

Simmons, Russell. 2009. *GlobalGrind.com.* September 25. Accessed August 9, 2013. http://globalgrind.com/2009/09/25/minister-louis-farrakhan-my-second-father-2/.

Simone, Nina. 2003. *I Put A Spell On You.* De Capo Press.

Staff, BET. 2005. "News Person of the Year 2005: Minister Louis Farrakhan." *BET.com.* December 19. Accessed August 10, 2013. http://www.bet.com/news/news/2008/02/11/newsarticlepersonofyearfa rrakhan.html.

Steinberg, Jeffrey. 1995. "March Signals Revolt Against Conservative Revolution." *Executive Intelligence Review,* October 27: 58.

Syed, Ibrahim. n.d. "An International Conference." *Islamic Research Foundation International, Inc.* Accessed August 10, 2013. http://www.irfi.org/articles/articles_51_100/an_international_islamic_ confere.htm.

Tabor, Daniel K. 1985. ". . . no, that's not the issue." *Houston Chronicle,* September 18: 11.

The American Prospect. 2002. "Lunatic League Formed." *American Prospect,* March 11: 7.

The Final Call. 1996. "World Friendship Tour Coverage-South Africa." *The Final Call,* February 14.

ThomasJr., Harry L. 1989. "In Praise of Louis Farrakhan: Mr. Thomas Replies." *Washington Post,* October 27: A18.